WHEN BAKERS COOK

Over 175 Recipes from Breakfast to Dessert
Simply Fabulous Food for Family and Friends

Marcy Goldman

Author of *A Passion for Baking*
and Host of BetterBaking.com

www.RiverHeartPress.Com
Montreal, Canada
Canada

WHEN BAKERS COOK

Text and recipes © 2013 by Marcy Goldman

River Heart Press
Montreal, Canada

Marcy Goldman is a cookbook author, master baker, and host of the website, **www.BetterBaking.com**, Est. 1997. Inquiries may be sent to **editors@betterbaking.com** or **marcygoldman@sympatico.ca**

Library and Archives Canada in Publication
ISBN-13: 978-0-9865724-0-1 Print book
ISBN: 978-0-9865724-8-7 E-Book
ISBN: 0986572403

Goldman, Marcy
When Bakers Cook/Marcy Goldman
1.Cooking l.Title

Printed in the United States of America by CreateSpace, a division of Amazon
Cover Photo Eva Kosmas

First Edition

Also by Marcy Goldman
A Treasury of Jewish Holiday Baking, 2007 Whitecap Books (Print, eBook)
The New Best of BetterBaking.com, 2007 Whitecap Books (Print, eBook)
A Passion for Baking, 2005 Oxmoor House (Print)
A Passion for Baking, 2013 Gibbs-Smith (eBook)

Dedication

To my sons, Jonathan, Gideon, and Benjamin, who make me feel that everything I cook is ambrosial. I dedicate this book to them, each recipe seasoned with love of family and our joyous times past, present, and future in the kitchen and at our table.

Table of Contents

CHAPTER THREE
Soup's On! Hot Stuff Coming Through 39

CHAPTER FOUR
Salad Days, Best of the Green Stuff. 75

CHAPTER FIVE
Cry Fowl: Chicken and Turkey. 91

CHAPTER SIX
It's Beef! It's What's for Dinner. 127

CHAPTER SEVEN
Catch of the Day, Fish and Seafood. 143

CHAPTER EIGHT
The Bistro Italiano, Pasta and Pizza. 157

CHAPTER ELEVEN
Baker's Bonus, or A Little Decadence. 221

Introduction

The Real Story Behind the Chef

I was born hungry: hungry with curiosity, hungry for learning and discovery, and hungry to create. Some people use paper and paints, some use a camera and others belt out a song or pick up a flute. Instead, others, like me, turn to the kitchen. The onions, the whisks, the fry pans and the hot stovetops beckon; the smells, tastes, and textures of food in all its guises have a siren's call. To a home or professional chef, each recipe is a performance, played out in soups and salads. Each entrée is a novel; side dishes are chapters or a verse of an inner food poem. We stir the pot, we stir our souls—*whatever* we make, whether elite or rustic, is comfort food for ourselves and those we serve.

Like many people, many of my colleagues, certainly, I chose the food profession as symptomatic relief for hunger pangs far greater than any physical sort. I am speaking of course of hunger pangs of the emotional kind. As a child, my home, which I shared with my parents, two older brothers, and my grandmother, was chaotic. Sometimes it was exciting, but other times, I experienced significant difficulties and challenges in our familial day-to-day life. Often

there was, for lack of a better phrase, a sense of "never-enough-ness". Clearly, among other things, I was famished for nurturing.

Sitting down to the table as a family was a rare occurrence in our house. We had wonderful parties (my parents were great hosts), as well as many interesting friends dropping by for homey conversations and coffee. But what we lacked was consistent table time, consistent meals, a consistently stocked pantry and fridge. We often had luxury foods (lobster, imported cheeses) but no regular staples such as I saw in other people's homes. Nowadays, times have changed and the transient, on-the-go family is now the norm, but in those days, it wasn't usual and I felt the gap. (And let the record state I still think sitting down to break bread together, to eat a meal and share the day is a centering, anchoring tradition that will never be outmoded or lacking in core benefit. I notice this every time my own family and I sit down for meals, either lavish or impromptu; the experience is always positive and bonding)

What we *did* have in our home were four pivotal things that made my life or career in food totally possible, if not inevitable.

First, my grandmother was blind and it often fell upon me to offer her meals, snacks, or warming cups of tea. I was happy to do so. I quickly and lovingly learned that although my grandmother couldn't see, she did indeed smell, taste and appreciate the most basic foods I made. She applauded my best and worst efforts—which is saying a lot considering I was about seven when I started cooking and I scored a hit for every miss! A granddaughter's love of a grandmother, evidenced by those early recipes I conjured up, is a fine place to learn about giving to others.

Second, my mother had a fine palate, but fluctuating interest in keeping the home fires burning. She experimented with ingredients and recipes and was both bold and adventurous when it came to food. She encouraged my brothers and me to do anything we wanted in the kitchen. That, in itself, was inspiring. Other mothers would shoo kids out of the kitchen or throw them a box of Kraft Dinner; my mother gave us carte blanche over the stove, pantry, sink and fridge. The usual concerns, such as the dangers of frying with oil or sugar (although she warned us), were never deterrents. There were no admonitions and little guidance and there was incredible freedom. We could make steaks at midnight or date squares at 6 a.m. She was never one to fret over mess or ineptitude, nor question our choices in recipe. Her only caveat was that we not waste ingredients.

This freedom extended to her entrusting me at 13 years old, to do the family grocery shopping and plan the meals for the week. I leapt at the chance to make things 'regular' and secure, if

only via the kitchen. I also learned how to spend modestly (I had a limited budget) and still create a feast. Such parameters teach you how to make the most of simple things and revere quality and value. I still think one needn't be a spendthrift to make terrific food. But I also don't, as it turns out in my chef's evolution, skimp on great ingredients. While there were traditional rules in my home, there were standards, especially in the kitchen. That meant few canned goods, no pretend orange 'shaker' cheese, no phony things, nor highly (and artificially colored) foods, and no "instant" anything.

Third, while I was growing up, we had a revolving door of live-in help. People came from all over the world, particularly immigrants who fled difficult countries where repression may have ruled or there was a lack of opportunities, to settle in Canada, in our home and with our family. There was the European connection, women who taught me how to prepare every type of roast potato and chicken and the finer points of stretch strudel and hearty bean soups. The Caribbean women who worked for us showed me how to spice something pure and simple with such an acute touch, a shaman's sensibilities. At the end of my tutelage, I could make shoe leather taste like a Cordon Bleu dish. The Argentinian (former dressmaker turned housekeeper), who came with her humongous white angora cat, taught me how to make *dulce de leche* and fritters (even, as my brothers and I recall, "fritter fritters": leftover fritters made into yet more fritters). Young French Canadian women from rural parts of Quebec taught me beautiful, rustic baking and our Greek housekeeper taught me a respect for lemons

I've never forgotten (nor her generosity in using her sewing skills to make my wedding dress). Each person came and went like temporary characters in our family cast. Their gift to me was that they imparted a rich culinary culture, which I gobbled up in big gulps and stored in my chef's brain.

Lastly, the fourth component to my early life in the kitchen was the Time Life series of cookbooks. Many food folks talk about which cookbooks got them on their path, and that series, along with the Good Cook Series, James Beard, Julia Child and The Joy of Cooking, were my in-house chef's correspondence course. With those books, page by page, I learned techniques and acquired foundation recipes. Nowadays, there is the Internet, with free recipes galore and YouTube with wonderful culinary instruction but in those days, there was also a warmth and coherence of 'voice' found in those cookbooks, those authors are still respected today.

A Baker Who Cooks

Why did I become a pastry chef and not a cook? That's simply because a part of me likes difficulty. I found baking more challenging than cooking and I dug in – for me, it could have been the Oregon Trail and I have a pioneer spirit. And then one day I fell in love with flour and the rest is history. Still, where I *began* in food was in cooking - with the onions, the garlic and all the savory things that end up in soups, salads, succulent roasts. I've never forgotten nor neglected my cooking roots and certainly as a mother of three sons, I've also earned my cook's stripes.

This book is a collection of my personal favorite recipes I've created over the years. They are the recipe "glue" of my own family times and the star attractions at our meals and also coincidentally the most beloved fan favorite of my original recipes I've shared at www.betterbaking.com.

So yes, I am a baker. I also happen to be a baker who cooks, because no one lives by bread alone. Happily, I love cooking as much as I love baking, which is a good thing because there's a limit to how many cream puffs you can have for dinner.

While I have written several baking books, now I am equally proud and happy to share my first *cooking* book with you. I've selectively culled my most treasured savory recipes that I've created over the years, from breakfast and main dishes to dessert. *When Bakers Cook* is a book I hope will be as grease-stained and well used as my baking books (unless of course you are viewing this in a digital form on some electronic device, but I think you get the point).

Some of Us Are Cooks, Some of us are Bakers (and some of us are both)

How often have you heard someone say, "I like to cook but I love to bake," or "I like to cook but I simply can't bake" There are bakers and there are cooks; on rare occasion, in the home kitchen as well as the professional one, the twain does meet. Isn't it true? How many people do you know who admit a preference for baking over cooking or vice versa? Competent cooks sometimes confess that baking isn't their strong suit. But bakers? They might *prefer* baking but they do it *all*, so to speak. In other words, while many good cooks are also good bakers, bakers, by necessity, are most assuredly excellent cooks, as well.

Cooking versus *baking* is a conundrum that began the first time a cave man/woman brought home freshly killed supper from a hunt. Someone probably wanted to roast it to perfection; someone else, (probably the village baker) thought about a great bread to mop up the sauce. It is a gusto-laced rivalry that's as old as time, even in the professional food trade and restaurant industry. Cordon Bleu trained bakers and cooks have long enjoyed this friendly kitchen duel of diverse as well as overlapping culinary abilities and sensibilities. Yes, it *all* has to do with food and the kitchen but a cook and a baker have widely different culinary mentalities.

Although, if I were to tip the rivalry just a bit more, I would mention that in days of old, it was also the village baker who minded *everyone's* cooking. The housewives of the village would take their casseroles and braising dishes to the baker's ample oven. There one was ensured to find a consistent, reliable heat source (nothing beat those big stone, wood-fired baking ovens) along with a generous professional chef to kindly pot watch and jockey around the savory dishes of pot au feu, beans and other homey comforts. Clearly, baking and cooking once shared a hearth in more ways than one.

As a flour girl who started her professional culinary journey learning to cook at home,

and then later on, training professionally as a pastry chef and baker (having taught myself the flour arts at home as my start), I know the baker/cook rivalry very well. As a pastry chef I can definitely bake a cherry pie, but I can also cook up a fine soup and conjure up a bistro-style pepper steak, seasoned just so, that would make a gourmand weep with pleasure. A great baker is as fine a captain at the helm of the stock and stew pot as they are manning a six-deck revolving oven and tending bubbling sourdough starters. As it is in the restaurant as well as in the home kitchen, we bakers happen to make superb cooks.

To *be* a baker means you are truly a master of the comprehensive culinary world because the baker's skill set is unrivalled. Under the baking umbrella, we walk the line of chef, short-order cook (because most bakers are family folks as well as pros), chemist, artist, sculptor, physicist, magician and nurturing mother. It's part of our overall training and professional pride and food curiosity. To this, we also bring the savvy of spices, flavorings, techniques and an intimacy with the oven and top range that carries over into our recipes and the flair with which we execute them.

In every restaurant I have baked in, I also did the cooking and I even trained many a cook before ducking out back into the bakery. I am thrilled if you put me near fresh herbs, a chopping block, a mound of onions, tomatoes and some prize-winning cookware. Add some eggs, and I can whip up a feast in minutes, which is why ever since I launched my website www.BetterBaking.com in 1997, I have featured a cooking recipe or two, as part of the monthly offerings. In fact, the feature column was called *When Bakers Cook.*

My Cooking Style

What do *I* cook when I cook and how has my style evolved? Well, first consider the broad-based experience of a mother of three (now grown) sons who is also a professionally-trained chef, restaurant consultant, newspaper food journalist, author of several cookbooks and website editor/personality. Then similarly consider that I'm lucky enough to live in Montreal which is largely a Francophone city, one that has long welcomed and enjoyed the input of diverse, international cultures. Montrealers take their food seriously and are extremely ardent about flavor. I think this emphasis on great taste is something, that if you live here, seeps into your blood, whether you are a chef or a gourmand. It also opens your mind and your palate to new and different foods that you soon embrace and adopt as your own or fuse to all else you do. I salute my own 'food city' and am grateful for the culinary inspirations it has afforded that has emerged in my cooking (and baking) and certainly the recipes in this book.

This all said, overall my style is minimal effort, maximal effect. I lean towards food with flair and true cachet, vibrant tastes and panache - food that is easy on skills and time, and uses common pantry and fridge ingredients. Plus I always give a big nod to nutrition and a huge salute to the global flavor table. This is especially evident in the *Soup* and *Chicken* chapters of this cookbook. Both chapters are disproportionately chock-full of recipes that offer a spunky world beat. Enjoying different foods, flavors, and ingredients is a wonderful way to see a bit more of the world without using your passport.

I believe I also have an appreciation of varied eaters (both adult and juvenile, both adventuresome palates and those that are more reserved). I feel that if something doesn't look good *and* sing out with flavor, you might as well buy take-out food. So I've tried with my cooking, as I do with my baking, to create recipes that are classic, yet contemporary; recipes that are fresh with a sense of now-ness, but timelessly appealing with tastes we all love. Last, they are each honed with an extra flair, dash or special cachet that puts them a cut above a back-in-the-day Sunday night dinner.

These recipes are what I make for my family and friends. When I making any of them, I am also thinking: would my readers also love this? Is it easy? Is it fun? Can you do it without breaking the bank or hauling out extra equipment or a run to the store for another ingredient your pantry doesn't have? Can you do it in short time and with little energy? Can you serve it to your kids, your beau, your best friend, or when your mother-in-law or older brother drops by? Is the food absolutely magical? It better be, because nothing less, when it comes from my kitchen to yours, will do!

When Bakers Cook is *my* cookbook that I am handing off to you, as my cooking friend. The recipes are lovingly created, tested, refined and painstakingly recorded because it's my mission to make *you* shine in your own kitchen. When you look good (and your family and friends beam), *I* feel happy. So, fire up the range, hone the knives, find an apron and get ready to let the good times roll - we have so much to do.

Bon Appetit,

Marcy Goldman

Author, Master Baker, and as always, a Cook

The Nitty Gritty Stuff

Ingredients

Equipment

Tools

Ingredients

I believe in pure, great tastes that come from simple but quality ingredients. In produce (vegetables and fruits), meats, chicken, and dairy products, that means becoming aware of quality and prices. It's true that you can take a pretty tough cut of beef and, together with a great recipe and slow cooking, make an ambrosial stew. But overall, it's best to start with superb, fresh ingredients, be it a well-trimmed, lean piece of perfectly-aged beef, nicely trimmed, organic chicken breast or a springy bunch of leeks. Make quality in the very basics your starting point. As with baking, mouth-watering cuisine is the sum of all its parts, so begin at an optimal level with both your main and minor elements to spiral up, through the cooking process, to a pinnacle of superlative taste, texture, and presentation.

Salt, Pure and Simple Kosher Salt, *Fleur de Sel*, Sea Salt, and More

What amazes me is how so often salt is taken as an afterthought. Considering salt is the spine of so many recipes, it warrants familiarizing yourself with the options, if not become an expert, in the palette of salt. In fact, as the foodie world broadens in the new millennium, salt is almost trendy with a plethora of wonderful choices in gourmet salt available to us. There was a time when our ancestors would have given their eyeteeth for something so essential and convenient. In fact, salt was once used as currency; so precious it was for curing, preserving, and flavoring food. Nowadays, the least discerning among us cannot help but be intrigued by the salt options (unless of course you are avoiding salt in your diet, in which case, find a salt substitute you like and be doubly sure to use fresh spices and herbs). Online and in gourmet shops and specialty food stores, you can find many fine choices in any one of these superb varieties of salts.

Kosher salt

Kosher salt is an iodine-free salt. It comes in fine table salt or coarse grain consistencies. Kosher cooks use it as part of their tradition, but because it is iodine free, it is perfect for soups and all other cooking. It's the salt I use in most of my recipes, whether cooking or baking.

Sea salt

Sea salt is, of course, from the sea. It varies in flavor, depending on where it comes from, but is always flavorful. The most popular brands are from Greece and, like kosher salt, come in coarse or fine consistencies. Most often, I use fine salt, but at the table, I prefer a salt grinder filled with coarse salt. There's just something fun about each person grinding his or her own salt at the table, and when it comes to food, there's something to be said for ceremony.

Fleur de sel ("flower of salt" in French) is a special sea salt, garnered by salt workers who collect only the top layer of salt before it sinks to the bottom of large salt pans. A lot of French *fleur de sel* is collected off the coast of Brittany, from the town of Guerande. This is one of the most costly salts in the world (due to hand collection and the skimming of the crème de la crème of this salt), but the flavor is delicate, pure, and incomparable. A little goes a long way. It is sold in little jars, sometimes slightly damp (in the jar), or in pretty gourmet canisters or tins. A touch on bagels or shortbread enlivens their flavor. When it comes to soup, of course, you could do no better than to use such a fine salt to heighten all flavors and make your soup flavor soar.

Himalayan Salt, also known as Himalayan Pink Salt

This salt comes from the ancient Himalayan Sea beds and purports to have 84 essential and beneficial minerals. It also is fine in cooking. Its pink hue is pretty and appealing, and it has a subtle, slightly smoky taste (depending on the brand). It is suitable in cooking and makes for a nice change as a table salt.

Sour Salt or Citric Acid The secret 'zap' and perk of so many soups

Sour salt or citric acid are interchangeable names for a dry, white, granular powder, much like salt or sugar, that I use in soups in particular, as well as in lemony things (like my Extra Lemon Bars and Lemon Meringue Pie). It's used when a recipe requires a real hit of acidic punch but on occasions I don't want to 'lemon' up in flavor nor add too much liquid to (such as extra lemon juice). A little citric acid or sour salt goes a long way! Sometimes, just a pinch will do. You can also find it in the kosher food section of some stores where it might be granular and free flowing or, occasionally, in small chunks. Tartaric acid is another granular substance that can be used. Similarly acidic, it is garnered from the inside of wine casks. It is the acidic residue that forms, becomes crystalline. This is then can be scraped off to be converted into tartaric acid and used whenever citric acid is called for. This is an ingredient well worth seeking out (even if you just use it to torque up your homemade lemonade or iced tea)

Pepper
Tellicherry, Pink, and Green Peppercorns

There are many types of peppercorns ranging from popular pink or green to the more common but delectable, all-purpose black pepper. Most often, I order mine from The Spice House or pick some up at Costco, which generally stocks a wonderful Tellicherry pepper in a super-size canister at a bargain price. But make no mistake: pepper, like salt, should never be an afterthought. Great pepper, like great salt, and all other spices and herbs, makes a dish. Great pepper can make an ordinary recipe blossom exponentially. So, take the trouble to seek out superb pepper (fresh, fragrant) and use a great pepper grinder (such as an Atlas Mill from Peppermill Imports). Do not, under any circumstances resort to pre-ground pepper. You can't know beforehand if it is fresh or what quality it is or how long ago it was ground and then packaged. If you can find them, I suggest you opt for organic peppercorns.

Spices and Herbs, Fresh and Dried

As I do in baking, I keep various tiers or choices of the same ingredients. I might have lemon juice, as well as lemon oil, lemon extract, and fresh lemons on hand. Having choices ensures my cooking and baking feature a lot of flavor dimension (plus if I am out of something, I have always backup options). In cooking, that means having fresh ingredients as my first option, but I also believe in those extra 'tiers,' like fresh garlic, as well as jarred crushed garlic and quality powdered garlic. As in baking, various options can be better or best, but combinations of things (fresh garlic and a pinch of garlic powder) might, in fact, make a better final dish. Here's how I stock my larder.

Herbs are the cook's perfumed palette, from fresh parsley, fragrant thyme, perky tarragon, earthy basil, zesty oregano, woody rosemary and everything in-between. All are happily available in most supermarkets' produce section and these garden greens bring freshness and dimension to cooking that will make you blink in pleasure. Nothing uplifts a recipe as much as the masterful use of fresh herbs.

But there are also occasions for using dried herbs, and I call for both fresh and dried in my recipes in either/or both scenarios. Fresh does seem like higher ground, but the truth is that dried herbs also have a different taste than fresh, and sometimes, a dusting of both dried and fresh oregano on a pizza achieves just the taste you want.

At any rate, it's always good to have a backup, and that is to me, an important role of dried herbs. For example, if you know well ahead that you're making Rosemary Chicken, do tote home some fresh rosemary (unless you have a green thumb and have some in your garden or windowsill herb pots). But it's also smart to have quality dried rosemary on hand just in case. Ditto with all of your herbs. Dried herbs, when mixed with fresh herbs, can add an extra dimension to your cooking.

Dried herbs are often said to have twice the oomph or power as fresh herbs. I don't think I agree. Dried herbs are to fresh herbs what eau de toilette is to *eau de parfum*: not only weaker (on many occasions) than the perfume (fresh herbs) but most often, a totally different fragrance and taste spectrum. Frankly, I often like to use both dried and fresh herbs in the same recipe for different taste effects.

Dried herbs also require the same great quality as all of your other ingredients; so don't rely on bulk food stores or bottled national brands for the best unless you've taste tested them and can endorse them. More often, it's best to find a spice and herb supplier (for many of us that means an online purveyor) and stock up on the dried herbs you use most often.

You can wash, dry, and freeze fresh herbs, but frankly, this has never worked well for me. I find they lose their color and flavor and then turn mushy so I prefer to rely on fresh and/or better quality dried herbs. The one exception to this is parsley. I've never found dried parsley good for much and so parsley, when I need it, (and that's often) is something I only buy fresh.

How to Reconstitute Dried Herbs

Fresh is best, but sometimes you might be out of fresh parsley or chives. It might be snowing and the dogsled is out of gas. What to do? As a first substitute, parsley in a tube is good to have on hand. The last resort, but still respectable (versus not cooking at all), is to put the dry spice in a bowl and cover it with very hot water or lemon juice, or even hot white wine. This allows the dry spice to swell and regain some of its vital flavor. Then add it to the soup, chicken, roast, or salad dressing. It's just a little trick to get the most out of dehydrated spices.

Basil

Dried basil is fine for many recipes, but fresh is a prerequisite in my kitchen. You can have a windowsill basil plant or buy fresh basil at the supermarket. Put it in water (like a bouquet of flowers—a large mug will do) and it will keep for a few days.

Garlic

I prefer California-grown or locally grown garlic, but Chinese garlic, which is often featured in my local supermarket, is also fine. Look for peeled fresh garlic—this is a wonderful boon. Christopher Ranch is a great resource for all sorts of superlative garlic products (including pickled, crushed, and fresh, peeled garlic) and their products are available all over North America.

Spices

As with dried herbs, do look for the freshest and best quality spices. Whenever I call for spices in this book, unless otherwise stated, please use ground spices (such as ground cinnamon, etc.)

Equipment and Tools

You can make great food with simple equipment—a good knife, good energy, and pure ingredients can result in a feast. But when comprehensively equipping a kitchen, there are some basics that help. Your equipment and tools are, in effect, your sous chefs, so hire well!

Mortars and Pestles

I love shortcuts but I also like taking the long way home, both in life and in the kitchen, which is probably why I like mortars and pestles. The mortar and pestle is likely the oldest cooking utensil known to man. In a singular way, no other utensil has been embraced, crossing culture, time, and even social strata, as pervasively as the mortar and pestle. It is one of those tools that reverberate with a special energy.

One person's mortar and pestle is another person's *molcajete* (Mexico) or yet another's *suribachi* (Japan). You can find mortars of almost any material from lava, volcanic rock, wood, especially olive wood ones, as well as brass, marble, granite, cast iron, vitreous pottery, ceramic, glass, soapstone, sandstone, jadite, and clay. Rougher finishes, such as Thai granite or

Mexican mortar, make short work of grains or garlic. A Japanese mortar, with its converging relief work of grooves on a shallow incline, invites you to grind garlic. Wood and brass mortars are more likely to feature flavor transfer, so take care what you use them for.

You're probably asking why bother with a mortar and pestle when there are chef's knives, food processors, blenders, and garlic crushers to do the job? Bereft of switches, timers, buttons, digital regalia, and whatnot, a mortar and pestle is the anti-appliance. But this kitchen workhorse is a model of design brilliance and Titian results. You can pulverize bittersweet chocolate or chocolate nibs, cinnamon sticks, garlic, Turkish coffee beans, bitingly hot chilies and black peppercorns, star anise, *Lebucken* spices, almonds, citrus zest, or vanilla beans into sublime, sweet and savory oblivion. Nothing releases more flavor, nor does so as expediently as a mortar and pestle. When it comes to garlic, pounding it in a mortar first bruises it and then extracts and disseminates its flavor in a way no Microplane, food processor, garlic crusher, mandolin, or knife can ever do. You can also, given you have a roomy mortar and pestle, make the whole vinaigrette in it, with the pulverized garlic in a state receptive to additions of herbs, salt, pepper, and oil.

Pepper Mills

A great pepper mill is an investment, and, for me, the very best are the brass mills from **www. PepperMillImports.com**. Nothing but nothing beats their pepper mills (and their salt mills). A close second choice, especially if you are looking for a wooden mill, would be anything in a Benton mill from **www.VicFirth.com**. They also make incredible rolling pins (and drum sticks).

Knives

I've tested a ton of knives and my top two picks are **www.Cutco.com** and Lamson and Goodnow knives from **www.LamsonSharp.com**. A third choice would be Wustoff Trident or Victorinox. Serrated knives, I should note, generally can't be sharpened, so in this case, inexpensive serrated knives aren't necessarily a bad bet. Just chuck them out when they don't do the job anymore. The exception to this is Cutco serrated knives. They stay sharper longer than others, and the company offers sharpening services for all of their knives, even the serrated ones.

Always have a few great essential knives on hand: A bread slicer, a chef's knife, and a few paring knives. Regardless of my suggestions, find a knife that feels good in your hand. Hone your knives between uses, and every once in a while, take it in somewhere for a professional sharpening.

Cookware

I have a gas stove and for my range, I need cookware with nice upward tilting handles. That means only one choice for me: All-Clad. I test all sorts of cookware and I keep coming back to All-Clad as the core of my pots and pans. Their nice, thick bottoms prevent burns and scorched spots and their durable (and gorgeous) roasting

pans are true investment pieces that you'll appreciate every time your roast a turkey. All-Clad pots and pans also clean up as if they were brand new, even years (and many pots of soup) later.

That said, there are still other good quality lines of cookware that might work better for your needs. I recommend that you buy a small starter set and then add in pots, a la carte, as it were, from brands you like. Cast iron from The Lodge, enamel-on-steel from Emile Henry or Chantal, nonstick from almost any manufacturer (I see nonstick as disposable cookware; no matter what the price and how you take care of it, nonstick rarely lasts well), enamel on cast iron from Le Creuset, or even no-name brands.

Batter Up: Choosing Skillets and Fry Pans
Cast Iron Versus Nonstick

A cast iron skillet is a usual suspect in most kitchens, and with good reason. It is extremely durable legacy cookware that has been around since the West was settled. It was on the Klondike Gold Rush and every wagon trail, and it's still a part of country cabin weekends and camping trips. Given a choice between nonstick pans, which make butter or oil unnecessary, or a cast iron pan, I would choose a "naturally nonstick," well-seasoned cast iron pan for my pancakes. First of all, cast iron skillets make the best pancakes—they cook up hotter and lighter, and just using the cast iron adds a welcome extra milligram of iron to your diet. And, oh, how brown and crisp they turn out! I have Lodge Cast iron in regular and their newer pre-seasoned, as well as vintage Wagner ware and no-name old cast iron pans in all sorts of sizes. They also make a good sandwich-grilling pan. Use a second cast iron pan as a top weight for a quick restaurant-style Panini.

Cast iron is inexpensive and gets passed from generation to generation. Just make sure to buy cast iron pans made in North America, which are generally the best quality. Vintage cast iron pans are great and come pre-seasoned (and with a ton of history), so if you see them at flea markets or garage sales, don't hesitate to invest!

Electrics

You don't need much to cook well, but you do need some electrics, aside from your stove, to do the job. Here are some of my essentials. Extras—such as waffle makers, deep fryers, popcorn makers, pressure cookers, and fondue makers—are up to you and your choices will depend on how often you make recipes requiring those tools. Otherwise, the basics are all you need.

Food Processor

A great food processor with ample capacity is my right hand in the kitchen. I so appreciate and use my food processor that it almost has equal billing to my mixer. A great food processor purees soups, makes great batches of vinaigrette, and turns a can of chickpeas into a silky, fragrant batch of hummus. I prefer KitchenAid food processors for their durability, design, ease of use, and performance. Choose a high-quality food processor that works for you. Don't skimp. Like great cookware, a good food processor is an investment in your own energy and labor.

Toasters

What's a whole paragraph on toasters doing in a cookbook? Just one glance at the breakfast chapter should convince you that breakfast, and therefore toast, is a big deal to me. Toast is my all-time comfort food and so I've always relied on a durable toaster, which is generally a commercial toaster. Although there are many choices on the market, I am a diehard Dualit toaster fan (**www.dualit.com**). A shiny, stainless 2- or 4-slice Dualit toaster like art for your kitchen counter (in fact, Dualit often appears in kitchen scenes in films). I also would recommend the heavy-duty toaster from Viking. If you want great performance and a somewhat leaner, prettier toaster, look to Breville, Cuisinart, Krups, or even a retro and colorful Bodum toaster.

Mixers

Nothing beats a KitchenAid stand mixer for looks, performance, and company reputation. Although mixers are primarily for baking, my mixer is a great hamburger meat mixer-upper. Aside from KitchenAid, opt for Viking, Cuisinart, or Breville. Either buy a great mixer or wait until you can afford one. Hand-held mixers fall in between two territories, being neither like stationary mixers nor like wooden spoons. I've never been a fan, but if you do like hand-held beaters, again, KitchenAid is your best bet.

Blenders

I tend to use a food processor instead of a blender, but blenders are handy, especially for soups and salad dressings or smoothies, of course. I recommend KitchenAid, Oster, and Bodum as my top three.

Coffee Grinders

Coffee grinders need to be burr grinders with burrs that actually pulverize or grind coffee rather than blade grinders (great for spices but not for coffee), which merely finely chop up the coffee. I recommend KitchenAid, Cuisinart, Breville, and Bodum as my best bets. I've tested them all (as well as many brands in between), and these are all high-performance grinders. Besides which, nothing is better natural aromatherapy than freshly ground coffee.

Coffee Drips and Single Coffee Makers

Since great coffee is my lifelong pursuit, I've tested tons of coffee makers (as well as coffee roasters and grinders). In the end, I have a few different approaches.

For single and second cups of coffee, I use either a Chemex glass carafe or, more often, a simple Melitta filter with unbleached paper filters.

For larger amounts of coffee, again, I use a Chemex (larger) carafe or, sometimes, a drip coffee maker. For that route, I go with KitchenAid drip makers, or Cuisinart, Hamilton Beach, Krups or Braun.

Teapots

I love tea just about as much as coffee. I recommend a classic Brown Betty or a pot from Chatsford. I purchase mine from **www.uptontea.com**

CHAPTER ONE

Good Morning!
Breakfast and Brunch Served All Day

Good morning to you and happy breakfast or brunch no matter the time of day. I think we can all agree breakfast is one meal you *can* serve any time of day.

Most people have a favorite meal and it's most often supper and on occasion, it's brunch. For some reason, people rarely vote for lunch. But my personal favorite choice is the first meal of the day - breakfast. I'm an early riser for one thing but I simply love everything about this time of day and the meal that come with it. Breakfast, like the fresh new day ahead, is open to a variety of so many good things—sweet preserves, salty-smoky bacon, strong smelling cheeses (or not), honey-laced hot cereals, iron-rich eggs, any sort of toast (bagels or sourdough bread), and/or welcome baskets of muffins.

Breakfast also reminds me of my dad who was the breakfast king. He would time the poached eggs just so or prepare kippers (yes, kippers!) so they were piping hot to serve alongside buttered warm, croissants. His coffee was scalding and pitch black, and he sipped it in short shots. I loved my dad, and I loved the ceremony he made of the first meal of the day and clearly, I've continued the tradition

I'm especially pleased to share my best breakfast and brunch recipes with you which are dishes that work any time. A home kitchen is a palace of comfort foods, and breakfast served 24/7 in your own abode is ample proof of that. Breakfast, (when done caringly) is both nutritious and hospitable (who doesn't love hot coffee and biscuits or all things golden and eggy?). It's also a good time to indulge, because you have the rest of the day to work off any excess calories.

So rise up and warm up the cast iron grill and get the coffee going – we have a lot of cooking to do!

Rise and Shine Stuffed Breakfast Biscuits

Egg McMuffin - move aside! Great, quick, wholesome, all-in-one breakfast sandwiches are easily managed at the home grill. They're also far less fat-laden and ten-fold more flavorful. This ingenious recipe starts with a buttery, flaky biscuit that holsters a stash of scrambled eggs and cheddar cheese. What's better than a tote-able snack with drive-thru convenience, homemade taste and superior nutritional value? The biscuit recipe alone is one of the best. (P.S. these freeze well and microwave when you want one on-the-run)

Biscuits
1/3 cup warm water
4 teaspoons instant yeast
5 cups all-purpose flour
2 tablespoons baking powder
1 teaspoon baking soda
1 ½ teaspoons salt
3/4 cup unsalted butter or shortening, or half and half combination
1 ½ cups buttermilk

Scrambled Egg Filling
2 tablespoons butter
8 eggs
¼ cup water, milk or whipping cream
Salt, pepper
Tabasco to taste
1 ½ cups shredded sharp orange cheddar cheese

Finishing Touches
Melted salted butter

* If using shortening, which offers that 'commercial' taste to your homemade biscuits, opt for a trans-fat free shortening, which is slightly healthier.

Preheat oven to 425 F.

Arrange the oven rack in the middle position. Stack two baking sheets together and line the top one with parchment paper.

For the biscuits, in a small bowl, mix the water and yeast together and let stand one minute. In a large mixing bowl, blend the flour, baking powder, baking soda, and salt together. With your fingertips, rub in the shortening and butter to make a grainy mixture. Make a well in the center, pour in the water-yeast mixture and mix with the dry ingredients a bit. Drizzle in the buttermilk and mix to make a soft, shaggy dough.

Knead the dough in the bowl with your hands until it holds together. It should be moist, but you will be able to roll or pat it out. Cover it while making the scrambled eggs. (The dough will rise very little, but the baked biscuits will be both flaky and have a bit of extra rise to them)

For the filling, melt the butter in a large nonstick fry pan. Whip the eggs in a medium bowl with the water or cream. Add the eggs to the pan, season with salt, pepper, and Tabasco, and cook gently to scramble the eggs. Add the cheese and cook for a bit. You want to end up with cooked eggs that are between the consistency of an omelet and scrambled eggs, but they should also remain moist since they will get another bake in the oven within the biscuits.

On a lightly floured work surface, roll out half of the dough into an 8- by 10-inch rectangle. Spoon on or arrange the eggs over the dough. Roll out the remaining dough and arrange on top of the eggs. Pinch the sides with the tines of a fork. Using a large knife or pizza cutter, cut into 10 to12 squares. Pinch the sides of the squares a bit with fork tines. They do not have to be sealed perfectly.

Put the biscuits on the baking sheet and brush them lightly with some melted butter. Bake until golden brown, 15 to 17 minutes. Brush again with butter as they come out of the oven for that drive-thru look and taste (but this is optional if you want to avoid extra butter).

Wrapped well, these can be frozen up until a month and then microwave to reheat.

Serves 10–12

Turkey Breakfast Sausage Patties

A pastry bag does quick work of filling sausage casings (available online), but more often than not, I simply make this recipe into patties. Fry what you need and freeze the rest of the patties. Then prepare what you need for your own breakfast sandwiches at home or for a scrambled egg breakfast. This recipe calls for ground chicken and veal in addition to turkey, but using all turkey meat would be fine too.

1 pound ground dark chicken meat
1 pound ground dark turkey meat
½ pound lean ground veal
1 cup peeled, shredded apples, lightly packed
1/3 cup minced onion
2 or 3 medium garlic cloves, minced
¼ cup minced fresh parsley, lightly packed
4–5 teaspoons salt
1–2 teaspoons pepper
2 teaspoons sage
½ teaspoon marjoram
1/8 teaspoon cinnamon
1/8 teaspoon nutmeg
1/8 teaspoon ginger
1/8 teaspoon allspice
1 tablespoon oil
2 tablespoons water or chicken broth
¼–½ teaspoon liquid smoke, optional

In a large bowl, gently blend the chicken, turkey, and veal. Once they are combined somewhat, add the apple, onion, garlic, parsley, salt, pepper, sage, marjoram, cinnamon, nutmeg, ginger, allspice, oil, water or broth and liquid smoke.

To test the seasoning, take a bit of the meat mixture and make a small patty. Fry up it up in a nonstick pan with a touch of oil. Once the test patty is cooked, taste it and adjust the seasonings in the uncooked portion as needed; you might want to add more salt, pepper, or a touch more liquid smoke.

Form the mixture into small patties or stuff, using a sausage stuffer (or attachment on your mixer), into casings or form small sausage logs by hand or into small patties, much like hamburgers. To cook, heat a bit of vegetable oil in a nonstick fry pan and brown well on each side until sausages are cooked through, about 8 to 12 minutes. (The best test is to taste a small piece). The sausages (or patties) will keep in the freezer for 3 to 4 months.

Makes about 12–20 sausages or patties.

Classic Eggs Benedict

Nothing beats this classic. It is a perky, tangy, gorgeous, golden Hollandaise sauce over perfectly poached eggs. So elegant; it turns a homey kitchen into the best restaurant on the block. Leftover Hollandaise is perfect over fresh, steamed spring asparagus.

Hollandaise Sauce

3 egg yolks
1 tablespoon fresh lemon juice
1 tablespoon water
½ cup unsalted butter, diced
Salt, pepper
Tabasco, to taste

Assembly Items

2 English muffins, split, toasted
4 thin slices Canadian bacon, smoked turkey, or
    smoked ham, cooked and kept warm
4 eggs, poached in vinegar water (1 quart water
    with 2 tablespoons vinegar)

Finishing Touches

Pepper, paprika, parsley, orange slices

For the Hollandaise Sauce, in a small saucepan, over low heat, whisk the egg yolks, lemon juice and water for 5 minutes. Whisk in the butter and cook, allowing mixture to thicken to a sauce and stirring all the while. Keep warm.

Poach the eggs and assemble the English muffins and other items.

To assemble the Eggs Benedict, place one toasted English muffin half on a plate. Top it with a piece of the bacon, then the poached egg. Spoon the Hollandaise sauce over the egg. Dust with pepper and paprika. Garnish with some parsley and orange slices.

Serves 4

Southwestern Tortilla Casserole

This is a stunning symphony of Southwestern flavors—creamy scrambled eggs, enlivened with hot peppers and Monterey Jack cheese (medium Cheddar or Colby are noble substitutes), and golden, crunchy, broken-up tortilla chips.

10 eggs
3 tablespoons half-and-half or light cream
Salt, pepper
2 tablespoons olive oil
1 small tomato, diced
1 small mild Serrano pepper, green or red, seeds removed, diced
1 small Scotch bonnet pepper, seeds removed, finely diced
1 small onion, diced
2 cups broken-up tortilla chips
2 cups shredded Monterey Jack cheese
2 tablespoons minced cilantro

Finishing Touches

Hot sauce
Sour cream
Diced black olives
Minced tomatoes
Minced cilantro

Whisk the eggs with the cream in a large bowl. Dust in salt and pepper.

In a nonstick fry pan, over low heat, warm up the oil and sauté the tomato, peppers and onion until they are softened and the liquid from tomatoes evaporates, about 6 to 10 minutes.

Add the eggs and cook until the eggs are nearly done. Add the tortilla chips and toss. Stir in cheese and cilantro.

Serve immediately, garnished with sour cream, olives, minced tomatoes and more cilantro.

Serves 4

Primavera Quiche

An herb-filled, mouth-wateringly tender tart bottom is the throne to a zesty filling. This is as sophisticated as you expect from quiche, but as fun and flavorful as a pizza. In a word, this is spectacular. Don't count on leftovers.

Savory Tart Pastry

2 cups all-purpose flour
¾ teaspoon salt
½ teaspoon sugar
¾ cup unsalted butter, in chunks
1 tablespoon minced fresh parsley
1 tablespoon minced fresh basil
1 egg
¼ cup ice water

Quiche Filling

2 tablespoons olive oil
2 garlic cloves, finely minced
½ teaspoon mixed Italian herbs
1 28-ounce can chopped plum tomatoes
1 tablespoon red wine
½ cup whipping cream
2 eggs
1 ½ cups shredded mozzarella
2/3 cup grated Parmesan cheese
Salt, pepper
8 cherry tomato halves

To make the Savory Tart Pastry, place the flour, salt, and sugar in a food processor and blend briefly. Add the butter and pulse to make a coarse, grainy meal. Add the herbs, then the egg and most of the ice water, and pulse to make a shaggy dough, adding in more water if required until dough holds together. Knead the dough gently on a lightly floured work surface. Pat into a disc, wrap, and refrigerate one hour or overnight.

For the Quiche Filling, in a nonstick fry pan, over low heat, gently sauté the garlic in the olive oil just to soften the garlic a bit. Add the Italian herbs and then stir in the tomatoes and wine and cook to meld the flavors and reduce the juice of the tomatoes, 15 to 25 minutes, until the tomatoes are slightly pasty and most of the liquid has evaporated. Remove from the heat and set aside to cool.

Preheat oven to 425 F.

For the crust, roll the chilled dough out to fit a 10-inch tart pan. Press the dough into the pan. Line a baking sheet with parchment paper. Place crust on the baking sheet and bake 10 to 12 minutes, just to brown it briefly. Remove from the oven. Lower the temperature to 375 F.

Spread the tomato mixture onto the crust. In a medium bowl, mix the cream with the eggs, dust with some salt and pepper, and fold in the mozzarella and half the Parmesan cheese. Drizzle the egg mixture over the tomato mixture, swirling with a fork a bit to get it dispersed around the tomatoes. Garnish with the remaining Parmesan cheese. Arrange the cherry tomato halves decoratively on top.

Bake 25 to 30 minutes, until the edges of the crust start to brown and the cherry tomatoes appear tender.

Serves 6–8

Restaurant Style Buttermilk Pancakes

These are restaurant-style pancakes with that special flavor and texture, but they are, of course, extra wonderful as they are made from scratch. Tender, but hearty, they are probably the best pancakes you'll ever whip up (the batter is also great for waffles). Malt powder, which can be found online or in health food stores, is another trick in this recipe. You can also experiment with other flour choices such as using part spelt, kamut, buckwheat or whole-wheat flour.

2 cups all-purpose flour
1–2 tablespoons corn flour* or cornmeal,
    optional
½ teaspoon salt
3 tablespoons sugar
1 tablespoon malt powder, optional
1 tablespoon baking powder
1 teaspoon baking soda
1 ½ cups, or more, buttermilk
2 eggs
1 teaspoon pure vanilla extract
3–4 tablespoons unsalted butter, melted (or
    canola oil)

Finishing Touches
Milk, as required
Butter for frying

* Corn flour is a finely ground cornmeal that is silky as flour instead of grainy. You can use cornmeal instead or leave it out.

In a medium bowl, blend the flour, corn flour, salt, sugar, malt powder, baking powder and baking soda. Make a well in the center; add a cup of buttermilk, the eggs, vanilla extract, and melted butter and stir, adding more buttermilk as required to make a thick, but loose batter. Let batter stand 10 minutes. If batter seems to thicken or rises up (the leavener can do that), stir it down and loosen with a bit more milk.

Heat a fry pan or skillet with a bit of butter until it is quite hot (not burning, but not low heat either). Using a soup ladle, spoon about ½ cup batter into the pan. Fry one side, wait until bubbles appear (about 1-2 minutes) and flip to fry the other side.

Makes 8–12, depending on size

Red Velvet Waffles with Cream Cheese Glaze

Red Velvet Cake done up in a waffle dress, just in time for breakfast, brunch, or as a fabulous dessert. I serve these just as often with fresh strawberries, ice cream, and fudge sauce as I offer them with the delectable Cream Cheese Drizzle. What's nice about this recipe, aside from it being a glamorous breakfast food, is that it uses more chocolate flavor than the usual Red Velvet recipe to get an especially rich chocolate-y taste. For baking powder, I recommend either Clabbergirl or Rumford – the results (high rising waffles) speak for themselves.

Waffles

2 eggs
1 ¾ cups buttermilk
1 tablespoon pure vanilla extract
¼ teaspoon almond extract
1 teaspoon white vinegar
¼ cup unsalted butter, melted, cooled
1/2 cup sugar
1/3 cup cocoa
1 teaspoon red food coloring
2 cups all-purpose flour
4 teaspoons baking powder
½ teaspoon baking soda
3/8 teaspoon salt
1 ½ teaspoons malt powder*, optional
1/4 cup finely chopped chocolate chips

Cream Cheese Drizzle

4 ounce package cream cheese, softened
3 tablespoons unsalted butter, softened
2 cups confectioners' sugar
1 teaspoon pure vanilla extract
Milk, as required

Finishing Touches

Vanilla ice cream
Sliced strawberries
Fudge sauce

* Malt powder can be found online or in health food stores.

Have a waffle iron nearby and already heated up.

In a large bowl, whisk the eggs, buttermilk, vanilla extract, almond extract, vinegar, and butter together. Fold in the sugar, cocoa, and food coloring and mix well. Fold in the flour, baking powder, baking soda, salt, malt powder and chocolate chips. Let batter rest for 20 minutes or refrigerate (for up to 2 days) until needed. Stir batter down a bit before using (it will rise a bit) and if it seems very thick, thin it with a few teaspoons of water or buttermilk.

Heat waffle iron and smear on some butter. Make the waffles and keep warm (lightly covered with foil).

For the Cream Cheese Drizzle, whisk the cream cheese in a medium bowl with the butter, confectioners' sugar, and as much milk as required to make a drippy glaze. Drizzle over the waffles before serving, or serve the waffles with ice cream, berries, and warm fudge sauce.

Serves 6

Blueberry Sour Cream Pancakes

These pancakes are so tender and light, they almost float away and are especially superb if you make them silver dollar-sized. They're just as delectable made with miniature chocolate chips or diced apples (and a touch of cinnamon) instead of blueberries, but even pure and simple, with nothing added to them, these are quintessential, heavenly pancakes.

1 cup all-purpose flour 1 ½ teaspoons baking powder

¼ teaspoon baking soda

1/8 teaspoon salt

1 tablespoon sugar

2 eggs

1 cup milk

1/3 cup sour cream

1 teaspoon pure vanilla extract

2 tablespoons melted butter

½ cup fresh or frozen blueberries

Finishing Touches

Butter for frying

Maple or blueberry syrup, agave syrup or brown sugar

In a medium bowl, whisk together the flour, baking powder, baking soda, salt, and sugar. Make a well in the center and whisk in the eggs, milk, sour cream, vanilla extract, and melted butter. Blend well, but don't over beat. Gently fold in the blueberries.

Let the batter stand for 15 minutes. Stir down (if it rises up a bit). The batter should be soft and loose, but if it is too loose, mix in in 1 to 3 tablespoons of flour.

Heat a griddle or skillet with a little butter. Using a soup ladle, spoon pancake batter into pan or onto griddle. Cook until the underside is browned and bubbles appear on the top surface of the pancakes. Once bubble appear all over, turn pancake to other side and cook 25 to 60 seconds to brown both sides.

Serve with drizzled with syrup or dusted with brown sugar.

Makes 6–12 pancakes, depending on size

Buttery Belgian Waffles

Batter up! Lots of butter, yeast and baking powder is what puts a taste of Old Europe in these mouth-watering waffles. One bite of these and you won't ever give frozen Eggos a second glance. These bake up deeply golden, with buttery crisp exteriors and soft, almost pudding-like interiors. They are great topped with maple syrup, whipped cream, or ice cream and fresh strawberries. This recipe makes a ton, but they freeze quite well, which is the added bonus of a great waffle recipe. I use the leftovers for my famed Waffle Bottom Cheesecake.

½ cup warm water
1 ½ teaspoons instant yeast
1 ¼ cups evaporated milk
1 cup warm milk
4 eggs
2 egg yolks
1 ¼ cup unsalted butter, melted
1 cup sugar
2 tablespoons pure vanilla extract
¾ teaspoon salt
4 teaspoons baking powder
1 tablespoon malt powder, optional *
5–6 cups all-purpose flour

* Malt powder is a secret ingredient and/or trick I am delighted to share. You can get malt powder at bagel shops, health food stores, bulk food stores, or online. Malt adds that special something to these wondrous waffles or any pancake recipe.

In a large bowl, whisk the water and yeast together and let stand 2 minutes. Briskly whisk in the evaporated milk, milk, eggs, egg yolks, butter, sugar, and vanilla extract and blend well. Fold in the salt, baking powder, and most of the flour to make a thick batter. Add remaining flour, as required, to make a thick pancake batter.

Cover and let stand for one hour. Stir down and then use as regular waffle batter with your waffle iron. Alternatively, cover and refrigerate overnight; stir down batter the next day and let it warm up for about 30 minutes. If it is too thick (i.e. you cannot spoon it easily as you would regular waffles), loosen it with some warm milk or water (or a bit of both).

Makes 10–15 waffles, depending on how you dispense batter and your waffle iron design.

Note: Baked waffles freeze well. Put them on a parchment paper lined baking sheet and allow them to freeze. Once they are frozen, pack them in Ziploc bags.

Cheesecake-Stuffed French Toast with Cidered Apples

This is a great company dish for brunch or New Year's breakfast and it's easily prepared the night before. One of my recipe testers said this recipe is worth the price of the whole cookbook, declaring: No matter what you say in the recipe headnote, it won't convey how extraordinary these are!

Cheesecake Filling

1 8-ounce package cream cheese, softened

2 eggs

1/3 cup sugar

2 teaspoons pure vanilla extract

¼ cup all-purpose flour

8 thick slices challah or brioche, about 1 inch thick

Egg Bath

6 eggs

½ cup cream or milk

¼ cup all-purpose flour

3 tablespoons sugar

1 teaspoon pure vanilla extract

½ teaspoon baking powder

¼ cup unsalted butter, melted

Cidered Apples

4 cups peeled, diced apples

½ cup (packed) brown sugar

¼ cup unsalted butter

½ cup apple cider or juice

Finishing Touches

Butter for frying

Apple or maple syrup

For the Cheesecake Filling, blend cream cheese, eggs, sugar, vanilla extract, and flour in a food processor until smooth.

Make a cut deeply into each slice of the bread to make a pocket. Alternatively, you can slather cheesecake filling between two thinner slices of bread (i.e. cut a thick slice in half, diagonally, and fill with filling, and gently top with the other half).

For the Egg Bath, in a large bowl, whisk the eggs, cream or milk, flour, sugar, vanilla extract, baking powder and butter to blend. Soak each French toast slice in the egg bath for about 10 to15 minutes.

Heat some butter in a large nonstick pan. Sauté or brown each French toast piece on each side. Place in a casserole dish and keep warm until ready to serve.

For the Cidered Apples, heat the butter in a medium pan. Stir in brown sugar and cider and mix well; then quickly add the apples and cook until they are softened, over low heat, for about 15 minutes. Keep warm and then spoon the apples over the French toast, drizzle with apple or maple syrup, and serve.

Serves 4–6

New Orleans Overnight French Toast

This recipe, also known as Pain Perdu, is essentially a French toast soufflé casserole. If you don't have some day-old, leftover croissants on hand, use challah or a thick white bread instead. This is a puffy, golden brown showstopper of a dish that impresses in a glance and wins devotees at first bite.

Bread Stuff
Unsalted butter, for pan
8 large, slightly stale croissants (or 8-10 thick slices leftover challah or white bread)

Egg Bath
8 eggs
1 cup milk
½ cup whipping cream
¼ cup unsalted butter, melted
2 teaspoons pure vanilla extract
½ cup sugar
3 tablespoons all-purpose flour
2 teaspoons baking powder
1/8 teaspoon salt
¼ teaspoon cinnamon

Finishing Touches
Pure maple syrup
Confectioners' sugar and cinnamon for dusting

Butter a 9-by-13-inch baking dish or a 5-quart oven-proof ceramic casserole.

Split the croissants horizontally almost, but not quite, all the way through.

For the Egg Bath, in a large bowl, whisk together the eggs, milk, cream, butter, vanilla extract, sugar, flour, baking powder, salt and cinnamon. Add the croissants to the egg mixture and let them soak for a few minutes. Remove the croissants gently from the bath and lay them in the prepared baking dish.

Pour the remaining egg bath mixture over the croissants. Cover lightly and refrigerate overnight or for at least a few hours.

Preheat the oven to 400 F. Bake for 25 to 30 minutes and then lower the heat to 350 F for the last 10 minutes. Bake until the croissants are browned wherever they are peaking out. Dust with confectioners' sugar and cinnamon. You can also garnish with fresh, sliced strawberries. Serve with maple syrup.

Serves 6–8

Apple Puff Pancake

Who can resist this easy brunch dish that is all about little effort that yields extraordinary results. Caramelized apples sit in an eggy batter that puffs up into a sweet soufflé during its brief stay in the oven. McIntosh, Cortland or Yellow Delicious apples are recommended.

Apple Part
2 tablespoons unsalted butter
4 medium to large apples, peeled, cored, cut
    in ½ slices
Juice of ½ lemon
3 tablespoons light brown sugar
½ teaspoon pure vanilla extract
2 tablespoons apple cider or juice

Pancake Batter
1 ¼ cups all-purpose flour
1 ½ teaspoons baking powder
¼ cup sugar
¼ teaspoon salt
4 eggs
½ cup milk
3 tablespoons unsalted butter, melted

Finishing Touches
Butter, about 2 tablespoons
Confectioners' sugar
Maple syrup

Preheat oven to 450 F. Butter a 10- or 12-inch layer cake pan or a 3-quart oven casserole or baking dish.

Meanwhile, for the Apple Part, melt the butter in a nonstick fry pan. Add the apples and sauté them over medium-low heat. As the apples cook and soften, add the lemon juice, brown sugar, vanilla extract, and apple cider (or juice). Cook until the apples are almost completely softened, about 8 minutes. Set aside to cool for 10 minutes.

For the Pancake Batter, in a medium bowl, blend the flour, baking powder, sugar and salt. Add in eggs, milk and butter and blend well.

Place the apples in the prepared pan. Pour on the pancake batter and dot with bits of butter.

Bake until puffy, about 15 to 17 minutes. Dust with confectioners' sugar. Serve with maple syrup.

Serves 2–4

Old Fashioned Irish Oatmeal

These are the real deal: true Irish steel-cut oats (they're the ones that look a bit like tiny barley). Make a big batch once a week and store it in the fridge. This is also bolstered with wheat germ and ground flax but you can leave those out if you like and sprinkle them on top on each single hot cereal serving o. Just scoop out as much oatmeal as you need, microwave for a minute, and lace it with milk, Greek yogurt, and maple syrup.

1 cup steel-cut Irish oatmeal, such as McCann's
Water, preferably spring water
2 tablespoons brown
¼ teaspoon salt
2 tablespoons wheat germ
2 tablespoons ground flax seed
1 cup regular or old-fashioned oats or oatmeal
(like Quaker)
2 teaspoons pure vanilla extract
¼ teaspoon pure maple extract
½ cup raisins, optional

Finishing Touches
Blueberries, cranberries, raspberries, diced apple
Hemp hearts
Flax seed (both ground and regular flax seeds)
Maple syrup
Agave
Honey

Place the oatmeal in a 3-quart saucepan and cover with water by about ½ inch. Stir in the sugar, salt, wheat germ and flax seed. Simmer, stirring often, adding more water as needed, over medium heat, for about 20 minutes until oatmeal is softened. It will be similar to cooked rice, but a little firmer. During the last 5 minutes of cooking, stir in the regular oatmeal.

Remove from the stove and stir in extracts and raisins.

Refrigerate what you are not using right away. To serve, scoop out what you require into a bowl and microwave for 1 to 2 minutes. Serve with whatever finishing touches you desire.

Serves 4–6

Cranberry, Sour Cherry, and Almond Granola

An exquisite gourmet granola blend, inspired by Dorset Cereals of the UK, who make stunningly good granola (when you can find it). This makes a noble cereal that tastes as beautiful as it looks. For holiday gifts, pack up a batch in a cello bag, tied with a scarlet ribbon, or use a large Mason jar.

4 cups toasted malt flakes*
1 ½ cups oatmeal, large flakes, toasted if possible
½ cup sunflower seeds
1 cup dried cranberries, coarsely minced
½ cup dried sour cherries, coarsely minced
½ cup raisins
¼ cup dried dates, finely minced
¼ cup dried minced mango, apricot, or
    pineapple
¼ cup slivered almonds
¼ cup dried coconut slivers, toasted, optional
1 ½ teaspoons pure vanilla extract, optional
¼ teaspoon pure orange oil, optional

* Malt flakes can be found in health food stores or online.

In a large bowl, toss the malt flakes, oatmeal, sunflower seeds, cranberries, cherries, raisins, dates, other dried fruits, almonds, coconut slivers, vanilla extract and orange oil (if using). Pack into jars and store in a dry place.

Makes 5–6 cups

Moist Blueberry Muffins

Whether you use butter or oil, this modest and moist little gem of a muffin should bring back memories of a New England B&B. This is one of those pure and simple muffins of yesteryear: small, moist little cakes that are delicious for breakfast or teatime and won't dent your diet.

½ cup unsalted butter, melted, or canola oil
1 ¼ cups sugar
2 eggs
1 ½ teaspoons pure vanilla extract, optional
2 cups all-purpose flour
2 teaspoons baking powder
¼ teaspoon salt
½ cup milk
2 cups blueberries

Finishing Touches
Sugar

Preheat oven to 350 F.

Line a baking sheet with parchment paper. Line 12 large muffin cups or 24 small muffin cups with muffin liners and place the muffin tin on the parchment-lined baking sheet.

In a mixer bowl, blend the butter or oil with the sugar, eggs and vanilla extract until well combined. Fold in the dry ingredients in batches, alternating with the milk, and, when almost blended, fold in the blueberries. To prevent the batter getting blue-hued, be very gentle while mixing in the fruit.

Using an ice cream scoop, scoop the batter into the muffin cups and dust each with a bit of sugar.

Bake on upper rack of oven, until lightly golden around the edges and muffins spring back when gently touched, 30 to 32 minutes.

Makes 12 large muffins or 24 small muffins

Multigrain Low-Fat Carrot Muffins

Nothing beats these fabulous, crusty topped, moist-interior muffins. These have all the goodness of applesauce, buttermilk, wheat germ, oat bran, and wheat bran along with precious little fat and only one egg. These are staying, rustic and good-for-you appetite zappers.

¾ cup (packed) brown sugar
3 tablespoons canola oil
1 egg
2 egg whites
1 cup buttermilk
½ cup unsweetened applesauce
1 ½ teaspoons pure vanilla extract
¼ cup wheat germ
½ cup oat bran
½ cup wheat bran
½ teaspoon cinnamon
¼ teaspoon salt
2 teaspoons baking powder
½ teaspoon baking soda
½ cup whole-wheat flour
1 ½ cups all-purpose flour
2 cups shredded carrots
¼ cup sunflower seeds
1 cup raisins or minced dried mango or apricots

Preheat oven to 375 F.

Line a baking sheet with parchment paper. Spray a 12-cup muffin tin with nonstick cooking spray, and line each cup with paper muffin cups. Place the muffin tin on top of the parchment-lined baking sheet. Arrange oven rack position to middle. Place muffin tin on parchment paper lined baking sheet.

In a large bowl, blend the brown sugar, oil, egg, egg whites, buttermilk, vanilla extract and applesauce. Fold in the wheat germ, oat bran, wheat bran, cinnamon, salt, baking powder, baking soda, whole-wheat flour and all-purpose white flour; blend well. Fold in the carrots, sunflower seeds and raisins or other dried fruit.

Let the batter stand 15 minutes. If the batter seems too loose, add up to ¼ cup additional all-purpose flour, as required. Using an ice cream scooper, spoon muffins into pan.

Bake until the muffins are puffy and nicely browned, 25 minutes or a bit longer. Let cool in the pan for 15 minutes before removing to cool completely on a wire rack.

Makes 9–12

CHAPTER TWO

Starter Up! Appetizers

What's there to say about appetizers? In keeping with what appetizers are all about, anything you say about them should be short and to the point, which is exactly what a good appetizer is supposed to be: short and to the point, but also wholly delectable and totally memorable.

Appetizers are also known as whets (or teasers) for the palate. They can either wake up an appetite or effectively suppress one in that they are meant to take the edge off hunger and prevent you from devouring the meal ahead. Appetizers are generally starters before a meal, especially a special or formal meal, but they can also be the main event. If you offer a selection of appetizers along with some cocktails, appetizers can be an extravagant, varied buffet.

How can exceptional appetizers end up being the meal itself? Because if you're a nibbler, appetizers are just up your alley. Have one or

two, a little or a lot, and you can call it a day (or a meal). What I like best about appetizers is that they tend to be intensely flavorful and are usually infused with spice, salt, and acidic notes, such as garlic and lemon, making them unusually addictive.

I am delighted to share some of my favorite appetizers that I've served many times to family and friends. The recipes in this particular collection, coincidentally but not surprisingly, are also the most "hit on" recipes at my website, BetterBaking.com, and you will find most of them have a bit of a world beat feel to them. These appetizers are perfect as a snack if you find yourself at loose ends around 4 o'clock or are feeling just a tad peckish and aren't sure what would suit. Ditto for the midnight snack hour—appetizers are just the thing and something in this batch of flavorful recipes is sure to please.

Red Beet Hummus

Since I'm pretty partial to hummus I'm not surprised to see it's morphed from an occasional dip to a mainstream trend. I've never met a hummus recipe I didn't like but this one I love, probably because I also love beets. The vibrant color of the beets also takes this usually blah-hued spread up a notch.

4 medium beets, peeled and cubed
5 tablespoons fresh lemon juice
2 tablespoons tahini or sesame seed paste
2 tablespoons extra virgin olive oil
1 medium garlic clove, finely chopped
1 tablespoon cumin
Zest of one large lemon, finely minced
Salt, pepper

Finishing Touches
2–4 tablespoons minced cilantro
Goat cheese, crumbled
Cucumber slices
Pita bread

Place the beets in a small pot of water and bring to the boil. Simmer until tender, about 20 minutes. Drain well.

Place the beets in a food processor along with the lemon juice, tahini, olive oil, garlic, cumin, lemon zest, salt, and pepper. Pulse and then process 1-2 minutes to make a smooth paste. Chill until ready to serve.

Serve alongside warm pita bread or spread on cucumber rounds or slices, topped with cilantro and crumbled goat cheese.

Makes 2 cups

Bissara North African Hummus

The typical garlic/lemon hummus might be what you're used to, but this North African spin on the chickpea spread is dynamite. It calls for canned fava beans along with touches of dried chili pepper, cumin, plenty of paprika and a kiss of lemon for a unique, spicy hummus. Use this spread on crackers, flatbreads or alongside grilled chicken. It's smooth as silk, a little hot and just outstanding.

1 19-ounce can fava beans, drained
4 garlic cloves, finely minced
1/3 cup extra virgin olive oil
2–3 tablespoons fresh lemon juice
4 sprigs parsley
¼ teaspoon dried red chili pepper
2 teaspoons sweet paprika
1-2 teaspoons cumin
Salt, pepper

Place the fava beans, garlic, olive oil, lemon juice, parsley, chili pepper, paprika, cumin, salt, and pepper in a food processor and process 1 to 2 minutes to make a smooth paste. Chill for at least an hour. Serve with flatbreads, crackers, grilled fish, or chicken.

This can be refrigerated up to one week.

Makes approximately 2 cups

Chevre and Sun-Dried Tomato Cheesecake

This is a fabulous savory cheesecake that serves a crowd. Silky chevre cheese, herbs, and a ribbon of sun-dried tomatoes make this both elegant and unique. Serve slivers of this delicacy with water crackers or hunks of fresh sourdough along with vegetable crudités to offset the creamy fare. Bring this to your next potluck or brunch and you'll be a legend.

Soda Cracker Crumb Crust

1 ½ cups fine soda cracker crumbs
¼ cup Parmesan cheese, grated
4 tablespoons unsalted butter, melted
½ teaspoon garlic powder

Cheesecake Filling

1 cup (or small jar) oil-packed, sun-dried
    tomatoes
1 ½ pounds cream cheese, softened
8 ounces Chevre
½ cup whipping cream
1 teaspoon salt
1/8 teaspoon pepper
1 teaspoon minced garlic
1 tablespoon minced parsley
4 eggs
¼ cup all-purpose flour
2 cups shredded cheese, either Brick or
    Monterey Jack

Preheat the oven to 350 F.

Line a baking sheet with parchment paper. Spray a 9-inch springform pan with nonstick cooking spray.

For the Soda Cracker Crumb Crust, place cracker crumbs, cheese, butter and garlic powder into

the crust the prepared pan and toss with a fork to combine. Press the crumb mixture into bottom of the pan. Bake to toast the crumbs, 15 minutes.

Meanwhile, drain the sun-dried tomatoes and then place them in a small bowl. Cover with boiling water and let them plump for 5 minutes. Drain and dry in paper towels; put the tomatoes in a food processor and pulse to make a paste. Set aside.

For the Cheesecake Filling, in a mixer bowl, cream the cream cheese with the chevre, cream, salt, pepper, garlic, parsley, and shredded cheese.

Add the eggs, blend well, and then fold in the flour. Scrape bowl sides and bottom to combine evenly. Spoon half the mixture into the prepared pan. Dollop half of the sun-dried tomato paste on top. Repeat with remaining batter and sun-dried tomato paste. Swirl with a knife. Place the pan on the prepared baking sheet.

Bake until just set, 35 to 50 minutes. Chill overnight before unmolding and serving. Serve in thin wedges with crackers or chunks of sourdough bread.

Serves 16–20, depending on portion size

Nippy Cheddar and Roasted Garlic Cheesecake

This is a delight of sharp cheddar cheese served up in a savory, creamy cheesecake with hints of roasted garlic and herbs—a party pleaser.

Roasted Garlic
1 large bulb garlic
Olive oil

Crust
1 ½ cups finely ground soda cracker crumbs
¼ cup grated Parmesan cheese
4 tablespoons unsalted butter, melted

Cheesecake Filling
1 ½ pounds cream cheese, softened
1 teaspoon salt
1/8 teaspoon pepper
2 teaspoons Dijon mustard
1 tablespoon minced parsley
4 eggs
½ cup whipping cream
2 cups shredded sharp orange cheddar
2 cups shredded sharp white cheddar
½ cup all-purpose flour

Preheat the oven to 425 F. Place the bulb of garlic in a shallow, small baking dish, drizzle with the olive oil and roast until softened, 20 to 30 minutes. Remove the garlic from the oven and reduce the oven temperature to 350 F. When the garlic is cool enough to handle, squeeze the cloves from the skin and mash with a fork.

To make the crust, line a baking sheet with parchment paper. Spray a 9-inch springform pan with nonstick cooking spray. Place the crackers, Parmesan cheese, and butter in the pan and toss with a fork to combine. Press crumbs into pan, place the pan on the prepared baking sheet, and bake for 15 minutes or until lightly browned or toasted.

To make the Cheesecake Filling, in a mixer bowl, cream the cream cheese with the salt, pepper, mustard, and parsley. Add the roasted garlic and then blend in the eggs and cream. Finally, add the cheddar cheeses and flour and mix to combine. Scrape bowl sides and bottom to combine evenly and then spoon into the prepared pan. Place the pan back on the baking sheet.

Bake until just set, 35 to 50 minutes. Chill overnight before unmolding and serving. Serve in thin wedges with crackers, cold green grapes, and toasted walnut halves. Serve with wedges of black bread, crostini, or fine crackers.

Serves 16–22, depending on portion size

Herbed Cheeses in a Crock

I love things that are both easy and snappily gourmet style. This oil- and-herb laced cheese starter fits the bill. Any semisoft, white cheese (Feta or Chevre) will do nicely. This makes a perfect hostess gift.

1 ½ pounds white cheese such as Feta or Chevre, cubed
Juice of one lemon
½-1 teaspoon each dried basil, oregano
Salt, pepper
4–6 garlic cloves, smashed
1 cup canola oil
¼ cup olive oil

In a clean 16-ounce jar (such as a mason jar or a decorative jar), combine the cubed cheese with the herbs, lemon juice, salt, pepper and garlic. Drizzle the oils over the top to cover the cheeses. Refrigerate for 3 to 4 days.

To serve, remove the cheese, letting the excess oil drizzle off into the jar. Serve with organic sourdough, French, or multigrain bread, whole-wheat crackers, or vegetable crudités.

Serves 10-14

Bake Brie in Filo with Cranberries

This is a classic that is also quick, easy and satisfying. It takes just minutes to create a buttery bundle, filled with oozing, warm Brie all topped with a vibrant, scarlet dash of cranberries. Provide pear or apple wedges or hunks of French bread for dipping.

4 sheets filo dough
¼ cup, approximately, unsalted butter, melted
1 8-ounce wheel Brie cheese
2-4 tablespoons cranberry sauce (homemade or canned)

Finishing Touches
Apples, pears, sliced
Crostini or French bread

Preheat the oven to 375° F. Line a baking sheet with parchment paper.

Brush each filo sheet with some butter and stack them on top of each other on the baking sheet. On the last layer, position the round of cheese, spread on the cranberry sauce. Gather the filo sheets around the cheese and press slightly to seal. Brush with more butter.

Bake 20 to 25 minutes until golden brown. Pull open with a fork, and serve warm.

Serves 6–8

Beer Batter Onion Rings

Nothing beats crisp and zesty homemade onion rings! Prepare the batter the night before or at least several hours ahead. Serve with a nice rib steak and green salad for a great bistro supper.

2 eggs
2 tablespoons oil
1 ¼ teaspoons salt
1 cup flat beer
2 cups all-purpose flour
¼ teaspoon baking powder
1 teaspoon garlic powder
1 or 2 very large Bermuda or Spanish onions

Canola oil for deep frying

In a medium bowl, for the batter, whisk together the eggs, oil, salt, beer, flour, and garlic powder until the batter is smooth and thin. Let the batter stand, covered, at room temperature for at least 4 hours, or refrigerate it overnight. Remove from refrigerator one hour before using.

Slice the onions about ¼- to ½-inch thick and separate into rings.

Fill a deep pot, such as a wok, or a deep fryer two-thirds full of canola oil and heat to 360 F. If you don't have a thermometer, test the oil temperature by dropping a little batter in. It should immediately begin to sizzle. Dip onion rings, a few at time, in the batter. Fry until golden brown on both sides. Drain on paper towels.

Serve immediately or keep warm by placing on a wire cookie rack on top of a cookie sheet in a 275 F. oven.

Onion rings can also be frozen and reheated in toaster oven as needed.

Serves 2

Artichoke Pesto

This is a bold, zesty and totally gourmet tasting satisfying dip. Makes a great gift too.

1 12-ounce can artichokes

2 medium garlic cloves
¼ cup pimento-stuffed olives
2 tablespoons finely minced onion
1 tablespoon capers
1 tablespoon fresh lemon juice
¼ teaspoon black pepper
Salt
2–3 tablespoons olive oil

Drain the artichokes and place them in a food processor with the garlic, olives, onion, capers, lemon juice, pepper, salt, and olive oil. Pulse once and then process to make a coarse paste.

Chill and serve with flatbreads, focaccia, or fine crackers.

 Keeps refrigerated 7-10 days.

Serves 4–6

Cranberry, Vidalia Onion and Apple Salsa

Great with Thanksgiving turkey or week night turkey burgers, or alongside a homey roast chicken.

¼ cup minced red onion
½ cup minced Vidalia onion
3 tart apples, cored and diced (you can peel them or leave the skins on)
2 tablespoons dried cranberries, minced
2 teaspoons minced fresh cilantro
1 hot pepper, such as Scotch Bonnet, seeded, finely minced
1 tablespoon red wine or balsamic vinegar
2 teaspoons apple cider vinegar
1 teaspoon light olive oil
1 teaspoon sugar
Pinch salt

In a medium bowl, mix the onions with the apples, cranberries, cilantro, hot pepper, vinegars, olive oil, sugar and salt. Combine well.

Refrigerate at least 2 hours before serving.

Makes about 2 cups (Keeps a week, refrigerated)

Golden Corn Fritters

Nothing compares to a tender, crispy, slightly sweet golden corn fritter. This is a summery morsel that that is almost addictive. Serve the fritters in a basket as a special appetizer or as a side dish and watch them disappear.

3 eggs, separated
1 ½ cups canned or freshly shucked corn kernels
½ cup all-purpose flour
1 tablespoon stone-ground cornmeal
1 tablespoon sugar
½ teaspoon salt

Canola oil for frying

Finishing Touches
Confectioners' sugar or maple syrup

In a medium bowl, beat egg yolks until light, about 2 to 3 minutes, and then stir in the corn, flour, cornmeal, sugar, and salt to make a soft batter. In another bowl, whip the egg whites until stiff and glossy. Fold in one third of the whites to lighten the batter. Then gently fold in the remaining whites.

Fill a Dutch oven or deep fryer about two-thirds full with canola oil and heat it to 375 F. Drop in dollops (I use a small ice cream scoop) of the batter and fry until golden. Drain on paper towels. Place on a baking sheet, cover lightly with foil and keep warm in a 250 F oven.

Serve in a basket dusted with confectioners' sugar or drizzled with warm maple syrup.

Serves 4

Baba Ganoush or Eggplant Caviar

In summer, I grill the eggplants for this recipe on the outdoor barbecue. In winter, I cover the eggplants in foil and grill them over the gas burners of my stove, turning them until the eggplants are softened and the outer skins get charred. Of course, a regular oven is fine for grilling eggplants. My trick is to add a touch of liquid smoke for that charred taste. This is a gorgeous, heavenly silky dip.

2 medium eggplants
¼–½ cup canola or light olive oil
¼–1/3 cup tahini or sesame seed paste
1 tablespoon finely minced onion
2–4 teaspoons cumin
½–1 teaspoon coriander
2–4 drops hot sauce
1/3 cup fresh lemon juice
¼–½ teaspoon liquid smoke, optional
2–3 large garlic cloves, crushed
1–1 ½ teaspoons salt, or to taste
¼ teaspoon pepper

Finishing Touches
Minced parsley
Minced tomatoes
Minced red pepper

Preheat oven to 450 F.

Prick the eggplant with fork tines. Place on a baking sheet that has been lined with foil. Bake the eggplant until the skin turns black or very dark brown and juices begin to ooze. Cool well and peel away (and discard) skin. Chop coarsely by hand or in a food processor, and then add the oil, tahini, onion, cumin, coriander, hot sauce, lemon juice, liquid smoke (if using), garlic, salt and pepper. Taste and adjust seasonings as needed. Chill until ready to serve.

Garnish with minced parsley, tomatoes, and red pepper and serve as an appetizer or spread, with dark bread wedges, crackers, or pita.

Serves 4

Retro Vegetable Dip in a Bread Bowl

This is brunch food, Saturday afternoon food, or if you're asked to bring something to a potluck, the perfect centerpiece nibble. Essentially, it's a vegetable dip in a hollowed-out rustic bread. The hollowed out bread bits are the "dippers" you use for enjoying the dip. Then you can eat the bread bowl it came in!

Bread Bowl
One large round bread such as Italian bread, black pumpernickel, or sourdough.
1/3 cup olive oil

Vegetable Dippers
Raw vegetables such as cut up (or baby) carrots, mushrooms, broccoli, cauliflower, etc., cut into bite-sized pieces

Filling
1 1/3 cups sour cream or plain yogurt
1 1/3 cups mayonnaise
1 10-ounce package frozen chopped spinach, thawed and drained
1 5-ounce can water chestnuts, minced fine
2 tablespoons finely minced parsley
2 tablespoons finely minced onion
1 ½ teaspoons finely minced fresh dill
1 package dry vegetable soup mix (such as Knorr)

Preheat oven to 375 F.

Slice the top off of the bread to use as a cover or lid. Hollow the bread out, reserving the inside for dipping. Line a large baking sheet with parchment paper.

Paint the hollowed bread inside and out with the oil and place on a baking sheet. Bake until crusty, about 15 minutes. Remove from the oven and set aside.

For the filling, in a medium bowl, mix the sour cream, mayonnaise, spinach, water chestnuts, parsley, onion, dill weed and soup mix and blend well. Refrigerate for at least an hour to allow the flavors to meld.

When ready to serve, set out bread pieces and raw vegetables. Fill the hollowed bread with dip. Place reserved bread cover on top. (Leftover serving bread "bowl" can be eaten when the dip is gone.

Serves 6–8

BBQ Roasted Garlic Peppers

For a smoky taste, grill over the barbecue. Peppers can also be roasted in a 450 F oven or broiled over a gas burner. This is one of those repertoire recipes that is simply delicious and great, stuffed in sandwiches.

6 large green peppers (or a variety of green, red, yellow, and orange)

Marinade
¼–1/3 cup white or balsamic vinegar
3 large garlic cloves, crushed
½ teaspoon salt
Pinch sugar
¼ teaspoon pepper
2/3 cup vegetable or olive oil
2–4 drops liquid smoke, optional

Prepare the grill or preheat the oven to 450 F. Prick the peppers all over with a fork. Grill as close to the heat source as possible, turning and rotating the peppers to evenly char (blacken) them on all sides. Peppers should be thoroughly blistered and scorched. Place peppers immediately in a plastic bag and close, allowing peppers to sweat for 15 to 20 minutes. Meanwhile, make the marinade.

For the Marinade, in a medium bowl, combine vinegar, salt, garlic, sugar, and pepper and then stir in oil and liquid smoke. Remove the charred bits from the peppers and cut them into strips about ½ inch wide. Leave the core and seed sections intact—this is the best part.

Toss the pepper strips and cores in the marinade. Using a slotted spoon, transfer the peppers to jars or storage containers and spoon the marinade over them to cover. Serve as an appetizer, in salads, or with cold roast beef and hot mustard.

To store the peppers, refrigerate 2-3 weeks.

Serves 4–6

Old-Fashioned New York-Style Potato Knishes

There are many versions of this standard pastry wrapped mashed potato entrée. This is a traditional Jewish delicacy and as good as any knishes you get from a New York food truck. In a hurry? Use prepared mashed potatoes and store-bought puff pastry; you'll still have outstanding knishes.

Dough

5 cups all-purpose flour
2 ½ teaspoons salt
¼ cup sugar
1 teaspoon baking powder
1 cup warm water
3 eggs
¾ cup canola oil

Filling

3 tablespoons oil
2 large onions, finely diced
2 cups mashed potatoes *
Salt, pepper

Finishing Touches

Egg, lightly beaten

* Prepare the mashed potatoes your usual way— salt, pepper, milk, butter, etc. If using boxed mashed potatoes, prepare 6 servings worth. Line one or two baking sheets with parchment paper.

For the dough, in a food processor or large mixer bowl, add the flour, salt, sugar, baking powder, water, eggs, and oil and mix until a soft dough forms. Wrap and refrigerate the dough while preparing the filling and sautéing the onions.

For the filling, in a medium nonstick fry pan, heat the oil and sauté the onions over low heat until well softened and gently browned, 20 to 30 minutes. Cook them slowly so they don't crisp.

Prepare mashed potatoes as per your preference. Season the potatoes with salt and pepper and then fold in the sautéed onions.

Preheat the oven to 350 F.

Divide the dough in two. On a lightly floured work surface, roll out each half to a 12- by 12-inch rectangle. Smear half of the mashed potatoes on one rectangle of dough and roll it up into a log. Cut into 10 to 12 pieces. Repeat with remaining dough and mashed potatoes.

Turn cut side down and press slightly down, gathering outer edges slightly inward to round edges (you can even slightly squish the knish inwards to its center for a more traditional 'knish' shape)

Place on the parchment paper-lined baking sheet. Spray the knishes with nonstick cooking spray and then brush with the beaten egg. Bake until golden brown, about 30 to 40 minutes.

Makes 2 dozen

Empanadas

You can make these calzone-shaped treats with prepared pie dough or pizza dough and either bake or fry them. Fillings can vary from sweet to savory. Empanadas are found throughout Latin America, with widely varied fillings depending on where you go. Adobo seasoning is available in Latin food stores or online. Alternatively, you can also use a combination of onion powder, chili powder, salt and pepper.

Dough

3 cups all-purpose flour

1 ½ teaspoons salt

4 teaspoons sugar

1 cup vegetable shortening or lard

1 egg, optional

4–6 tablespoons ice water

Filling

2 medium onions, chopped

2 tablespoons oil

1 pound lean ground beef

1 clove of garlic, peeled and mashed

1 teaspoon cumin

Salt, pepper

Dusting garlic powder

3 tablespoons Adobo seasoning

5 eggs, hard boiled, finely minced

1 cup pimento-stuffed olives, finely minced

Egg Wash

1 egg

1 egg yolk

For the dough, place the flour, salt, and sugar in a food processor and blend briefly. Break in the shortening or lard and pulse to make a grainy mixture. Add the water and egg and pulse to make a rough dough. On a lightly floured work surface, knead the dough to make it cohesive. Wrap and refrigerate for at least 2 hours or up to 3 days.

For the filling, in a medium nonstick skillet, sauté the onions in oil until softened, about 5 to 8 minutes. Brown the meat, adding the garlic, cumin, salt, pepper, garlic powder and Adobo seasoning. Remove from the stove and place in a bowl. Toss the meat with the eggs and olives.

Preheat the oven to 350 F. Stack two baking sheets together and line the top one with parchment paper.

For the egg wash, in a small bowl, whisk egg and egg yolk together.

To fill the empanadas, roll out the dough to ¼ inch thick or a bit thinner. Cut in circles of 5 to 6 inches in diameter. Place 2 tablespoons or so of the meat filling onto one half of the circle. Brush egg wash around the edges of the circle. Fold over to make a half moon shape and press the edges with the tines of a fork to seal. Place the pastries on the sheet, brush each with egg wash, and poke some holes with a fork to allow steam to escape.

Bake until nicely browned, about 25 to 35 minutes.

Makes 2–3 dozen, depending on size

CHAPTER THREE

Soup's On!
Hot Stuff Coming Through

Oddly, it was Ludwig van Beethoven who is quoted with, "Only the pure in heart can make a good soup." I agree (and I also happen to like his music). For a pastry chef, I have put in more than my share of culinary flying hours creating and cooking up a symphony of amazing soups.

As fate would have it, when I first began in food professionally, despite my pastry chef training and the job mandate I was also frequently pressed into service in the other side of the kitchen. The "other side" was the *non*-baking side, the cook's side. It was the domain of chopped onions, the reception area for the daily produce order, salad prep and main plates place. It was a world alive with the scent of garlic and onions and something sizzling in oil. In short, it was a totally different world from the calm of the one of flour, vanilla, and butter that I usually resided in.

But more often than not, the "other side" implored the resident baker for assistance.

"Help, the soup tastes like water!" was an urgent plea I heard often. There I would be, in the bakery or pastry kitchen mixing muffins or breads and I would be frantically yanked away to rescue the cooks (in what were usually startup restaurants). I was flattered and more than capable; if you know how to fiddle with vanilla and lemons (i.e. you know your flavors), you can create magic with soup. Pretty soon, I became adept at tweaking humongous drums of soup into flavorful bouquets.

Meat-based or vegetarian, I soon learned new and applied all sorts of my own chef's tricks of the trade, fixing or otherwise rescuing pallid soups or inventing new ones. It is far easier to make a great formula from the start than to tweak 40 quarts of an unseasoned mongrel broth. Pretty soon, I had a varied and large repertoire. And as time goes on, I like soup more than I ever did.

Soups are so satisfying. They are low-tech, feed crowds, and are as flavor-packed as they are densely nutritious.

"What You Need Is a Bowl of Hot Soup!"

Who doesn't agree that the true meaning of the term *comfort food* refers to specifically to soup? Who would contest that hot soup is the tonic, regardless of the season and regardless of the impulse that creates the appetite for it? *"What you need is some hot soup"* is an expression that is *so* part of our collective awareness that the phrase should be soup's official tagline.

As comfort food and as a comfort itself, nothing beats a hot bowl of chicken soup or vegetable or hearty beef and barley soup. No matter how tepid your palate, there's always *something* from the repertoire of soup to tempt you. Whether vegetarian or bolstered with beef or chicken stock, soup knows what you need even when you don't.

There are soups that are dinner party starters, and then those that are made for sneezes and sore bones, heartbreak, or fatigue or when you need might need a hug or want to remember the special feeling, and recipe, of a loving parent or grandparent. Memory food! No wonder soup comforts. There are soups for when you decide you are going to eat light ("the diet starts tomorrow") or have an unsettled tummy. There are soups to cuddle up with, soups to sip with a special someone with candlelight, and then those soups that you want to slurp on your own, curled up with *When Harry Met Sally* and all you want is soup, a handful of crackers, quiet time alone, and yes, more….hot soup.

And if it's not comfort you are after or think you need, why then, in essential culinary terms, soup plays the role of the elegant starter to a fine meal. A great soup rounds things out just so and teases the diner with what's up ahead. Leek soup, a fine vegetable potage, or French bistro-style onion soup—you choose. Or consider Hot and Sour or cumin-laced Coriander and Carrot soup to announce an Asian-themed dinner party. A country chicken soup might precede grilled cheese sandwiches in a diner-style meal that becomes a banquet. Soup is renowned for bumping up even a simple meal into a feast. Soup sets the tone; it also effectively shears off the brute force of appetite (so you can slow down and enjoy the rest of the dishes) and/or allows the host to finish some last tasks in the kitchen while diners are stalled, so to speak, on that soup first course. In fact, forget the meal. Supply a hunk of cheese, a warm loaf of bread, tack on a salad and that pot of homemade soup and presto! Soup *is* a more than a meal; it's a banquet.

What's also nice about soup is that while most soups like simmer time, they don't all need hours and hours on the stove. You can plan ahead, of course, especially for bean soup or a classic chicken soup, but just as often, there's a soup recipe in this collection that takes but minutes of prep time and under an hour on the stove. Moreover, many a soup (by recipe or new invention) is simply made with simple ingredients, generally things most pantries and fridges stock: potatoes, barley, carrots, a can of corn, onion, a beef bone, a leftover turkey carcass. Almost anything can become part of a great soup.

The How-To's of Becoming a Soup Legend

There are but a few things great soup demands:

- Taste, fragrance and flavor
- Best quality ingredients

Contrary to the notion that inferior quality ingredients "might as well" go into a soup, superb soup demands quality from the get-go. Sure, vegetables that are not picture perfect are fine enough in soup and a bruised eggplant won't hurt it a bit for you can always trim away random cosmetic bumps and such, but that's about it. Don't even think about using rotting, mushy vegetables, or flavorful-less, un-fragrant ingredients, and inferior spices (dried *or* fresh) in a stock pot and still expect ambrosia to result. It's a qualitative process from its beginning steps all the way through.

The second criterion to great soup and it primarily appeal is its aroma as it cooks - that amazing flavor and fragrance of fresh soup. Stellar soups are known by the great flavor they waft while they are simmering and then emphatically deliver once they are done. For arguments sakes, all recipes being equal, this is a matter of knowing how to balance sweet, sour, salty, and spicy, along with the thematic flavors at hand, i.e. the very theme flavor and even its roots (what country, what tradition, what occasion?). *This* is the flavor litmus test. Nothing marks the fine palate of the chef as his soup signature, and a great soup can make one legend.

Best Quality Ingredients
Spices and Herbs

All in all, many soups are called but few, as they say, are chosen. Great soups start with great recipes and to those great recipes, you do have to learn to add that discretionary touch of taste and adjust. What assists you is relying on the freshest ingredients possible, especially in terms of fresh herbs and fine spices. If using dried herbs or spices make sure they are fragrant and fresh. Never assume a year-old jar of oregano is anything other than finely ground grass! Even dried herbs, which look like they last forever, *do* have a shelf life. And there are also varying qualities of such things, so smell, inhale, taste. Don't just dump stuff into the stock pot.

Salt and Pepper to Taste?

Salt and pepper are so ubiquitous in recipes, especially for soup, that we can take them for granted. But there are so many salts: Kosher, sea salt, and *fleur de sel,* and there are also pungent Tellicherry peppercorns. Since soup is all about savory perfection, take the time to consider which salt and which pepper you want to cook with. It does make a difference! If you are in any doubt about which is best, just do your own taste test. Grind up some salt or have a few fine salts on hand and taste them. You will be amazed at the character in this ancient ingredient (which in fact, was once used a currency, such was its value). The same is true for quality pepper. Try a supermarket pepper alongside a specialty spice house pepper. Invariably, it is the difference between freshly ground pepper "dust" and totally vibrant, brisk, zest, heat, and spice-laden great pepper. Soups, like everything else in the wholesome food kitchen, are a series of little things done well. So make sure the basic elements, like using spring water in your soups, are chosen with care. It is those touches that separate good homemade soup from superlative elixirs and gourmet potions!

Pure Spring Water

For the best soups, I always use spring water. Spring water is chemical free and tastes best in soups, where the fresh clean taste of pure water marries well with the flavors of the ingredients to make the best possible soup. There's no aftertaste of chlorides or anything else to interfere with the flavors and seasonings in your soup. Since water is the major and certainly integral ingredient in soup, why not start with the best possible choice in wholesomeness?

Broth, Chicken, Beef, or Vegetable

For the sake of convenience, these soup recipes call for prepared chicken or beef broth (when they call for broth). I use liquid broth, under the Bovril name, available in supermarkets here in Canada, but there are other comparable brands, such as Campbell's and Swanson in the United States. Sometimes I find all-natural, broth pastes in jars that are far better quality and feature more flavor and less salt. You can substitute canned broth or powder or cubes of

broth (also called bouillon), as long as you know the conversion, i.e. a can of chicken broth is probably one cube, or one tablespoon powder broth with hot water, or 1 tablespoon liquid broth concentrate to one cup of water. When in doubt, hold back on fully salting the soup until you see how salty the soup is, given broth, regardless of its source is often quite salty. Of course, if you have quarts and quarts of fresh, homemade (frozen) broth, that would be ideal.

Quick Fixes in Packets and Cans

And now, having just talked about fresh ingredients and fresh broth, I offer a detour or something else—dry soup mixes. Of course, in all cooking, and particularly in soup making, nothing beats from-scratch recipes, fresh ingredients, sumptuous spices, and a slow hand. But there are days when nothing beats, for nostalgia the least, a can of mushroom soup or that Warhol famous can of tomato soup. Who can argue with the comfort of the familiar and convenient? Not me. But you also, always have the option of tweaking the can or the packet. For instance, cream of tomato soup can take some added real cream, or a spritz of fresh parsley, rosemary, basil leaves, and dash of white wine. Canned cream of mushroom welcomes a lashing of wine or brandy or generous anointing of Worcestershire and a goodly amount of freshly ground black pepper. Canned minestrone or vegetable can also be enlivened with red wine, a shower of imported Parmesan cheese, or garlic croutons and made *au four,* in the oven. You can pop a can of cream of chicken soup, in a pinch, into a home-assembled chicken pot pie (leftover chicken, prepared pie dough, pre-chopped carrots, cans of corn and peas), or oven-poach fish fillets in cream of celery soup with added fresh herbs. Or add a can of tomato soup to cabbage borsht or homemade minestrone to bulk up the body and tomato flavor notes. Even a plain old can of chicken broth goes uptown if you load it with Asian vegetables, fresh ginger, garlic, lemon grass, cilantro, and slivers of chicken.

Dry soups, such as Knorr, for example, fortify cream soups or make something exceptional even better, as in **The Best Vegetable Soup Ever**. Or with some white wine, poultry spices, and a packet of mushroom or cream of chicken dry soup mix, you have near-instant gravy for a family turkey or Sunday night roast chicken dinner.

See? The trick is not to make convenience foods (or soups) the enemy but to take the best of what they offer (convenience, some flavor, texture, thickening agents) and partner them up with fresh flavors or make them an integral part of your recipe. They might speed things up on days when you are short on time or offer another dimension of flavor that is simply tasty, but also, simply…fun!

Roux the Day for Best Cream Soups
A roux is a base from which chefs make gravies, sauces such as classic béchamel, and creamy soups. A roux can be used to hold a soup together (even a light cream soup). Essentially it is the liaison preparing chefs use to fuse things. A roux is made by warming up butter (or sometimes olive oil) and cooking a few tablespoons of flour in it. It makes a light brown, crumbly mixture that is really just evidence that

the flour (which will bind things later) is cooked, versus being "raw"—both in flavor and raw on the palate and our tender stomachs (tummies don't like raw flour). Milk or broth is then added to the browned flour to finish up the roux. The biggest tip I can give you here is to use a good whisk to keep the flour and fat from lumping up too much and then, again, to whisk in the milk or milk and broth, and ensure it is smooth. This is not the time to use a wooden spoon; a whisk is *the tool* for the job.

Soup and Stock Pots
A great soup needs a great broth or soup pot to match your efforts. Make sure the pot you have fits the amount of soup you are making. You don't want a small pot that might result in overflow; nor do you need a 12-quart vat for a small batch of carrot soup. There are dedicated soup pots such as the proverbial stock pot, which is somewhat conical in shape, or a classic Dutch oven that comes in a variety of materials. One of my favorites is cast iron or enamel-over-steel pots. Whatever you do, invest in a quality stock pot.

Heavy Bottomed Stock Pots Best Choice in Bean Soups
Bean soups, pea soups, soups with barley in them, and some potato soups are wonderful, but those starchy ingredients are also the first things to burn when making or reheating a great soup. This is the perfect rationale to invest in a superb stock pot, a classic 8-quart, or a 6-quart, in a 3- or 5-ply sandwich or cladded-style pot. A cladded pot is one that features several layers of metal, cladded or sandwiched or otherwise fused

together. You can get 5-ply stainless steel or stainless steel with a copper or aluminum core for remarkable conduction, even cooking, and stable heat. In essence, cladded pots use a few fused layers of metal of one sort of another (or in conjunction with each other) for best looks and performance). The technology has changed making all ranges of cookware incredibly high performance.

Whatever you do, don't waste time, ingredients or money on a pot that is thin stainless steel or thin aluminum with but a veneer of copper to it. These might have been the workhorses of your grandmother's kitchen, and are suitable for things like chicken soup, but so many great and better pots are now out there.

Start Your Blenders or Rev Your Processors or Immersion Blender? What's Your Preference?

I like those Waring retro-looking blenders—you know, those glass ones with the brightly colored bases—to look at, but nothing beats a great KitchenAid or Oster for superb soup blending. For sheer performance, a commercial blender, slightly more costly, is unbeatable, but there are plenty of great, high performance, and well-priced blenders out there, perfect for making soups, especially cream soups, as smooth as silk. Personally, I prefer two other appliances for creaming soups. I use a large food processor (make sure you have a large one; you don't want to have overflow with hot soup leaking out between the work bowl and base). Alternatively, I use another implement, similar to what chefs use in hotel and restaurant kitchens, called an

immersion blender. It is a small appliance— Braun, KitchenAid, Cuisinart, and other companies make them—and it features a long stem with a rotary blade on the end. Without skipping a beat or necessitating the transfer of hot soup to another vessel (blender or food processor), you simply pulverize the soup as it sits on the stove. Do take care to go slow to avoid splattering hot soup.

Serving the Soup

Lastly, *how* you serve soup says you care. It says you care not only about what is *in* the bowl, but about your dinner. It says you are mindful of aesthetics and know, as most chefs do, that people eat first with their eyes. So make soup pretty. Find nice bowls and shiny soup spoons that gleam. Source out little breadboards to offer warm, mini breads to go with your soups, and tiny crocks of butter to serve nearby. Add rustic or elegant finishing touches (a swirl of sour cream in Russian Borsht or a fine sprig of rosemary in the potage). Check out estate sales or housewares stores for a tureen or use a classic Le Creuset pot to both simmer and serve the soup.

Soup Storage

Most soups freeze well. You can freeze soup in single-portion containers or in larger ones, if you want a rainy day batch of soup for a company or family meal.

For liquid, broth-y soups such as traditional chicken soup, you can actually freeze the whole kit and caboodle in the stock pot (providing you won't be needing that stock pot for a month or two). This is a really great trick if you know you will want a big batch of Tortilla Soup or Chicken Soup on hand for a crowd or a traditional holiday dinner when you always serve a certain soup. On the day of serving, just take the pot out of the freezer, pop the soup on the burner perhaps and hour or two beforehand, heat the soup on low until it is piping hot and ready to eat, just in time for the first course. I find this really a boon when serving a dinner with a few courses; the soup is done and photo-shoot ready, and it's one less item on my menu to be concerned about.

Soups generally refrigerate well for five or six days, allowing you to store it for a few days' servings or ladle out a lunch time portion or two.

Bean soups reheat well but do need care. Starchy soups with beans or potatoes in them prefer slow and gentle reheating so they do not scorch. You might have to add some broth or water, too, as the soups reheat to loosen the thickened soup, as is the case with bean, corn and potato-based soups.

Bistro-Style Butternut Squash Soup

Is this a bisque or a soup? It's creamy and slightly thick, but refined and elegant at the same time. Squash soup recipes are plentiful, but this one is flavor-tweaked to perfection. It's so creamy and yet there's not a drop of cream in it. This is gourmet chef-quality soup, but it will be exclusively your creation to crow over as you ladle it out.

1 small butternut squash, peeled and diced
    (about 6 cups diced squash)
1 medium sweet potato, peeled and diced
2 tablespoons olive oil
1 tablespoon unsalted butter
Salt, pepper
Pinch of nutmeg
¼ teaspoon coriander
¼ teaspoon cumin
1–2 teaspoons curry powder
Juice of ½ lemon
3 cups chicken broth
3 cups milk

Finishing Touches
Minced cilantro
Lime zest

In a 6-quart stock pot, heat the oil and butter, add the squash and sweet potato, along with a dusting of salt, pepper and nutmeg and gently sauté over low to medium heat. If the vegetables stick, add a bit of water. Sauté to soften the vegetables, stirring often, about 15 minutes. Stir in the coriander, cumin, curry, lemon juice, broth, and milk. Simmer over low heat until the vegetables are completely soft, about 30 to 45 minutes.

Purée in a food processor or using an immersion blender until smooth, about 2 minutes or as long as it takes.

Return the soup to the pot and add some minced cilantro and lime zest. If soup needs thinning, add equal parts of chicken broth and milk.

Serves 6–8

Carrot-Coconut Soup with Fried Kale

The kale is just an extra touch (and you can also use spinach) on top of this sublime soup of carrots, cream of coconut and the sultry spices of cumin, and coriander. Coco Lopez, available in Latin food markets, is a common brand of cream of coconut, used in this recipe.

1 medium onion, finely minced
2–3 tablespoons vegetable or light olive oil or
    unsalted butter
2 pounds carrots, peeled and thinly sliced (about
    5 cups)
Salt, pepper
4 cups chicken broth
2 cups cream of coconut (Coco Lopez is a
    common brand)
1 cup milk (2% or low-fat)
2–4 teaspoons curry powder
½–1 teaspoon cumin
½–1 teaspoon coriander
1 teaspoon minced fresh ginger
1 teaspoon minced fresh garlic
Pinch ginger
Pinch cardamom
1 tablespoon fresh lime juice
2 tablespoons minced cilantro
Pinch crushed red pepper flakes, optional

Fried Kale
4–6 large kale leaves
2 tablespoons light olive oil

In a 6-quart stock pot, heat the oil and sauté the onions over low heat until softened, about 10 minutes. Add the carrots and season with salt and pepper. Sauté the carrots until softened, about 15 minutes. Add the chicken broth, cream of coconut, milk, curry, cumin, coriander, ginger, garlic, cardamom, and lime juice. Heat to a gentle simmer and cook until the carrots are completely softened, about 30 to 45 minutes.

Transfer to a food processor or use an immersion blender to purée the soup. Return to the pot, if needed, season to taste, and add the cilantro.

Before serving, heat the kale leaves in a nonstick pan in 2 to 3 tablespoons of oil. Fry until crisp. Drain on paper towels, crumble, and garnish individual bowls of soup.

Serves 6–8

Ribolitta or Rustic Tuscan Vegetable Soup

Peasant soup that is pure sunshine and a Nona's love in each spoonful. This is not just vegetable soup, this is an operetta. Don't throw out the heel or final hunk of Parmesan cheese; it's just one of the things that make this soup outstanding. This recipe calls for dried beans, which need a few hours' (or overnight) soak. Kale can be quite sandy, so be sure to wash it very well.

3–4 tablespoons olive oil
1 cup chopped celery
½ cup chopped onion
1 cup finely chopped carrots
3–4 garlic cloves chopped
1 28-ounce can Italian San Marco tomatoes, ground
6–7 cups chicken broth
1 large heel of Parmesan cheese
2 bay leaves
Pinch of thyme
½ cup diced pancetta or chorizo, optional
3 tablespoons red wine
2–3 cups diced stale Italian bread
1/3 cup dry beans such as cranberry or cannellini, soaked for a few hours
1 cup chopped zucchini
1 cup thinly sliced cabbage
Salt, pepper
4–5 cups shredded or chopped black kale (or Swiss chard)
1 cup chopped squash (acorn or butternut)

Finishing Touches
Grated Parmesan cheese

In a medium skillet, over medium heat, heat the oil and sauté the celery, onion and carrots until softened. Stir in the garlic and cook for just a few minutes to soften. Transfer the mixture to a 6-quart stock pot. Add the ground tomatoes, chicken broth, Parmesan cheese, bay leaves, thyme, pancetta or chorizo, if using, red wine, bread, beans, zucchini, cabbage, salt, and pepper.

Simmer over very low heat until the beans are cooked, 2 to 3 hours. About 30 minutes before serving, fold in the kale and squash and simmer a bit longer.

Serve with Parmesan cheese on top.

Serves 5–6

The Paprika Restaurant Cream of Cauliflower Soup

A local quaint little Hungarian restaurant, aptly called The Paprika, used to serve a specialty cauliflower soup such as this one. Possibly they had other soups on the menu but this seems to be the only soup everyone ordered. On a busy night, they must have gone through 60 quarts of this simple, satisfying, best-way-I-know-to-use-up-fresh-cauliflower soup starter. If you have some sweet, imported Szeged Hungarian paprika (it comes in that pretty red and white tin), that would be the perfect touch.

1 large cauliflower, cut into small chunks and florets
2 tablespoons unsalted butter
1–2 tablespoons canola oil
1 medium onion, finely diced
1 medium garlic clove, finely minced
1 large potato, peeled and diced
1 small carrot, finely shredded
3 tablespoons all-purpose flour
1 tablespoon sweet paprika
Salt, pepper
¼–½ teaspoon dill weed or fresh dill
1 cup warm milk
4 cups chicken broth
2 cups water
½ cup sour cream

In a large pot, blanch the cauliflower in boiling water about 5 minutes, remove and drain.

In a 6-quart stock pot, melt the butter with the oil over medium heat. Add and sauté the onions to soften, 5 to10 minutes. Add the garlic and cook briefly to soften, but not brown, 2 to 3 minutes. Add the cauliflower, potato, and shredded carrots. Cook to soften the vegetables, about 12 to 15 minutes.

Sprinkle on the flour and paprika, salt, pepper and the dill weed, tossing to cook the flour, about 5 minutes. Slowly drizzle in the milk, chicken broth, and water and stir.

Cook over low heat for about 45 minutes. Purée in a food processor or use an immersion blender. Return to the pot, if needed. Using a wire whisk, briskly whisk in the sour cream. Adjust seasonings and serve

Serves 6–8

Old World Italian Restaurant Minestrone Soup

Some restaurants make this a pretty ho-hum recipe which is a pity when can be as exceptional as this recipe. Don't forget when cooking with dried beans and legumes, they must be presoaked.

1 cup mixed dried beans (Romano, kidney, fava, pinto, cranberry, etc.) soaked
3 tablespoons extra virgin olive oil
4 medium garlic cloves, crushed
½ cup diced onions
1 ½ cups sliced carrots
1 cup chopped celery
2 cups finely shredded cabbage
1 cup diced zucchini
1 28-ounce can crushed tomatoes
16 cups water
¼ cup whole dried peas
1 to 3 tablespoons pearl barley
1 ½ tablespoons salt (or taste)
1 teaspoon pepper
½ teaspoon original Tabasco
¾ teaspoon garlic powder
2 bay leaves
2 teaspoons oregano
2 teaspoons basil
1 teaspoon celery seed
¼ cup minced fresh parsley
¼ teaspoon crushed red pepper
2 tablespoons red wine
¼–½ teaspoon citric acid or sour salt or 2-3 tablespoons lemon juice

Finishing Touches
Grated Parmesan cheese, cooked bite-sized pasta, garlic croutons

A few hours or the night before, cover the beans with water and let soak. Drain before using. Discard soaking liquid.

For the Chicken Broth, in an 8-quart stock pot, add the oil and sauté the garlic, onions, carrots, celery, cabbage, and zucchini until the vegetables are softened, 8 to 10 minutes. Add water, crushed tomatoes, beans, peas, barley, salt, pepper, Tabasco, garlic powder, bay leaves, oregano, basil, celery seed, parsley, red pepper, wine and citric acid. Simmer, partially covered, for 2 to 3 hours until the beans are soft. Adjust seasonings.

Serve with fresh Parmesan cheese, cooked bite-sized pasta, and homemade garlic croutons or Italian bread.

Serves 12–16

Restaurant-Style Chicken Vegetable Soup

You know that soup you get at cafeteria- or family-style restaurants? It is hugely comforting but offers just a bit more edge than home-style? This is the one. Kosher salt is a must in this heartwarming soup.

Chicken Broth

1 5–6 pound chicken, cut into 8 parts
Water just to cover the chicken (approximately 12–14 cups)
1 large stalk celery with a few leaves
1 large carrot, cut into 3-inch chunks
1 medium onion, trimmed, peeled, and cut in four
2 garlic cloves, peeled and smashed
2 parsnips, peeled and cut in chunks
1/3 cup finely minced parsley
4 sprigs fresh dill, broken in half
2 teaspoons whole peppercorns
Salt (preferably kosher), pepper
1 teaspoon onion powder
¼ teaspoon celery seed powder
½ teaspoon garlic powder
¼–½ teaspoon marjoram
¼–½ teaspoon thyme
¼–½ teaspoon rosemary
2 tablespoons white wine, optional
2–3 tablespoons pearl barley

Soup Add-Ins

2 cups diced carrots
1 cup finely slivered cabbage
2 cups diced celery
2 cups frozen peas
1–2 tablespoons minced fresh parsley
2 cups cooked, flat egg noodles or cooked pasta shape of your choice

For the broth, rinse the chicken well. Place chicken in an 8-quart stock pot. Cover with cold water that should just cover top of chicken.

Bring the water to a boil, skimming off any foam that forms. Reduce to a medium simmer. Add the celery, carrot, onion, garlic, parsnip, parsley, dill, peppercorns, salt, pepper, onion powder, celery seed powder, garlic powder, marjoram, thyme, rosemary, wine and barley. Partially cover the pot and simmer for 2 hours. When the soup is done, let it cool until you can strain it.

Strain the soup into a clean pot. Reserve choice pieces of meat (bones removed) for chicken salad or chicken pot pie. Discard the bones and other solids from the broth.

When reheating the soup add the Soup Add-Ins, i.e. diced carrots, cabbage, celery, peas, and a bit more minced parsley. If adding cooked noodles, add them last, just before serving.

Let simmer until barley is tender. (The fresh vegetables are to be eaten in the soup as it simmers whereas the discarded ones were used to flavor the soup, i.e. they did their duty for the cause).

Serves 8–12

August Moon Cauliflower Chick Pea Soup

Nothing is as satisfying as the simple flavors of garden fresh cauliflower, a hefty offering of sweet paprika and some protein-packed chick peas. The trick of only pureeing half the soup results in a soup that is staying and hearty but a homogeneous glop. Ancho spice is a sweet pepper spice that looks like, but is not as hot as chilli and is somewhat smoky and sweet. Online spice stores sell it if you don't see it in your local supermarket. You can also omit it and will still find this an extraordinarily good soup. Why August Moon? I invented on a full August moon night.

1 medium cauliflower, coarsely chopped (about 6 cups)
¼ cup olive oil
1/2 cup water
1 medium onion, finely minced
3 garlic cloves, finely minced
1 medium carrot, finely shredded
1 rib celery, finely chopped
¼ cup parsley, finely minced
Salt, pepper
2 tablespoons paprika
1 tablespoon smoked paprika
1 teaspoon ancho spice
2 tablespoons chicken stock liquid concentrate
7 cups water
2 tablespoons white wine
Juice of one lemon
Half 19 ounce can chick peas

In a large stock pot, over medium heat, sauté the cauliflower in the olive oil and water to soften cauliflower, about 15 minutes, adding a bit more water if necessary to allow cauliflower to cook.

Add in onion, garlic, carrot, celery and dust with salt and pepper and stir another 3-5 minutes. Then stir in the sweet paprika, smoked paprika and ancho spice to coat the mixture and toss for a few minutes. Add the chicken bouillon concentrate, water, wine and lemon juice.

Cook over very low heat, 45-55 minutes. Remove half the soup and puree in a food processor. Return to the pot and stir to blend and adjust seasonings. Stir in chick peas and simmer 20-30 minutes.

Serves 6-8

Shaika Lentil Soup

I once had a business meeting at a delightful outdoor café on an early spring day. My lunch date had this soup and as soon as I got a whiff of its tantalizing aroma, I knew I had to recreate it. What's nice about this soup is that it is not heavily spiced in one tradition or another, but instead is an appetizing flavor crossroad that is between gourmet health food café and Eastern Europe. It's sublime.

3 tablespoons olive oil
3 garlic cloves, finely minced
1 small onion, finely minced
1 ½ cups finely minced carrot
½ cup finely minced celery
1 cup dried lentils, either brown or green
2–3 tablespoons barley
3 tablespoons tomato paste
Small handful celery leaves, coarsely chopped
1 bay leaf
2 cups spinach (or Swiss Chard), coarsely chopped
1 teaspoon garlic powder
1 teaspoon onion powder
1 tablespoon paprika
¼ cup minced parsley
Salt, pepper
8–10 cups chicken broth or vegetable broth
1 tablespoon balsamic or red wine vinegar
1 tablespoon lemon juice
2 small potatoes, peeled and cut in ½-inch dice
½ cup canned chickpeas
1 cup small cubes (peeled) squash (any type, optional)

In a 6-quart stock pot, heat the olive oil and sauté the garlic, onion, carrots, and celery for 5 to 10 minutes on low.

Stir in the lentils, barley, tomato paste, celery leaves, bay leaf, spinach, if using, garlic powder, onion powder, paprika, parsley, salt and pepper.

Stir briefly and add the chicken broth, vinegar, and lemon juice. Simmer 1 to 2 hours, until the barley is almost softened. Add the potatoes, chickpeas, and squash, if using, and simmer until the barley is softened. Season to taste and serve.

Serves 5–6

Cream of Asparagus Soup

Most cream soups begin the same way: simmered vegetables go into a broth where eventually they are amalgamated with a cream base, usually made with a classic roux (a flour and fat mixture), to which cream or milk (or both) is added . The soup is seasoned, the softened vegetables and creamy broth get puréed, and voila: fabulous cream soup in any flavor you choose! You can play around with the herbs and spices but this is just the quintessential recipe that suits whatever vegetable you prefer or what the local market or season offers.

4–6 cups chopped asparagus
¼ cup finely minced celery
2 tablespoons finely minced onion
2 tablespoons unsalted butter
2 tablespoons olive oil
2 tablespoons flour
Salt, pepper
1 teaspoon finely minced garlic
4 cups chicken or vegetable broth
2 tablespoons white wine, optional

Roux
3 tablespoons flour
2 tablespoons unsalted butter
1 ½ cups milk
¼ cup whipping cream
1–2 teaspoons each, fresh parsley, chives, or
basil, as desired, and to taste
¼–½ teaspoon *herbes de Provence*

In a 4- to 6-quart stock pot, sauté the asparagus, celery ,and onion in the butter and olive oil to soften, about 15 - 20 minutes, over low heat. Stir in the 2 tablespoons of flour, and season with salt, pepper and garlic. Add the chicken broth and wine and simmer for 15 minutes. Cool slightly, transfer to a food processor or blender, and purée.

In the same stock pot, make a roux by cooking the flour with butter for about 3 minutes. Slowly stir in the milk and whipping cream and whisk to make a smooth, creamy broth. Add the pureed vegetables and whisk, over low heat, to blend. Adjust salt and pepper and stir in herbs as desired.

Serves 5–6

Thai Hot and Sour Soup

This is the Asian chicken soup remedy, good for what ails you and even when nothing seems like it will help – this soup is the tonic. You can vary the add-ins and feel free to make this vegetarian or leave out the tofu if it's not your thing. What's important to know is that this soup is only as good as the broth used. The sesame oil called for is the toasted, full-flavored type.

Marinated chicken

1 cup shredded, Chinese-style smoked chicken or leftover roast chicken
6 tablespoons soy sauce
1 tablespoon toasted sesame oil
1 tablespoon cornstarch

Soup

3–4 Chinese dried black mushrooms or fresh mushrooms
6 cups homemade or canned, quality prepared chicken broth
1 8-ounce cake firm tofu, cut into small cubes
½ cup minced bamboo shoots
1 teaspoon salt, or to taste
White pepper
1 teaspoon sugar
2 tablespoons soy sauce
2 tablespoons rice vinegar
2 teaspoons sesame oil
1 teaspoon finely minced garlic
1–2 teaspoons finely minced fresh ginger
1 2-inch chunk lemongrass, slivered or minced
1 tablespoon cornstarch dissolved in ¼ cup water
1 egg, beaten
2 green onions, finely chopped
¼ cup coarsely minced fresh cilantro
Hot chili oil, to taste, optional

For the Marinated Chicken, shred the chicken and set aside in a bowl. In another bowl, whisk the soy sauce, sesame oil, and cornstarch and pour over the chicken. Let marinate for 20 minutes.

Reconstitute the dried mushrooms by soaking them in warm water for 20 minutes. Rinse, and cut into thin pieces.

In a 6-quart stock pot, bring the broth to a high simmer. Add the tofu, bamboo shoots, and mushrooms. Return to a boil and add the shredded chicken along with the marinade.

Stir in the salt, pepper, sugar, soy sauce and vinegar, sesame oil, garlic, ginger and lemon grass. Taste and adjust seasonings.

Mix the cornstarch and water. Slowly pour the cornstarch mixture into the soup, stirring while it is being added. Let the broth come back to a boil. As soon as it is boiling, remove the broth from the stove.

Slowly drop in the beaten egg, stirring all the while and then add the green onion, cilantro, and the white pepper to taste. Drizzle with chili oil if desired.

Serves 4–5

Potage Bonne Femme

Rustic and yet refined, this is the quintessential French cream of vegetable soup. It's the sort of soup you had in a fine restaurant. It is delicate, flavorful and oh-so-French.

2 tablespoons unsalted butter
1 cup sliced leeks
2 cups finely chopped onion
1 cup diced carrots
5 cups peeled, diced potatoes
8 cups boiling water
½ cup frozen peas
4 generous cups shredded cabbage
1 garlic clove, minced
2 ½ cups half-and-half or light cream
½ cup finely chopped parsley
1–2 teaspoons each fresh chervil and chives
½ teaspoon, or to taste, *herbes de Provence*
3 tablespoons white wine
Salt, pepper

In a 6-quart stock pot, melt the butter and sauté the leek, onion, carrots, and potatoes over low heat, about 10 minutes. Make sure you do not brown the onions. Add the water and gently simmer for 30 minutes. Add the peas, cabbage, and garlic and simmer another 20 minutes.

Let the soup cool a bit and then slowly drizzle in the half-and-half. Add the parsley, herbs and wine. Season with salt and pepper.

In a food processor or using an immersion blender, purée the soup. Return to the pot, if needed, and reheat over low heat. Season with salt and pepper to taste.

Serves 6–8

Santropol Famous Ratatouille Soup

Santropol is a socially conscious, community-oriented Montreal landmark and the place to go for the most flavorful soups and mile-high sandwiches. This is one of their trademark soups that is as epic as soups come.

¼–1/3 cup olive oil
1 medium onion, finely diced
3–4 garlic cloves, minced
1 medium or large eggplant, peeled, trimmed, and diced
1 large red or green pepper, diced
4 medium small zucchini, diced
1 large carrot, peeled and finely diced
6–8 cups water
1 28-ounce can ground Italian plum tomatoes
1 28-ounce can plum tomatoes, finely diced (juice reserved)
½ 10-ounce can condensed tomato soup
1 tablespoon chicken broth concentrate
3 tablespoons red wine
¼ teaspoon each oregano and basil
¼ cup minced fresh parsley
½ teaspoon crushed red pepper
½ teaspoon garlic powder
½ teaspoon onion powder
Salt, pepper

Finishing Touches
Parmesan cheese for serving

In an 8-quart stock pot, sauté the onion, garlic, and vegetables over low heat in olive oil to soften, about 12 to15 minutes. Add the water, canned tomatoes with their juice, canned tomato soup, broth concentrate, wine, oregano, basil, parsley, red pepper, garlic powder, onion powder, salt, pepper and simmer for about an hour.

Serve with freshly grated Parmesan cheese or garlic croutons on top.

Serves 12–16

Italian Wedding Soup

Oh my goodness—how good can soup get? A robust and rustic meal in a soup bowl: delicately seasoned little meatballs of minced chicken breast and a touch of smoky pancetta, all gently poached in chicken broth enlivened with fresh greens and a shower of imported parmesan. Mangia bueno!

Meatballs

1 small onion, finely grated
1/3 cup finely minced Italian parsley
1 egg
1 teaspoon finely minced garlic
½ teaspoon onion powder
½ teaspoon garlic powder
1 teaspoon salt
1/8 teaspoon pepper, or more to taste
1 slice fresh white bread, crust trimmed, bread torn into small pieces
½ cup grated fresh Parmesan
1 pound ground chicken breast
½ cup cooked pancetta, finely minced (about 2 ounces before cooking)

Soup

12 cups chicken broth
½ pound curly escarole, coarsely chopped
3 cups coarsely chopped spinach
2 eggs
4 tablespoons freshly grated Parmesan, plus extra for garnish
Salt, pepper

To make the meatballs, place the onion, parsley, egg, garlic, onion powder, garlic powder, salt, pepper, and bread in a medium bowl. Fold in the cheese, ground chicken, and pancetta. Shape the meat into small balls and refrigerate until needed.

For the soup, in a 6- or 8-quart stock pot, bring the broth to a gentle boil and then add in the meatballs, escarole, and spinach and simmer until the meatballs are cooked and the greens are tender, about 8 minutes.

Whisk the eggs and cheese in a medium bowl to blend. Gradually drizzle the egg mixture into the broth, stirring gently with a fork to form thin strands of egg, about 1 minute. Season the soup with salt and pepper to taste.

Ladle the soup into bowls and serve garnished with additional Parmesan cheese, if desired.

Serves 8–10

Tex-Mex Tortilla Soup

There are countless versions of this wonderful soup. It's only all the more appealing because it's also a simple soup to make. This is rustic and heartily Latin and given the heft of sliced chicken breast simmering in the zesty broth, this is also a complete meal in a bowl.

¼ cup olive oil
8 ounces boneless chicken breast, cut into strips
Salt, pepper
1 small onion, finely minced
3 garlic cloves, finely minced
6 cups chicken broth
4 cups canned, coarsely chopped, or stewed plum tomatoes in their liquid
1 tablespoon cumin
1 tablespoon chili powder
1 tablespoon minced dried hot chili, preferably chipotle

Add-Ons
6 corn tortillas, cut into strips
Oil for frying
Chopped hard-cooked egg
Crumbled or small chunks of orange cheddar or Monterey Jack cheese
Canned corn
Minced cilantro
Thin slices of lime or lemon
Sour cream
Avocado, cut in chunks

In a nonstick skillet, heat 2 tablespoons of the oil and sauté the chicken breast. Set aside. Add the rest of the oil and sauté the onion. Then add the garlic and sauté over low heat to brown slightly. Place the chicken and onions in a Dutch oven or stock pot. Dust with salt and pepper and then cover with the chicken broth. Add the tomatoes, cumin, chili powder and chili and simmer for 30 minutes.

Fry the strips of corn tortilla in hot oil and drain.

To serve, ladle the soup into bowls and top each with fried tortilla strips and garnishes, as desired.

Serves 6–8

The Best Vegetable Soup I Ever Made

Once, on a cold, winter day, I happened on one of those delis that offer everything from 99-item salad bar choices to take-out entrees, cold beer and exotic fruits. I had no time but to buy some soup which I gulped as I sped off. One sip and I was hooked. My own version of that great soup calls for fresh ingredients as well as "a package of this" and "a can of that," but it is mostly scratch soup made with fresh vegetables. It's the best, fastest and most satisfying soup you will ever have.

12 cups of water
¼ cup extra virgin olive oil
2 ½ teaspoons salt
2 large garlic cloves, finely minced
1 large or two medium leeks, thinly sliced
1 large carrot, thinly sliced
1 large rib of celery, thinly sliced
2 tablespoons freshly minced parsley
Pepper
1 10-ounce can condensed tomato soup
2 packages dry soup mix *
1 potato, diced
2 tablespoons pearl barley
1 tablespoon chicken bouillon concentrate
¼ cup white or red wine

*For the dry soup mix, you can choose something like Knorr brand in Cream of Cauliflower or Broccoli and one such as Cream of Vegetable, Carrot or Leek.

Place everything in an 8-quart stock pot and bring to a boil. As soon as the soup reaches a boil, reduce the heat to low so that soup is just simmering. Let simmer, almost covered, for 45 minutes to an hour, stirring occasionally.

Serves 8–12

Old-Fashioned Chicken Soup with Matzoh Balls

The classic deli style chicken soup, a proven cold remedy is the quintessential comfort soup. Kosher chicken makes this unbelievably good, but if you can't find it in a kosher section of a regular supermarket (Costco often sells it in the frozen food section) or a kosher food mart, then a grain-fed or a quality regular chicken will still shine in this wonderful elixir. If you don't have matzoh meal, you can substitute ground up unsalted soda crackers.

Soup

1 4–5 pound chicken, preferably kosher
Water just to cover chicken (approximately 12–14 cups)
1 medium or large onion, peeled and trimmed
2 large stalks celery with a few leaves left on
2 large carrots, cut into 3-inch chunks
2 parsnips, peeled and cut in 3-inch chunks
1/3 cup finely minced parsley
4 medium sprigs fresh dill, broken in half
2 teaspoons whole peppercorns
Salt, pepper

Matzoh Balls

4 eggs
4–6 tablespoons chicken broth or water
4 tablespoons vegetable oil
1 cup matzoh meal
¾ teaspoon salt
Pepper

Rinse the chicken well under cold, running water. Place the chicken in an 8-quart stock pot. Add enough cold water to just cover the chicken. Bring water to a boil, skimming off any foam that forms. Reduce to a medium simmer. Add onion, celery, carrots, parsnips, parsley, dill, peppercorns, salt and pepper. Cover partially and simmer for 2 hours. Stir in additional dill and parsley

to finish the soup (1-3 tablespoons each). When the soup is done, let it cool somewhat and then strain it. Strain out all of the solids, including the vegetables and fat. Select the choice chicken pieces and return them to the broth (reserve the rest of the cooked chicken for chicken salad or chicken pot pie). Discard the remaining solids. If you like, add one cup each fresh, finely diced carrots and celery and a bit more minced parsley.

For the matzoh balls, whisk the eggs with the chicken broth (or water) and oil to blend. Add the matzoh meal, salt, and pepper. Cover the mixture and refrigerate for 1 hour.

To poach the matzoh balls, fill a 6-quart pot with water and 1 teaspoon of salt. Bring to a rolling boil. Drop rounded spoonfuls of the matzoh ball mixture into the boiling water (the mixture will make anywhere from 12 to 20 matzoh balls, depending on the size). Reduce the heat, cover pot, and simmer over low heat for about 30 minutes. Gently remove the matzoh balls from the water, drain, and set aside.

To serve, ladle the soup into bowls and add the matzoh balls.

Serves 8 –12

French Restaurant Onion Soup

When is the last time you had real French onion soup au gratin? This classic and dramatic soup is over the top - brazen with caramelized onions in a rib-sticking beef broth, and crowned with toasted sourdough bread, heavy with a trio of melted cheeses.

2 tablespoons unsalted butter
2 tablespoons olive oil
8 large onions, peeled, trimmed, cut into ¼-inch slices
Salt, pepper
2 garlic cloves, finely minced
4 teaspoons Dijon mustard
3 tablespoons red wine
1 teaspoon Worcestershire sauce
¼ cup brandy or cognac, optional
10 cups beef broth

Topping*
3 to 4 thick slices of toasted sourdough bread (one slice per serving)
Olive oil
1 cup shredded Gruyère cheese
1 cup shredded medium or mild Cheddar cheese
1 cup grated Parmesan or shredded American Asiago

*Each bowl requires a slice of bread and a few tablespoons of the cheeses.

In a large nonstick skillet, heat butter and oil. Add onions and sauté them over very low heat, stirring often, until they are deeply caramelized, 20 to 30 minutes. Dust with a bit of salt and pepper. When almost done, stir in the garlic, mustard, wine, Worcestershire sauce and brandy or cognac.

Heat the broth in a 6- to 8-quart soup pot. Stir the onion mixture into the hot broth and allow to simmer for 30 to 45 minutes.

To serve, preheat broiler. Brush the toasted bread lightly with olive oil. Place the soup bowls on a large baking sheet and fill generously with soup. Place a slice of bread on top of each and cover it with the cheeses. Place the bowls under the broiler and heat until the cheese melts and begins to brown a bit. Serve immediately.

Serves 3–4

Pub-Style Cream of Mushroom Soup with Worcestershire

Leave the can opener in the drawer! Once you make this, you will never go back to canned cream of mushroom again. The Worcestershire sauce and touch of wine, not to mention tons of fresh sautéed mushrooms, makes this special.

2 pounds mushrooms, sliced
1 cup diced onions
2–3 tablespoons butter, preferably unsalted
3 tablespoons all-purpose flour
4 cups hot water
2 cups hot milk
¼–½ teaspoons black pepper
Salt, pepper
1 tablespoon minced parsley
1 tablespoon Worcestershire sauce
2 teaspoons tamari
2 tablespoons white wine, optional

In a 6-quart stock pot set over low heat, sauté the mushrooms and onions in butter until softened. Sprinkle on the flour and cook another 3 minutes. Slowly add the hot water and hot milk and stir. Add the pepper, parsley, Worcestershire sauce, tamari and salt. Simmer for about 45 minutes, making sure the soup does not boil or milk will curdle. In a food processor or using an immersion blender, purée the soup until smooth.

Adjust seasonings and whisk in the wine, if using. Reheat over very low heat just before serving.

Serves 4–6

Country Pea and Carrot Soup

This is a nice change from ham bone-based pea soups. Serve with country bread and butter. One of my all-time favorite, go-to recipes, it's fast, easy, and satisfying (and vegetarian if you use olive oil), and I consider this soup a gift from my mother-in-law, Shirley Posluns.

12–14 cups water
2 cups yellow or green split peas
¾ cup finely minced onions
2 cups sliced carrots
1 cup chopped celery
¼ cup minced fresh parsley
1–2 tablespoons fresh dill or 1 tablespoon dried dill
1–2 teaspoon celery seed
2–4 teaspoons salt
¾ teaspoon pepper
3 medium potatoes, peeled and cubed
2 tablespoons unsalted butter, optional

Finishing Touches
Cooked noodles (any shape or size), optional
Fresh minced parsley

Fill a pot with the water and add in the peas; bring to a boil. Skim off any foam and reduce the heat to low. Add the onions, carrots, celery, parsley, dill, celery seed, salt and pepper. Cook until the peas are softened, about 45 minutes, then add potato cubes and continue cooking over low to medium heat until the peas are completely dissolved, about 90 minutes more.

Stir the soup to blend. Adjust seasonings, stir in butter, if using, and reheat over very low heat just before serving.

Serves 12–14

Atwater Market Roasted Garlic Tomato Soup

This outdoor, market-inspired soup is brilliant-hued and flavorful. It features fresh garlic, roasted garlic, sun-dried tomatoes, and herbs to make this light cream soup sing. Very ripe plum tomatoes from the garden are best, but any in-season tomatoes are fine.

¼ cup olive oil, or more, as required
2 large heads or bulbs of garlic, separated but not peeled
6 very large tomatoes, tops off, washed and diced coarsely
2 tablespoons minced onion
3 small garlic cloves, peeled and minced
1 small red pepper, finely minced
4 drained, sun-dried tomato halves, minced
2 tablespoons minced parsley
Pinch dried basil
Salt, pepper
1 tablespoon white wine
1 tablespoon balsamic vinegar
2 cups chicken or vegetable broth
2 tablespoons unsalted butter
2 tablespoons flour
1 cup light cream or half-and-half

Finishing Touches
Fresh minced parsley

In a small, heavy-bottomed skillet, heat the olive oil. Add the garlic and brown over the lowest heat possible for 20 minutes or so, until the garlic is golden and soft. Be careful not to scorch it. Remove the garlic from pan and save the oil for later. Drain the garlic on a paper towel before removing the garlic flesh from the paper-y shell. Garlic is easily squeezed out once softened by simply snipping a bit of the outer husk or dry casing.

In a 6 or 8-quart heavy bottomed pot, heat a few tablespoons of the oil left over from roasting the garlic. Over low heat, slowly sauté the diced tomatoes, onions and minced garlic for 7 to 10 minutes. Add the red pepper, sun-dried tomatoes, parsley, basil, salt, and pepper and Sauté until the tomatoes dissolve, about 10 minutes on medium or low, then stir in the wine, vinegar, and broth. Simmer for 10 minutes.

In a food processor, process until soup is well blended, about 1 to 2 minutes.

Meanwhile, over low heat (in the same pot, no need to wash it out), heat the butter and whisk in the flour to make a pasty mixture or roux. Add one cup of half-and-half to make a smooth sauce. Stir in the hot, pureed tomato mixture and blend well to make a cream soup, over low heat. Simmer for 10 minutes, adjust seasonings, and dust with parsley.

Serves 4–6

Classic Cream of Leek and Potato Soup

Is this mere soup? Mais non, this is truly a potage. No matter what you think about leeks, to cook with them is to acquire instant sophistication. Yet in this soup, leeks are as comforting as they are a class act. Leeks, shallots, chives, and potatoes get sautéed and "brothed" to perfection in this smooth, but chunky celebration of a garden soup.

1/ 4 cup unsalted butter (or half olive oil)
2 large garlic cloves, finely minced
6 large leeks, trimmed and sliced into ½-inch slices
2 scallions, finely diced
1 tablespoon minced chives
2 large shallots, finely minced
4 medium potatoes, peeled and diced
3 tablespoons flour
2 cups warm chicken broth
3 cups warm milk
¼ cup white wine
2–4 tablespoons finely minced parsley
Salt, pepper

In an 8-quart stock pot, melt the butter. Sauté the garlic, leeks, scallions, chives and shallots until softened, over low heat, for about 10 to 15 minutes. Add the potatoes and sauté to soften them, another 15 to 20 minutes. Stir often and dust with salt and pepper. Dust on flour and stir to coat, 2 to 3 minutes.

Add the chicken broth, warm milk, wine, and parsley. Simmer over the lowest possible heat (or milk will curdle) 30 to 45 minutes Adjust seasonings.

In a food processor or using an immersion blender, purée the soup. Reheat over low heat. Add more salt or pepper, to taste, and serve.

Serves 8–10

Carrot, Ginger and Cilantro Soup

A flavorful, refreshing, and colorful soup that is the darling of many restaurants, whether a sandwich café or upscale bistro. Fresh ginger is best, but jarred, minced ginger works well. Fresh cilantro, otherwise known as fresh coriander, is a must and the hint of orange makes this more than a trend soup.

1 tablespoon vegetable oil
1 cup finely chopped onion
2 medium garlic cloves, finely minced
2 tablespoons minced ginger
1 medium potato, peeled and shredded
2 pounds baby carrots, trimmed and finely diced
2 cups water
2 cups chicken broth (vegetable broth or water)
1–2 tablespoons sesame oil
1–2 cups orange juice
Salt to taste
Pinch of white pepper
Pinch of crushed red pepper

Finishing Touches
Orange shreds or zest
Toasted sesame seeds
Minced cilantro

In a 6-quart stock pot or Dutch oven, over low heat, sauté the onions, garlic and minced ginger in oil just to soften (not brown), 8 to 12 minutes. Stir in the potatoes, carrots, water and broth. Bring to a slow boil, then reduce the heat and simmer to tenderize the carrots, about 20 minutes.

In a food processor or using an immersion blender, purée the mixture. Reheat over low heat, and stir in the sesame oil, orange juice (enough to make soup a soupy consistency), and seasonings. Adjust seasonings and serve garnished with orange zest, sesame seeds, and minced cilantro.

Serves 6

Cuban-Style Black Bean Soup

A hearty recipe, this soup takes well to different seasonings, but it shines with a smoky accent. Serve with hard rolls or homemade Cuban sandwiches for a feast.

2 cups dried black (or turtle) beans, pre-soaked
¼ cup vegetable oil
1 cup finely chopped onion
3 large garlic cloves, minced
¾ cup chopped celery
1 cup finely chopped carrots
16 cups water
2 bay leaves
1–2 tablespoons cumin
1 tablespoon oregano
1 tablespoon salt, or to taste
1 ½ teaspoons pepper
1–2 teaspoons liquid smoke
¼–1/8 teaspoon crushed red pepper
2 tablespoons unsalted butter, optional
¼ cup lime juice

Finishing Touches
Fresh minced parsley
Minced cilantro
Lemon or lime slices
Chopped egg or corn kernels

Place the beans in a plastic or ceramic bowl and cover with water. Soak overnight. Drain and discard soaking liquid.

In a 6- or 8-quart stock pot, sauté the onion, garlic, celery and carrots in oil to soften. Stir in the soaked beans, water, bay leaves, cumin, oregano, salt, pepper, 1 teaspoon of the liquid smoke, and crushed pepper. Bring to a boil, skim if necessary, and then simmer for several hours until beans are thoroughly mushy.

Remove the bay leaves. Using a slotted spoon remove about 1 cup of the beans from the soup and set aside. In a food processor or using an immersion blender, purée the remaining soup. Return the reserved beans to the soup. Adjust seasonings and add more liquid smoke, if needed. If the soup is too thick, stir in a bit more water. Stir in butter and lime juice. Garnish with parsley, cilantro, lemon or lime slices, chopped egg, or corn kernels.

Serves 12–16

Deli-Style Mushroom, Bean and Barley Soup

After Chicken Soup with Matzoh Balls, this is a deli staple. This is soul-warming, comfort soup.

½ cup dried lima beans
4 tablespoons (about ½ ounce) imported dried mushrooms
4 tablespoons butter or light olive oil
2 garlic cloves, finely minced
1 cup minced onions
½ cup chopped celery
½ cup finely chopped carrots
8 cups chicken or vegetable broth (or water)
½ cup pearl barley
Salt, pepper
1 tablespoon minced parsley
½ teaspoon paprika

Cover the beans with spring water in a medium bowl and let stand overnight or for at least a few hours. Meanwhile, in a small bowl, soak the mushrooms in approximately ½ cup water for 30 minutes.

In a 6- or 8-quart stock pot or tall Dutch oven, melt the butter or heat the oil over low heat and sauté the garlic, onion, celery, and carrots until lightly browned and softened. Stir in the broth or water, barley, soaked lima beans, salt, pepper, parsley, paprika and the mushrooms along with their soaking liquid. Bring to a boil, and then reduce heat to simmer.

Cook, stirring occasionally, until the beans are cooked, 3 to 4 hours.

Adjust seasonings and add more water if soup has thickened too much. You may have to add more water and spices later if the soup thickens after being refrigerated, as well. Reheat soup over low heat just before serving.

Serves 6–8

Russian Sweet and Sour Cabbage Soup

This soup can scare away the chill of winter in one ruddy, gorgeous spoonful. Pair it up with Russian black bread or a fragrant loaf of pumpernickel bread for a meal that is as hearty as you could wish for. To make this meatier, add chunky beef bones or some strips of flank steak or leave it vegetarian.

11 cups water, divided, plus more as needed
3 tablespoons canola oil
1 medium cabbage, finely shredded
2 medium onions, thinly sliced and minced
1 large garlic clove, finely minced
1 large carrot, finely minced
1 cup light brown sugar
¼–½ cup white sugar
1 28-ounce can crushed tomatoes
1 10-ounce can condensed tomato soup
2 tablespoons tomato paste
1–2 tablespoons caraway seeds, optional
1–2 tablespoons salt
½–1 teaspoon pepper
1–2 teaspoons citric acid (or sour salts or 3 tablespoons lemon juice)

Finishing Touches
Sour cream or thick style Greek yogurt
Minced parsley
Caraway seeds

In a 12- to 16-quart stock pot, add about a cup of the water and the oil. Over medium heat, sauté the cabbage, onions, garlic, and carrot with the brown and white sugars until lightly golden and softened.

Stir in the remaining 10 cups of water, crushed tomatoes, tomato soup, tomato paste, caraway seeds, salt, pepper and citric acid, tartaric acid, sour salts, or lemon juice. Simmer on medium, reducing the heat to low as required, for 2 to 2 ½ hours.

Adjust seasonings and add additional sugar, salt, citric acid or lemon juice and caraway seeds for a more pronounced sweet and sour taste.

Serve with a dollop of sour cream or yogurt; dust with parsley and caraway seeds.

Serves 14–16

Indian Lentil Dhal

This soup is the classic Indian lentil soup you'll find in neighborhood Indian restaurants. It's not unbearably hot so no worries on that score. It's not hot but spicy; anyone would enjoy it. Try it once and it'll be in your repertoire forever. Super with warm naan bread and tandoori chicken.

1/3 cup light olive or canola oil
2 cups dried lentils, any color
½ cup diced onions
½ cup shredded carrots
1 medium tomato, diced
½ cup diced celery
1–2 garlic cloves, finely minced
¼ cup minced parsley
3–4 tablespoons curry powder
2 teaspoons coriander
1 tablespoon cumin
2 teaspoons turmeric
¼ cup fresh lemon juice
1 tablespoon salt, or to taste
10–12 cups water
2 tablespoons unsalted butter

Finishing Touches
Yogurt
Cooked basmati rice
Chopped fresh cilantro

In an 8-quart stock pot, over low heat, lightly sauté the lentils, onions, carrots, tomatoes and celery in oil for about 5 to 8 minutes. Add the garlic, parsley, curry powder, coriander, cumin, turmeric and lemon juice and sauté 1 to 2 minutes before adding the water and salt to the pot.

Bring to a gentle boil. Skim, if necessary, reduce the heat, and simmer until the lentils are tender, about 2 hours. Remove half the soup and purée it in a food processor or blender. Return the puréed soup to the main soup and stir to combine. Reheat over the lowest possible heat.

Adjust the seasonings, adding more water as needed for the desired consistency, and stir in the butter, if using. Serve with a dollop of yogurt and lemon slices and a spoonful of cooked basmati rice.

Serves 12–14

Village Vegetable-Lentil Soup with Asiago Cheese

Lakeside walks on a winter's day generally results in a hearty appetite for soup. Such was the case when I happened on a nook of a bakery in a small village near my home while out for a brief and nippy winter walk. Here is the soup as best as I can recreate the sheer fabulousness of it. I serve it topped with garlic bread rounds and a pile of Asiago cheese shavings. Pop it under a broiler for a few minutes until the cheese bubbles.

10 cups water
1 ½ cups dried green lentils
2 medium carrots, finely sliced
1 red pepper, diced
2 ribs celery, trimmed of leaves, finely chopped
1 small onion, peeled and finely chopped
3 garlic cloves, finely minced
1 12-ounce can corn
1 19-ounce can diced tomatoes
1 cup very finely chopped eggplant, optional
1 tablespoon liquid beef or vegetable broth concentrate
2 tablespoons red wine
¼ cup extra virgin olive oil
2 tablespoons minced parsley
1 tablespoon finely minced dill
1 ½ teaspoons garlic powder
1 teaspoon onion powder
1 tablespoon paprika
Salt, pepper
½ cup diced chorizo, optional

Finishing Touches
Toasted garlic bread
Asiago cheese

Place the lentils and water in an 8-quart stock pot. Bring to a boil and reduce the heat to a simmer. Stir in the carrots, red pepper, celery, onion, garlic, corn, tomatoes, eggplant, wine, oil, parsley, dill, garlic powder, onion powder, paprika, salt and pepper. If using chorizo, add it after an hour.

Simmer the soup, stirring occasionally to ensure the lentils cook and soften, 45 to 90 minutes on very low heat. Check for seasoning, adding more salt or pepper as required.

To serve, ladle the soup into ovenproof bowls. On top of each portion, place a toasted slice of garlic bread and top it with cheese. Broil until the cheese melts.

Serves 8–12

Sweet Paprika Smokey Bean Soup or Bableves

A hearty pinto bean soup that sticks to your ribs. You can use almost any sort of dried beans for this soup and add one or two tablespoons of barley to make it a bit more rustic. When I make this soup without meat, I add a few drops of liquid smoke for flavor.

1 cup dried pinto beans
6 cups water
1 medium onion, finely minced
1 green pepper, diced
2 garlic cloves, finely minced
1 large carrot, thinly sliced
2 medium ribs celery, finely chopped
1 tablespoon sweet paprika
¼–½ teaspoon Liquid Smoke, optional
3–6 drops hot sauce
Salt, pepper
3 strips smoky bacon or 1–2 smoked sausages, optional
2 tablespoons butter or olive oil
3 tablespoons all-purpose flour
1 tablespoon vinegar

Place beans in a medium saucepan and cover by one inch with cold water. Bring to a boil and let boil gently for 12 to 15 minutes. Drain the beans.

Place the beans in a 4- or 6-quart pot. Add the 6 cups of water along with onion, green pepper, garlic, carrot, celery, paprika, liquid smoke, if using, hot sauce, salt and pepper. Bring to a gentle boil, reduce the heat, and let simmer until the beans are softened. Add the strips of bacon or sausages, if using, and simmer 20 to 30 minutes to develop the flavors. Remove the strips of bacon or the sausage.

In a separate skillet, make a roux by heating up butter or olive oil and adding the flour. Stir to cook the flour and allow it to thicken and brown. Stir the mixture into the warm soup, along with the vinegar. Adjust seasonings and add a touch more water, if necessary.

Serves 8–10

CHAPTER FOUR

Salad Days, Best of the Green Stuff

Sometimes I don't know what I'm in the mood to eat. Carbs or protein, sweet or salty, soft or crunchy? But I *always* seem to be in the mood for salad. Maybe that's because a great salad can be all those things: carbs, protein, sweet, salty, soft *and* crunchy. Whether I'm starved or only slightly hungry or any point in-between, salad hits all the right notes. It's a great appetite waker-upper, and just as soup is, a magnificent flavor magnet – almost anything goes in a creative salad. You can be inventive or go classic; salads can be modest afterthoughts, or if you invest in them, they can rise to a new level such as Asian Chicken Salad or Restaurant Style Chicken Caesar Salad, which are landmark events, or at the least, meal-makers. Treated with care, even garden greens and a squirt of fresh lemon can be a feast. Just make sure you use great oils, especially extra virgin olive oil, superb vinegar, (especially when using balsamic), wonderful sea salt and fresh ground

gourmet-quality pepper. Things will only go up from there. Salad days, however modest, can be the best days of all.

Salad Dressing Trick

This is not a recipe but a recipe trick that is just as crucial in your repertoire of salad knowledge and it's something I learned in pastry chef school that still makes so much sense. When you make vinaigrette, recipes usually say to add salt, spices, etc. to the oil. In other words, you mix vinegar and mustard and garlic (most often) and then blend in oil, spices, salt and pepper. The thing is, salt will *never* dissolve (nor dried herbs hydrate) in oil. The salt is there but stays suspended, so to speak, in the oil. It's like a fine grit (that fine grit used to be unwashed lettuce until they solved that). So, the trick is simple. The best way is to blend vinegar (or lemon juice), salt, pepper, mustard, and dried herbs (or fresh) together. That dissolves the salt at the least. Then blend in the oil —all at once or in a stream (with that faint hope we all have that it will emulsify). I was training as a pastry chef in hotel school when I learned this trick from the master chef of the *cook's* class who occupied the kitchen beside us. Therein my erroneous contention that a cook couldn't teach a baker anything lies - because years later, it's a trick that has stayed with me and served me well. It's the same trick that makes me write recipes that instruct you to add the salt to the water (where it can dissolve) in a pie dough versus directly into the flour (where it doesn't dissolve); same logic and same success via better technique.

No Fat, All Flavor Vinaigrette

The trouble with most store-bought low or non-fat salad dressings is that they lack flavor. To make matters worse, these salad dressings, just like regular store-bought vinaigrette, unless they are cream style, have a tendency to separate. Moreover, making your own vinaigrette can get tiresome if you enjoy salad every day and lastly, salad is low in fat only until you add the dressing and then calorie hell breaks out. So what are you going to do? Hence, this wondrous recipe. This recipe is very low fat, robust of flavor, and has a magic ingredient that holds it (it's the honey mustard) so there's no separating –just sheer enjoyment..

1 cup honey mustard
¼ cup balsamic vinegar
¼ cup red wine vinegar
3 tablespoons water
3–4 garlic cloves, finely minced
½ teaspoon onion powder
1 teaspoon dried oregano
1 teaspoon dried basil
½ teaspoon salt
Pepper

Whisk together the mustard, vinegars, water, garlic, onion powder, oregano, basil, salt and pepper. Transfer it to a bottle, refrigerate (up to a month) and use it to dress salads whenever you like.

Makes 1 cup

Greek Restaurant Vinaigrette

I lured this out of a Greek restaurateur whose staff made 80 gallons of this every three days. It stays creamy due to the trick of slowly drizzling in the oil. For a bit of salad heaven, serve this superb vinaigrette on a chilled green salad, top with cubed tomatoes, feta cheese, black olives and a dusting of oregano.

¾ cup fresh lemon juice
¼ cup white vinegar
1 teaspoon pepper
1 tablespoon salt
1 tablespoon sugar
20 garlic cloves, finely minced
2 teaspoons dried oregano
2 ½ cups canola oil
½ cup olive oil

Process the lemon juice, vinegar, pepper, salt, sugar, garlic and oregano in a food processor. Drizzle in the oil(s) in a very thin stream until incorporated and the mixture thickens.

Makes 4 cups and keeps refrigerated 2 to 3 months

Variation
Use ¼ cup red wine vinegar or balsamic vinegar with ½ cup of lemon juice, or use ¾ cup red wine vinegar to replace all the lemon juice for a different sort of flavor.

Creamy Feta Dressing

I like this notion of combining the flavors of Greek Salad right into the dressing so the flavor is bold and coats every lettuce leaf.

4 ounces, about 1 cup, minced Feta cheese
¼ cup mayonnaise
½ teaspoon salt
Pepper
1 tablespoon lemon juice
1 tablespoon red wine vinegar
1 teaspoon oregano
½–¾ cup olive oil, plus more if needed

In a food processor, blend the Feta cheese with the mayonnaise until smooth. Add the mayonnaise, salt, pepper, lemon juice, vinegar, oregano and oil and blend until smooth, adding a bit more oil if required (for salad dressing consistency).

Chill, shake, and use on salad, especially Boston and romaine lettuce.

Makes approximately 1 cup

Layered Picnic Icebox Salad

What's easier for summer or picnics or anytime at all than an already bite-sized salad that serves up like a dream? No need to toss this garden extravaganza. You can fiddle with the ingredients as you like or add finely chopped bacon and smoked turkey for a Layered Cobb Icebox Salad. All you need is a clear serving dish (a glass trifle or salad bowl) to keep the visual drama.

Salad Layers
5 hard-boiled eggs, peeled and finely chopped
6 cups, finely chopped mix of green lettuces
½ cup sliced radicchio, finely chopped
1 head, Belgian endive, thinly sliced
1 medium cucumber, finely chopped
1 stalk celery, finely minced
1 cup shredded carrots
2 medium red peppers, finely chopped
4 medium tomatoes, finely chopped
1 small red onion, finely chopped
2 scallions, finely chopped
¾ cup black pitted olives, coarsely chopped
1 ½ cups (canned) boiled beets, finely chopped

Vinaigrette
¾ cup creamy onion or Italian dressing,
preferably homemade
¼ cup red wine vinegar
¼ teaspoon salt
1/8 teaspoon fresh black pepper
2 garlic cloves, finely minced
½ teaspoon mixed dried Italian spices
2 tablespoons olive oil

Finishing Touches
Minced parsley

Using a large serving dish or portable (Tupperware or Glad plastic dishes with cover) 2- to 3-quart dish, layer the ingredients in the order given: eggs, lettuce, radicchio, endive, cucumber, celery, carrots, peppers, tomatoes, onion, scallions, olives and beets. Using a plate, lightly press ingredients down.

For the vinaigrette, blend the salad dressing, vinegar, salt, pepper, garlic, spices, and olive oil in a small bowl with a whisk. Drizzle the vinaigrette over the salad, cover, and refrigerate for 4 hours or overnight. Dust with fresh parsley before serving.

Serves 6

Tuscany Bread Salad

Bread salads are popular these days and there are many varieties that bear this name. This is a salad that is definitely more than the sum of the parts.

Vinaigrette
3 tablespoons red wine vinegar
1–2 tablespoons balsamic vinegar
1 teaspoon salt
¼ teaspoon sugar
¼ teaspoon pepper
3 to 4 garlic cloves, finely minced
¼ cup olive oil
¾ cup canola oil

Salad
1/3 cup olive oil
3–4 slices Italian bread or rustic-style French bread
1 pound green beans, trimmed and steamed, warm
2-4 ounces prosciutto or pancetta, cooked
3-4 plum tomatoes, cubed
2 carrots, finely shredded
1 cup canned white pinto or kidney beans
1 small red onion, thinly sliced
½–1 cup Asiago cheese, shredded
4–6 cups mixed baby greens

Prepare the vinaigrette by combining the vinegars, salt, sugar, pepper and garlic in a medium bowl. Slowly drizzle in oils after and combine well. Set aside.

For salad, drizzle olive oil on the bread slices and bake at 350 F. for 12 to 18 minutes. Cool, and then break into pieces. Set aside.

In a large bowl, combine the green beans, prosciutto or pancetta, tomatoes, carrots, beans, onion, and cheese. Add the greens on top. Just before serving, pour on the vinaigrette and toss.

Serves 3–4

Asian Chicken Salad a la Ramen

Sure to please the most finicky eater—it's what to serve when you are having a brunch or lunch with friends. It is easy, fast, and serves up a relatively light bite that is still satisfying. Add a tablespoon of peanut butter if you like, or more hot sauce and ginger. This is such a good dish—it lasts for a few days in the fridge, is fresh and salad-y, and yet is packed with protein. You can even forgo the chicken and use roasted tofu for a vegetarian version.

Soy Marinade

½ cup soy sauce
2 tablespoons toasted sesame oil
1 tablespoon honey
3 garlic cloves, finely minced
2 tablespoons finely minced ginger or jarred ginger paste

Chicken

4 chicken boneless breasts, sliced horizontally in two
Canola oil

Salad

3 packets ramen soup and noodles, any flavor
2-4 tablespoons toasted sesame oil
1 large package cellophane noodles
6–12 cups of greens, such as Bok Choy, Romaine, Napa cabbage, radicchio
1 cup red peppers, slivered
1 ½ cups steamed, chopped broccoli
2 cups bean sprouts
2 cups sliced mushrooms
½ cup chopped scallions
1 can baby corn, drained and diced

1 cup coarsely chopped cilantro
2 tablespoons toasted sesame seeds

Peanut-Ginger Dressing

2/3 cup canola oil
½ cup rice vinegar
2 seasoning packets from ramen noodles
¼ cup soy sauce
2 tablespoons toasted sesame oil
2 tablespoons peanut butter, optional
½ teaspoon sugar
4 garlic cloves, finely minced
2 teaspoons minced ginger
2 tablespoons fresh lemon juice

For the Soy Marinade, in a large bowl, whisk together the soy sauce, sesame oil, honey, garlic and ginger paste. Add the chicken and toss to coat. Let chicken marinate one hour or longer (if more than an hour, refrigerate up to overnight). Drain chicken and discard marinade.

For the Chicken, in a large nonstick skillet, sear the chicken in a little canola oil and drizzle on additional soy sauce and a bit of sesame oil.

Cook to sear one side, reduce the heat and cook the other side (about 5 to 8 minutes). Remove and set aside.

Have a large bowl ready. Break up ramen noodles and sauté them in 2 tablespoons sesame oil until slightly browned. Remove from heat and put aside.

Prepare cellophane noodles by boiling in salted water until barely tender, about 5 to 6 minutes. Drain and rinse with cold water.

For the Peanut-Ginger Dressing, in a medium bowl, blend the oil, rice vinegar, ramen seasonings, soy sauce, sesame oil, and peanut butter well. Put one-third of the dressing in the bottom of the glass serving bowl.

To assemble the salad, place the cellophane noodles on top and then layer the salad ingredients in order given: greens, red peppers, broccoli, bean sprouts, mushrooms, scallions, corn, and cilantro. Top with the sautéed ramen noodles. Sliver the cooked chicken and place on the salad as the top layer. Drizzle the remaining dressing over chicken and let it seep through the salad. Dust with the sesame seeds. Chill for a few hours.

Serves 6-8

Chicken Caesar Salad with Asiago Cheese

This classic restaurant offering, done right, is a gourmet event. Unfortunately, too often restaurants offer this with cold, flavorless, strips of chicken breast and top it with a gloppy dressing with barely a hint of garlic. By contrast, this home recipe is a 5-star, stellar salad that hits all the right notes. Quality fresh Parmesan is a must and use Wisconsin or American Asiago cheese (not imported). Homemade garlic croutons are the crowning touch.

Chicken

2 chicken breasts, boned, skinned, cut into 2- by 4-inch strips
½ cup fresh lemon juice
2–4 garlic cloves, finely minced
½ teaspoon salt
¼ teaspoon pepper
1 tablespoon minced parsley
1–2 tablespoons olive oil

Dressing

1 ½ cups mayonnaise
1/3 cup olive oil
1 teaspoon red wine vinegar
1 teaspoon balsamic vinegar
5–8 garlic cloves, finely minced
2 tablespoons fresh lemon juice
Salt, pepper
1 teaspoon Dijon mustard
1 tablespoon Worcestershire sauce
¼ teaspoon hot sauce
½ cup freshly grated Parmesan cheese

Greens

6–8 cups romaine lettuce, in bite sized pieces

Finishing Touches

Garlic Croutons
Additional Parmesan cheese and/or grated Asiago
Thin slices of lemon

Prepare the chicken by tossing it in a medium bowl with the lemon juice, garlic, salt, pepper and parsley. Refrigerate at least 30 minutes or overnight.

In a nonstick pan, briskly sauté the chicken in the oil to cook it through and char it slightly, 5-10 minutes. Keep warm while preparing the dressing and salad.

For the dressing, whisk together the mayonnaise, olive oil, vinegars, garlic, lemon juice, salt, pepper, mustard, Worcestershire sauce, hot sauce, and Parmesan cheese.

Place half of the dressing in the bottom of a very large bowl. Toss the greens with the dressing. Divide the dressed greens equally among four serving plates. Top with equal portions of grilled chicken, croutons, and lemon slices. Sprinkle with additional Parmesan cheese and offer more dressing on the side. Can be stored in the refrigerator for up to 7 days.

Serves 4

Persian Cucumber Salad

Cool as a cucumber is the phrase for this salad. Fresh herbs, including cilantro, mint, and parsley on a bed of diced cucumbers, summery tomatoes, and some olive oil make a heavenly side salad. This is good also stuffed in a pita bread sandwich. Sumac, a tangy spice, red in color, is available in most Middle Eastern food shops.

1 cup yellow grape tomatoes, sliced in half
1 large red, ripe tomato, cubed
1 large cucumber, peeled, seeded, and diced
1 small onion, finely chopped
2 tablespoons sun-dried tomatoes, plumped and finely minced
3 scallions, finely chopped
2 garlic cloves, finely minced
¼ cup finely minced mint
¼ cup minced parsley
1 tablespoon minced cilantro
¼ cup extra virgin olive oil
2 tablespoons fresh lemon juice
2 tablespoons fresh lime juice
Salt, pepper

Finishing Touches
Sumac
Minced mint
Minced parsley

In a large bowl, toss the tomatoes, cucumber, onion, sun-dried tomatoes, scallions, garlic, mint, parsley and cilantro.

Drizzle on the oil, then the lime and lemon juices. Add salt and pepper to taste.

Chill well. Dust with sumac, mint, and parsley just before serving.

Serves 4

Quinoa, Mixed Grains and Cranberry Salad

Mixed grains, pine nuts, cranberries, and that great feeling that comes with good food are wrapped up in this simple recipe. Feel free to swap out any type of cooked grains you prefer or happen to have on hand, or use black beans in place of the chickpeas. This is a blue ribbon recipe, according to the five testers who each made it repeatedly after they tested it. This salad is a great accompaniment for chicken or broiled fish or with hummus, hard-boiled eggs, and cheeses.

1 cup cooked quinoa
1 cup cooked couscous
1 cup cooked wild rice
½ cup pine nuts
1 cup dried cranberries, plumped and dried
3 tablespoons light olive oil
3 tablespoons orange juice
2 teaspoons cumin
½ cup minced parsley
½ cup minced cilantro
1 cup canned chickpeas
Salt, pepper

Combine the quinoa, couscous, rice, pine nuts, cranberries, olive oil, orange juice, cumin, parsley, cilantro, chickpeas, salt and pepper in a large bowl. Taste and adjust seasonings as needed.

Chill before serving.

Serves 6–8

Adirondack Coleslaw

One of my website visitors, Louise Chadwinski, a B&B host, shared her favorite sweet and tart coleslaw idea. Once I knew the basic ingredients, I created my own version of this unique coleslaw, chock full of apples, toasted almonds, and a hint of maple syrup and orange. It is perfect with barbecued chicken or ribs or alongside grilled salmon. Use apples of various colors, with the skins left on, for the prettiest slaw.

Dressing
1 cup sour cream
½ cup mayonnaise
¼ cup maple syrup
Salt, pepper

Salad
6 cups finely shredded cabbage
3–4 apples cored finely chopped
1 cup dried cranberries
Zest of one medium orange, finely minced
½ cup sliced almonds

For the dressing, in a medium bowl, whisk together the sour cream, mayonnaise and maple syrup. Season with salt and pepper.

For the salad, place the cabbage, apples, cranberries, zest and almonds in a bowl and toss slightly. Add the dressing and toss well to coat the cabbage and apples.

Chill for at least 3 hours. Keeps 3 to 4 days in the refrigerator.

Serves 6–8

Fattoush Salad

Bread salads such as this traditional pita bread, aka fattoush salad are always welcome. Given the bold, zesty tastes and textures of this salad, it's no wonder. I top for grape tomatoes slice in half, otherwise in-season, local summer tomatoes, plum or otherwise, are ideal. Sumac is available in Middle Eastern groceries or by mail order from specialty spice stores.

Salad
4 pita breads
4 cups romaine lettuce, minced or cut in thin strips
1 cup minced cucumber
1 cup sliced tomatoes or halved cherry or grape tomatoes
½ cup slivered white onions, very thin
1 cup fresh parsley, very finely minced
Salt, pepper
1/3 cup light olive oil
2–4 tablespoons fresh lemon juice

Finishing Touches
Minced fresh parsley
Minced fresh mint
Sumac

Toast the pita breads, break them into pieces, and set aside.

On a large serving platter, layer the lettuce, cucumber, tomatoes, onions and parsley. Season with salt and pepper and drizzle with the olive oil and lemon juice.

Garnish with the toasted pita bread pieces, sumac, mint, and parsley.
Toss just before serving.

Serves 4–6

Bosc Pear, Blue Cheese and Bibb Salad

Bartlett, Anjou, Bosc, Comice, or any pear would be as sweet and natural on this wonderful, trendy salad. Pretty, pleasing, and an especially wonderful perk on a winter's day.

Salad
1 large head Bibb lettuce, leaves washed and separated
2 medium pears, cored and thinly sliced
½ cup crumbled blue cheese
½ cup toasted walnut crumbs

Vinaigrette
3 tablespoons red wine vinegar
1 tablespoon balsamic vinegar
1 tablespoon Dijon mustard
Salt, pepper
½ cup corn, canola, or olive oil

In a small bowl, whisk together the red wine and balsamic vinegars, mustard, salt and pepper. Add the oil, whisking constantly, in a slow, steady stream until the mixture is thickened and all the oil is used up.

To serve salad, arrange the lettuce leaves on four serving plates. Top each with some pears and crumbled cheese, and then last, the walnuts. Drizzle on some dressing.

The dressing will keep in the refrigerator for 3 to 4 days.

Serves 4

CHAPTER FIVE

Cry Fowl: Chicken and Turkey

Cry foul? I don't think so, especially if you spell it fowl in which case we are talking about a most versatile ingredient and meal-maker, i.e. chicken or turkey.

Chicken (and turkey) in all its guises (whole, cut-up parts, ground up, boned, or skinless) works for me, no matter what the meal or occasion. I'm a protein girl who appreciates quick, easy and adaptable recipes; chicken and turkey suits on all of those counts. I also like intense or high flavor dishes and here again, chicken is the perfect delivery system for exotic spice and herb combinations. Of course, what was once exotic (in terms of spices, condiments and other ingredients) or hard-to-find is now, given the ease of online shopping as well as supermarkets carrying broader choices of ingredients, very accessible. These days, neither miles nor borders nor even the seasons impede

the myriad and exciting possibilities of cooking with fowl.

You can up the ante by starting with a free-range, organic bird. Grain-fed chicken makes even a simple roast chicken (or any simple chicken dish), taste that much better. Kosher chickens, too, are known for excellent quality and cooked results. Here's to you as you wing your way through these recipes!

Favorite Spicy Lemon-Garlic Roast Chicken

I've made chicken this way for years and it's based on the recipe and method taught to me by a Barbadian cook who made incredible chicken by literally and liberally dumping every spice in the pantry on the chicken. It's the most succulent roast chicken I know and my hands down go-to chicken recipe.

1 whole chicken, about 3–4 pounds
Extra virgin olive oil
Coarse salt, pepper
Worcestershire sauce
1 large lemon, cut in half
1 bulb garlic, cloves separated (skins on)
¼ cup each minced parsley and chives
1–2 tablespoons paprika
1-2 tablespoons garlic powder
1-2 tablespoons onion powder
½ teaspoon cumin
½ teaspoon celery seed powder
1/3 cup white wine
¼ cup water
¼ cup chicken broth
2 tablespoons barbecue sauce

Preheat oven to 400 F. Place the chicken in a roasting pan.

Smear some olive oil generously all over the chicken. Dust with salt and pepper and squirt with 4 to 6 squirts of Worcestershire sauce. Squeeze both halves of the lemon over the chicken.

Put one lemon half in the roasting pan and stuff the other one, along with half of the garlic cloves, into the chicken cavity. Sprinkle the remaining garlic cloves in the roasting pan around the chicken. Dust the chicken very generously with the parsley, chives, paprika, garlic powder, onion powder, cumin and celery seed powder. Pour water, wine, chicken broth, and barbecue sauce into the roast pan. Make sure the chicken is thoroughly covered with spices; if you see any uncovered spots, dust on more paprika and garlic powder.

Roast, basting a few times, for 1 hour. Reduce the temperature to 375 F and cook until done, without basting, for another 30-45 minutes.

Serves 4-5

Apple-Brined Chicken

This is a great way to fix a deeply-flavored chicken when you want a great chicken dish or as a road-test recipe if you intend to brine and cook a large, whole turkey this way. Brining a chicken allows you to try things out on the smaller bird first. It needs an overnight stay in the fridge, but no other TLC is required. A favorite from my website and hands-down winner among my recipe testers. It's even more wonderful with apple cider if you have some on hand and want to donate a quart to the brine.

1 whole chicken, 2 ½ –3 pounds
½ cup apple cider vinegar
2 ½ cups white vinegar
4 cups apple juice
1 ½ cups water
2/3 cup sea or kosher salt
½ cup brown sugar
6 garlic cloves
2 tablespoons peppercorns
1 orange, sliced (washed but unpeeled)

Seasoning for Chicken

Paprika
Garlic powder
Salt, pepper
Olive oil
Soy sauce
Worcestershire sauce
2 tablespoons barbecue sauce

In a large bowl, stir together the vinegars, apple juice, water, salt and sugar. Stir until sugar and salt are dissolved. Then add the garlic, peppercorns, and orange slices. Place the chicken in a bowl that will fit it and the marinade (not too large a bowl just enough to have chicken in marinade). Pour the mixture over the chicken and refrigerate overnight (or for at least 8 hours).

Preheat oven to 400 F. Remove the chicken from the brine and discard the liquid.
Place chicken in a roasting pan to fit snugly. Dust with paprika, garlic powder, salt and pepper. Then drizzle on a bit of olive oil, soy sauce, Worcestershire sauce, and the barbecue sauce.

Place in the oven and immediately lower the temperature to 375 F. Roast until done, about 90 minutes, or until the chicken is well browned and seems tender.

Serves 4

Bistro Roast Chicken with Rosemary

A few herbs, fresh butter, salt, pepper, and scorching heat make this an outstanding chicken dish and a classic roast chicken that everyone should have in their repertoire.

½ cup minced parsley
3 sprigs fresh rosemary, finely minced or hand crumbled
6 sprigs fresh thyme, finely chopped
4 tablespoons unsalted butter
½–¾ teaspoon salt
½ –¾ teaspoon pepper
1 whole chicken, 3–4 pounds, rinsed and patted dry
1 medium bulb garlic, cut in half, across
1 lemon wedge
1 scallion, coarsely chopped
¼ cup extra virgin olive oil

Preheat oven to 450 F.

In a small bowl or using a mortar and pestle, blend half of the parsley, rosemary, thyme, 1/8 teaspoon each of salt and pepper and the butter to make an herbed paste. Lifting up parts of the chicken skin (from neck opening through to breast), push some herbed butter all over chicken as best you can. Have a casserole large enough to roast the chicken nearby.

In the cavity of the chicken, smear the remaining herbed butter and insert the garlic bulb, lemon wedge, and chopped scallion.

Heat the olive oil in a large nonstick or heavy stainless steel pan. Sear the chicken a few minutes per side and then place it in the casserole.

Place the chicken in the oven, reduce the heat to 425 F, and roast for 45 to 60 minutes, basting occasionally, until the juices run clear when the thigh area is pricked. Let stand 10 minutes before serving.

If you like, remove about 1 cup of the pan juices (or add some broth to make up one cup), add two tablespoons white wine or brandy, whisk, and serve as a side sauce.

Serves 4

Best-Ever Buttermilk Fried Chicken with Buttermilk Pecan Waffles

This is really exceptional fried chicken; it's tender, crisp, and oh-so-Southern. You can use a deep fryer but I use a wok, which is both roomy and deep. But a good Southern cook would argue (and they'd be right) that nothing beats a well-seasoned, deep cast-iron chicken fryer. Serve this with the usual fixins' (biscuits, gravy, corn) or go all out by offering it with Pecan Waffles.

Chicken

2 pounds chicken parts (legs, breasts, and wings)
4 cups water
4 cups buttermilk
1/3 cup hot sauce
5 teaspoons salt

Southern Coating

2 eggs
2 cups milk
4 cups all-purpose flour
2 tablespoons salt
½ teaspoon onion powder
½ teaspoon garlic powder
1 ½ - 2 teaspoons pepper

Canola oil for frying

In a large bowl, stir water, buttermilk, hot sauce and salt together. Add chicken and let it soak in the marinade overnight (or for at least 1 to 2 hours refrigerated). Drain well.

For the coating, whisk the eggs and milk in one bowl. Stir together the flour, salt, onion powder, garlic powder, and pepper in another large bowl.

Dredge the chicken first in the flour mixture, then in the egg mixture, then back into flour, pressing in to make stuff stick.

Fill the fryer two-thirds full of oil and heat to about 375 F. Cook a few pieces of chicken at a time until done, about 12 to 15 minutes. (To test, you can remove out a piece from the fryer and make a slit to see if it is cooked through). If you don't have a deep fryer, regular frying might take longer. Regulate the heat to ensure that the chicken doesn't burn, but does cook through. Drain chicken on paper towels.

Serves 3 or 4

Buttermilk Pecan Waffles

These are just the thing for breakfast, brunch or to tuck under a hot batch of Southern Fried Chicken. Brown sugar, maple, toasted pecans and a bit of buttermilk make these waffles a symphony of flavor. Top them with Best Ever Buttermilk Fried Chicken and warm maple syrup for a 'Diner's, Dives and Drive-ins' style feast. Served on their own, these are quintessential brunch waffles that score perfect 10's in sheer bliss appeal.

Pecan Waffle Batter
¾ cup pecans, toasted and finely chopped
1 ½ cups all-purpose flour
1/4 cup white sugar
3 tablespoons brown sugar
¼ teaspoon salt
2 teaspoons baking powder
½ teaspoon baking soda
1 egg
1 cup milk
½ cup buttermilk
1 1/2 teaspoons pure vanilla extract
1/4 teaspoon pure maple extract
2 tablespoons unsalted butter, melted

Finishing Touches
Butter for griddle
Maple syrup

In a large mixer bowl, stir the flour, white sugar, brown sugar, salt, baking powder and baking soda. Make a well in the center and add the egg, milk, buttermilk, vanilla, maple extract and butter. If mixture seems too thick, drizzle in more milk. Fold in the pecans and blend gently.

Have waffle griddle ready and warmed and brushed with some butter. Prepare waffles as per manufacturer's directions.

Makes 6 waffles

Moroccan Chicken

One of my New Jersey friends always inspires me to cook or bake something new. She makes this Moroccan Chicken her way and passed on her recipe. I added the garlic and paprika and, if you have it, sumac. Nothing is faster or easier than this chicken, or zestier. Huge wedges of Yukon Gold potatoes soaked in garlic and olive oil (or couscous with spices) completes the feast.

1 chicken, cut in half and flattened
2 teaspoons cumin
2 teaspoons cinnamon
2 teaspoons coriander
2 teaspoons turmeric
1 teaspoon sumac, optional
½ teaspoon garlic powder
½ teaspoon paprika
Sea salt, pepper

Finishing Touches
Lemon juice
Olive oil

Preheat oven to 425 F.

Line a baking sheet with parchment paper and place the chicken on it.

Blend the cumin, cinnamon, coriander, turmeric, sumac, garlic powder, paprika, salt and pepper in a bowl and then rub the mixture all over the chicken.

Bake the chicken for 30 minutes and as it bakes, spritz with lemon juice and drizzle on olive oil while it roasts until done, about 75 to 90 minutes.

Serve with couscous, garlic potato wedges, or saffron rice.

Serves 3–4

Chicken Vesuvio

Chicago, Chicago, you tumbling town, you also make great chicken dishes. This recipe is a Chicago legend and a great example of how a little technique and simple ingredients makes a heavenly dish. Here you have the choice to use dry or fresh herbs –it is a great dish either way.

1/3 cup flour
1 ½ teaspoons dry or fresh basil
¾ teaspoon dry or fresh oregano
½ teaspoon salt
Pepper
Pinch dry or fresh rosemary
Pinch dry or fresh sage
1 3-pound chicken, cut up into 8 pieces
½ cup light olive oil
4 large baking potatoes, cut lengthwise into six wedges each
3 garlic cloves, finely minced
¼ cup minced parsley
¾ cup dry white wine

Preheat oven to 375 F. Have an ovenproof casserole ready.

In a medium bowl, mix the flour with the basil, oregano, salt, pepper, rosemary and sage and press chicken pieces into the mixture to coat.

Heat the oil in a large nonstick skillet and cook the chicken on each side, until evenly browned all over, 5-8 minutes a side. Remove chicken pieces to the casserole.

Then, using the same pan, fry the potato wedges lightly just to brown, 8-10 minutes. Add the potatoes to the chicken.

Drain off all but 2 tablespoons of the oil from the pan. Stir in the garlic, parsley and wine and cook for 2 to 3 minutes. Spoon this over chicken.

Place in oven and bake until completely done, about 25 to 35 minutes.

Serves 4

Classic Coq au Vin

This is definitely something to crow over! Does anything this simple and classic taste so good and always impress as much as Coq au Vin? This is a great starter recipe for new cooks and Old Faithful for everyone else – it's one of my top-ten go-to chicken dishes any night of the week. Red or white wine is fine –just have a nice heavy casserole to make and serve this dish in, such as a vintage orange Dutch oven by Le Creuset.

1 4-5 pound chicken, cut in eights
Flour
Salt, pepper
¼ cup light olive oil or canola oil
2 cups mushrooms, sliced
1 cup finely minced onions
1 cup sliced leeks
1 cup baby carrots
2 bay leaves
3 medium cloves garlic, finely minced
1 cup white or red wine
1 cup chicken stock
1/3 cup parsley, finely minced

Lightly dredge the chicken pieces in flour and dust generously with salt and pepper.

In a 5-6 quart oven-proof casserole, heat the oil. Sauté the chicken, a few pieces at a time, skin side down until they brown, about 5-8 minutes. Turn and lightly cook the other side, 3-4 minutes. Drain each piece on paper towels. Preheat oven to 350 F.

In the chicken pan, pour off all but 2-3 tablespoons of the fat or oil and chicken bits left in the pan (if there is undue flour or sentiment from the cooking, wipe it out with a paper towel).

Over medium heat, sauté the mushrooms and onions to soften, 5-8 minutes. Add the chicken and then scatter in the leeks, carrots, bay leaves, garlic, wine, chicken stock and parsley.

Cover and cook for 60-75 minutes.

Serves 3-4

All American Chicken Pot Pie

The average frozen pot pie is a travesty, if not a crime, against all that great home-cooking stands for. By contrast, a Norman Rockwell perfect pot pie is a pinnacle of where the baker (top crust) meets the cook (the pot pie interior). It's all a matter of little things, done right, the whole way through. Use homemade pie crust or my preference, puff pastry (store-bought is fine) as the top crust. Inside? Fresh herb poached chicken breasts. This is a crowd pleaser, pot-luck legend-maker and reheats (and freezes before or after baking) like a dream.

1 9-inch pie crust or ½ pound prepared puff pastry

Filling
1 ½ pounds skinless, boneless chicken breasts
4-5 cups chicken stock
¼ cup white wine
Salt, pepper
1/2 teaspoon celery seed powder
1/2 teaspoon poultry seasoning
2 teaspoons fresh minced dill
3 tablespoons fresh minced parsley
1 cup small mushrooms (no stems), optional
1 ½ cups diced carrots, steamed
1 ½ cups cooked frozen peas, steamed
1 12-ounce can corn, drained
2 cups cooked cubed potatoes (skins peeled)
1/4 teaspoon celery seed powder
1/4 teaspoon poultry seasoning
2 teaspoons fresh minced dill
3 tablespoons fresh minced parsley

Herbed Béchamel
4 tablespoons unsalted butter or olive oil
4 tablespoons flour
1 1/4 cup milk
1 cup chicken reserved stock
3 tablespoons white wine
1 10-ounce can cream of chicken or mushroom soup
Salt, pepper
½ teaspoon garlic powder
½ teaspoon onion powder
¼ teaspoon poultry seasoning
2 tablespoons minced parsley
Milk, for brushing pastry

For the Filling, in a 3 quart sauce pot, place the chicken breasts, chicken stock, wine, salt, pepper, celery seed powder, poultry seasoning, dill and parsley. Bring to a simmer and cook the chicken about 20 minutes or until thoroughly cooked through. Cool 20 minutes. Reserve 1 cup of the chicken poaching stock. Cut the chicken into bite-sized pieces and place in a large bowl and dust generously with salt and pepper, then add the (second amount of) celery seed powder, poultry seasoning, dill, and parsley. Fold in the mushrooms, carrots, peas, corn and potatoes and toss. Taste to adjust seasonings.

Preheat oven to 375 F. Have a 4-5 quart casserole nearby.

For the Herbed Béchamel, heat the butter or oil in 6 quart stock pot; add the flour and whisk to make a roux or pasty mixture, 3-5 minutes on low-medium heat. Slowly add in the reserved stock, milk, and wine, whisking all the while to make a thickened sauce, 2-3 minutes. Remove from the heat and stir in the canned soup, salt, pepper, garlic powder, onion powder, poultry seasoning and parsley. Pour over the chicken and vegetables and stir to combine. Spoon filling into casserole.

On a lightly floured work surface, roll out pie crust or puff pastry to a size that would cover the casserole with some overlap. Place dough gently on top of filling and sides of casserole. With a paring knife, make some air vents. Brush pastry with milk as a glaze. Place casserole on parchment paper lined baking sheet.

Bake until filling begins to bubble through the vents and top crust is nicely browned, 45-55 minutes.

Serves 6

Thai Chicken Curry

Thai cuisine is so flavor-rich and exotic, making it especially satisfying. This classic Thai dish relies on fresh ginger, basil, Kaffir lime leaves, fish sauce and coconut milk, available in Asian markets or most big supermarkets. What I especially like about this dish is the creaminess of coconut milk which binds all the flavors together just so.

2 tablespoons Thai red curry paste
2 tablespoons vegetable oil
2 tablespoons fish sauce
1 tablespoon minced fresh ginger
2 garlic cloves, finely minced
3 hot red chilies, cored, stemmed, trimmed, and split lengthwise
½ teaspoon finely minced lime or lemon zest
¼ teaspoon salt
4 boneless, skinless chicken breasts
1 14-ounce can coconut milk
2 teaspoons Asian chili sauce
2–3 teaspoons curry paste (such as Patak's)
Pinch Asian red pepper

Finishing Touches
1 mango, peeled and diced
1 tablespoon lime juice
¼ cup minced fresh basil
¼ cup minced cilantro
1 teaspoon minced mint

In a large bowl, blend the curry paste with one tablespoon of the oil and the fish sauce, ginger, garlic, chilies, zest, and salt. Add the chicken (you can also put this all in a Ziploc bag at this point). Stir to coat and refrigerate for at least 1 hour or overnight.

In large nonstick skillet or wok, heat the remaining oil over medium-high heat. Brown the chicken all over and then place on a serving plate.

Stir the coconut milk into the pan and add the chili sauce. Bring to a gentle boil and simmer for 5 minutes or until mixture thickens. If you require it, add in more coconut milk and curry paste to make more sauce. Add a touch of Asian red pepper if you enjoy more heat in your food.

Return chicken to the pan to coat and simmer 15-20 minutes, ensuring chicken is cooked through and infused with the flavors. Meanwhile, place the mango on a dish, drizzle on the lime juice and then dust with basil, cilantro, and mint. Serve with steamed rice or vermicelli noodles.

Serves 4

Quick Pad Thai

There are as many versions of Pad Thai as there are versions of marinara sauce. Pad Thai is quick and filling although it's not a heavy meal. Just add chopsticks and a tumbler of iced mango juice and you have a banquet. Palm sugar is a typical Thai cuisine ingredient found in Thai markets but in a pinch, light brown sugar is an acceptable substitute.

2 boneless, skinless chicken breasts

Marinade
4 garlic cloves, finely minced
1 tablespoon cornstarch mixed with 3 tablespoons soy sauce

Cooking Sauce
1 tablespoon tamarind paste
¼ cup warm water
2 tablespoons fish sauce
1 tablespoon Asian chili sauce
2 tablespoons palm sugar or light brown sugar

Wok Stuff
1 tablespoon sesame oil
2–3 tablespoons canola oil
1–2 red chilies, finely minced
2 garlic cloves, finely minced
2–3 teaspoons finely minced ginger (or jarred ginger paste)
4 cups bean sprouts
4 green onions, sliced
1 tablespoon finely minced lemongrass
½ cup minced cilantro
1/3 cup chopped peanuts, optional
¼ cup vegetable or chicken broth
Salt, pepper

Pinch Asian red pepper
2 eggs, beaten
8 ounces cellophane or vermicelli noodles, soaked and set aside

Finishing Touches
Minced fresh cilantro and basil
Chopped roasted peanuts

Prepare the chicken by smearing with the garlic and the soy sauce-cornstarch mixture. Set aside.

Prepare the cooking sauce combining the tamarind paste and warm water in a small bowl. Stir in the fish sauce, chili sauce, and sugar. Set aside.

In a wok, heat the sesame seed and canola oil to medium hot. Add the chicken and sear to cook through, a few minutes each side. Remove the wok from the heat, remove the chicken and cut in slivers.

In the wok, add a touch more oil and add the chilies, garlic, ginger, bean sprouts, green onions, lemongrass, cilantro, peanuts and broth and cook over medium-high heat to soften the bean sprouts, about 3 minutes. Add the cooking sauce and cook for another 2 minutes. Season with salt, pepper and Asian red pepper.

In a small separate skillet, heat 1 tablespoon sesame seed oil, some oil and add the eggs. Cook briskly and then remove and thinly slice. Fold the cooked eggs into chicken mixture, along with the prepared vermicelli.

Serve, garnished with cilantro, basil and chopped peanuts.

Serves 3–4

Apple Cider Chicken

A bottle of bubbly cider and a heady mix of apples help braise plump pieces of golden brown chicken. A brief oven sojourn and 45 minutes later: ambrosial chicken. Use a mix of soft and tart apples or whatever is "in" at the market. Change the apples as the season progresses. If you are out of cider, try a mild beer. Is this good? Over 2,200 people downloaded this recipe at my website when it first appeared as the Free Recipe-of-the-Month.

2 chicken breasts, cut into two pieces each
2 legs and thigh pieces, cut at the joint
Flour for dredging the chicken
Salt, pepper
2–3 tablespoons light olive or canola oil
1 large shallot or onion, minced
1 small garlic clove, finely minced
1 cup chicken broth
4–6 apples, pared, cored, and cut in wedges
1 ½ cups apple cider
¼ cup light cream, optional

Dust the chicken pieces with flour and season with salt and pepper. Heat the oil in a Dutch oven, add the chicken pieces, and brown the chicken over medium-low heat, turning once, about 5 to 8 minutes per side.

Drain on paper towels and set aside while preparing the rest of the recipe. Drain most of fat out of Dutch oven.

Preheat oven to 375 F.

Sauté the shallot or onion in the (same) Dutch oven. Then add the garlic and the remaining 2 tablespoons of flour. Stir to cook shallot and brown the flour, about 2 to 3 minutes. Add the chicken broth and simmer 1 to 3 minutes to allow broth to thicken.

Place the chicken in the broth in the Dutch oven. Scatter the apples on top and drizzle the apple cider over the chicken.

Cover and place in oven, reducing heat to 350 F. Bake about 30 minutes, and then reduce heat to 325 F. Pour on the cream, give things a stir and allow another 15-20 cooking, uncovered, until the sauce thickens a bit.

Serve with wild rice or basmati rice.

Serves 3–4

Chicken Under a Brick

A little chicken, a little garlic, and a little muscle make for an outstanding chicken. Using weights to compress marinating foods is not new, but it's gaining ground as a nifty technique that produces New York Bistro style chicken. The only special equipment you need is two foil-wrapped bricks and a cast iron skillet.

1 chicken, 2–3 pounds, cut in half, semi-frozen
2 tablespoons minced rosemary
2 tablespoons minced parsley
2 tablespoons minced thyme
2 tablespoons minced chives
Juice of ½ lemon
6 large garlic cloves, finely minced
1 cup extra virgin olive oil
Salt, pepper

Remove any cartilage (attached to bone) under each chicken half. Pry out most of fine rib cage.

In a large bowl, whisk together the rosemary, parsley, thyme, chives, lemon juice, garlic and olive oil. Place the chicken in a plastic bag and pour the herb-oil mixture over it. Refrigerate for at least 4 hours or overnight.

Preheat the oven to 450 F.

Place a few tablespoons of the marinade in the bottom of an ovenproof skillet. Place the skillet in oven for 10 minutes.

Remove the skillet from oven and discard the marinade. Keep the oven on.

Place the chicken halves in the hot skillet, skin-side down. Season the chicken well with salt and pepper. Place foil-wrapped bricks on top of each chicken half.

Place the skillet on a burner over medium heat for 20 minutes. Transfer the skillet back into the hot oven and roast for another 15 minutes or so. If the chicken is well-browned, turn it over, put the bricks back on and continue roasting until done, 10 to 20 minutes, depending on the size of the chicken. Place the chicken on a platter to serve.

Serves 2–3

Portuguese Chicken

Roast this in a hot oven or grill it on the barbecue, either way, you won't find a finer bird. Portuguese restaurants serve various versions of this vinegar-infused chicken and each one is oh-so-good! An overnight marinade is best, but even 8 hours ahead is fine. This makes a tender, deeply-flavored chicken that is as good cold as it is fresh off the grill. It's best to make at least two birds; one to eat immediately and an extra one for great chicken sandwiches.

Chicken

1 whole chicken, about 3–4 pounds
White vinegar to cover chicken
½ cup hot sauce
1 cup water
1/3 cup salt
2 tablespoons garlic powder
1 tablespoon paprika

Before Roasting

2 teaspoons paprika
2 teaspoons garlic powder
Salt, pepper
2–3 teaspoons olive oil

If you plan to barbecue the chicken, split it in half.

The night before you plan to cook this, put the chicken in a large bowl and cover it with vinegar until almost submerged. Add the hot sauce, water, salt, garlic powder, and paprika and stir. Weigh down the chicken to submerge it and refrigerate overnight (or for at least 8 hours).

To roast the chicken, preheat the oven to 400 F. Drain the chicken and pat it dry. Put two halves in a roasting dish. Dust on the paprika, salt, pepper, and garlic powder and drizzle with olive oil. Roast 1 hour and then reduce to 350 F and finish roasting until the chicken is tender and juices run clear if you pierce chicken, another 20 to 30 minutes.

To barbecue/cook outdoors, cook the chicken over indirect heat and when it is close to being done, move it closer to grill heat source and let it finish cooking and get just a little bit charred.

Serves 3–4

Little Italy Chicken Cacciatore

I always think of the Billy Joel song when I make this dish. Chicken Cacciatore has gone from classic to cliché and is trendy all over again. Is it thanks to National CC Day, October 15th? No, it's more likely deserved respect for this rustic, rib-sticking, casserole that is chicken with a pizza vibe. I revamped the recipe with a bit more garlic, smoky pancetta and sun-dried tomato puree (and omitted the capers) for a dish that is simply Italian soul food. An Italian baguette and tossed pasta would frame this dish nicely.

Chicken Part
3-4 pounds chicken legs and breasts (or parts you prefer)
Flour
3 tablespoons olive oil
Salt, pepper

Tomatoes and Vegetable Part
2 tablespoons olive oil
8 thin slices pancetta
1 cup diced onions
3 large finely minced garlic cloves
1 large red pepper, cored and cut in strips
Salt, pepper
1 cup mushroom caps, optional
2 tablespoons sun-dried tomato puree or tomato pesto
1/4 teaspoon dried basil
½ teaspoon dried oregano
¼ teaspoon dried rosemary
1/8 teaspoon dried fennel
¼ cup fresh minced basil
¼ cup fresh minced parsley
½ cup red wine
1/3 cup chicken stock
1 14 ounce can ground tomatoes
1 cup marinara sauce

Dredge the chicken parts in flour and dust generously with salt and pepper. In a large non-stick fry pan, heat the oil and add the chicken, skin side down, over medium heat. Brown chicken on one side, 5-10 minutes, turn over and brown the other side. Remove the chicken and drain on paper towels. Preheat oven to 350 F.

Meanwhile, in a 5-6 quart Dutch oven, heat the oil one minute and add the pancetta. Over low heat, let the pancetta cook 3-5 minutes until crisp. Remove, drain on paper towels and then mince. Set aside.

To the pan, add the onions and cook 3 minutes and then add the garlic, red pepper and dust with salt and pepper. Let cook 3-4 minutes on medium and then add in mushrooms, sun-dried tomato puree, basil, oregano, rosemary, fennel, fresh basil and fresh parsley and stir to combine ingredients one minute.

Add the red wine, chicken stock, ground tomatoes, marinara sauce and minced pancetta. Stir and then add the chicken pieces.

Cover and bake until chicken is thoroughly tender, 60-75 minutes.

Serves 4-5

Popover Chicken

An easy dish with a dramatic and unique presentation that is wonderfully inviting, this is one of the first recipes I ever did that got published (Harrowsmith Cookbook, 1996). Browned chicken pieces are tucked into a casserole and then a special, savory popover batter is poured over the chicken. The batter puffs up and the result is golden hunks of chicken, nested in a crispy, tender golden popover crust. This recipe still and always makes everyone say "wow!"

Chicken
2–4 tablespoons oil
1 chicken, 2 ½–3 pounds, cut into 8 or 10 pieces (wing tips removed)
Salt, pepper

Batter
3 eggs
1 ½ cups milk
2 tablespoons oil
½ teaspoon salt
¼ teaspoon pepper
1 ½ cups all-purpose flour
1 tablespoon minced parsley
¼ teaspoon garlic powder
¼ teaspoon onion powder

Mushroom Sauce
1 cup homemade or canned cream of mushroom soup
½ cup white wine
1 tablespoon minced parsley
¼ teaspoon garlic powder
½ cup thinly sliced fresh mushrooms
Salt, pepper

Preheat oven to 350 F. Have a 9- by 13-inch casserole nearby.

In a large, preferably nonstick pan, heat the oil to medium. Season the chicken with salt and pepper and add it, a few pieces at a time, and sauté, turning each piece once, until just brown all sides, about 5 to 8 minutes. Remove the cooked chicken pieces to the casserole.

For the batter, in a medium bowl, whisk the eggs, milk, oil, salt, pepper, flour, parsley, garlic powder and onion powder. Pour the batter over the chicken, mostly drizzling extra batter into the spaces between the pieces.

Bake 55 to 60 minutes, or until the chicken is well browned (the exposed parts will be deeply browned and the chicken more crisped) and the batter has puffed up and turned golden brown.

Meanwhile, prepare the Mushroom Sauce. In a saucepan, combine the mushroom soup, wine, parsley, and garlic powder, and whisk or stir over low heat to combine. Stir in the sliced mushrooms, season with salt and pepper, and cook to soften the mushrooms a little, about 5 to 10 minutes.

To serve, pull the chicken apart with surrounding popover crust so that each diner gets some chicken and some crust. Offer the sauce on side for drizzling.

Serves 4

Cuban Grilled Chicken

This is one of my own favorite standby chicken dishes of summer. It is punchy with great taste. You will love the intense flavor of cumin, lime, orange juice and cilantro, all grilled to perfection. Grilled or oven baked, it's an outstanding dish.

¼ cup minced cilantro
¼ cup minced parsley
6 garlic cloves, finely minced
1 teaspoon cumin
1 teaspoon oregano
1 teaspoon thyme
½ cup orange juice
6 tablespoons lime juice
6 tablespoons extra virgin olive oil
Salt, pepper
4 chicken pieces (breasts or legs)

In a large bowl, combine the garlic, cumin, oregano, thyme, cilantro, and parsley and mix well. Stir in the orange juice, lime juice, oil, salt and pepper.

Make small cuts or scores on the chicken pieces. Add the chicken to the bowl that allows some room between the chicken pieces and pour the marinade over the chicken. Place in fridge and marinate one hour to overnight, turning the chicken to coat every once in a while. You can also marinate it for just 30 minutes, but do not refrigerate.

Heat the grill to medium and grill the chicken over indirect heat until almost cooked, and then allow to char slightly as it finishes cooking.

For oven preparation, roast at 400 F, basting every once in a while, until done, about 45 minutes. Broil for the last few minutes to char slightly.

Serves 4

Sticky Chicky

Sticky Chicky is an Asian-inspired luscious dish that has as many variations as there are chickens. Given my druthers, I would make this with bone-out, but skin-on, chicken breasts. If you have time, marinate the chicken overnight. But if not, it's still stupendous—sticky, sweet, garlicky, tangy – simply addictive chicken!

2 ½ to 3 pounds pieces (drum sticks and breasts)
1/3 cup ketchup
¼ cup orange juice
¼ cup honey
3 tablespoons soy sauce
2 tablespoons cornstarch
2 tablespoons finely minced garlic
1 teaspoon crushed ginger
Salt, pepper
Tabasco

In a large bowl, mix the ketchup, orange juice, honey, soy sauce, cornstarch, garlic, ginger, salt, pepper and Tabasco. Toss chicken in the mixture and marinate overnight for deep flavor or, if you didn't plan ahead, you can bake right away.

Preheat the oven to 350 F.

Place chicken in a roasting pan and bake, basting often, for 1 ½ hours, or until the chicken is nicely browned and tender.

Serves 4

Diner-Style Chicken and Herb Dumplings

Comfort food at its best—satisfying, moist, and incredibly flavorful chicken. Don't be discouraged by the number of ingredients. This is awesome diner food that turns your kitchen into a 5-star American bistro. Soda Cracker Dumplings are also good with this.

Chicken

1 chicken, 4–5 pounds, cut into 8 or 10 pieces
8 cups water
1 large onion, halved
2 carrots, sliced
2 ribs celery, cut in sticks
Celery leaves
6 sprigs parsley
1 bay leaf
1 tablespoon salt
¼–½ teaspoon pepper

Gravy and Vegetables

1 ½ cups frozen peas
1 cup corn kernels
½ cup finely sliced carrots
½ cup sliced celery
4 small onions, quartered
1 medium potato, peeled and chopped
1 large leek, sliced in ¼-inch rounds
1 garlic clove, finely minced
½ teaspoon thyme
¼ teaspoon sage
¼ teaspoon savory
1 tablespoon finely minced fresh parsley
2 teaspoons finely minced fresh dill
Salt, pepper
2 tablespoons unsalted butter
1 tablespoon oil
1/3 cup all-purpose flour

2 tablespoons white wine
1 ½ cups milk or light cream

Herb Dumplings

1 ½ cups all-purpose flour
2 teaspoons baking powder
¼ teaspoon salt
1/8 teaspoon pepper
½ teaspoon minced dill
1 teaspoon minced parsley
3 tablespoons shortening
¾–1 cup milk

To poach the chicken, place the chicken, water, onions, carrots, celery, celery tops, parsley, salt, and pepper in an 8- to 10-quart stock pot or Dutch oven. Bring to a boil, reduce heat, cover, and simmer until the chicken is tender, 45 to 60 minutes. Let cool, and then remove the chicken. Strain the broth, reserving the carrot and celery, as well as the poaching liquid. (At this point, you can refrigerate the meat and broth overnight or for several hours. After soup is well chilled, remove the fat that may have solidified on top of the broth).

Preheat the oven to 325 F.

Place the chicken in a large ovenproof casserole (a 12-inch x 3-inch brazier or paella-style pan works well—anything that can hold a lot of food and liquid). Place the peas, corn, carrots, celery, onion, potato, and leek, as well as the reserved carrots and celery from the poaching liquid, all around and on top of the chicken. Sprinkle the garlic, thyme, sage, savory, parsley, dill, salt and pepper over the top.

In a saucepan, make a roux by heating the butter and oil. Add the flour and cook, stirring, to brown the flour somewhat, a couple of minutes. Whisk in 3 cups of the reserved poaching liquid, white wine, and milk or cream. Pour this over the chicken, spooning on as evenly as possible.

For the Herb Dumplings, in a medium bowl, combine the flour, baking powder, salt, pepper, dill, and parsley. Cut in the shortening, and then add milk. Stir to make a moistened, thick batter. Drop the batter by spoonfuls into the chicken and gravy. Cover and bake for 30 to 45 minutes. Check once in a while to make sure there is sufficient gravy. Add more of the reserved chicken broth, if required. If casserole is bubbling a lot, reduce the heat to 300 F.

Serves 5–7

Soda Cracker Dumplings

I like this soda cracker crumb dumplings as an alternative to matzoh meal or regular flour dumplings.

2 eggs
½ cup chicken broth or water
2 tablespoons oil
1 cup soda crackers crumbs, or a bit more
½ teaspoon baking powder
1 ¾ teaspoon salt
Pepper

Whisk the eggs with the chicken broth and oil to blend. Add the cracker crumbs, baking powder, ¾ teaspoon of the salt, and pepper. The mixture should be stiff; add more cracker crumbs, if necessary. Refrigerate the mixture for 1 hour.

Fill a Dutch oven with water and the remaining teaspoon of salt. Bring to a rolling boil. Scoop spoonfuls of the dumpling mixture and drop into the boiling water. Reduce the heat to low, cover the pot, and simmer the dumplings 30 minutes.

Gently remove the dumplings from the water and drain. Serve 1 or 2 dumplings in a bowl of chicken soup.

Serves 6–8

Buffalo Girl Chicken Tenders with Sweet and Hot Sauce Drizzle

Crisp, hot, tangy chicken tenders—totally irresistible. I serve these with a hot mango salsa. When you have three sons, you get to be a chicken tender expert – trust me.

Chicken Hot Sauce Brine

¾ cup hot sauce
2/3 cup white vinegar
4 teaspoons salt
1 tablespoon sugar
3 pounds skinless, boneless chicken breasts, cut into 4–5 inch strips, 1 ½ inches thick
6 eggs

Seasoned Coating Mix

5 eggs
4 cups all-purpose flour
1/3 cup sesame seeds
3 tablespoons cornmeal
2 teaspoons kosher salt
2 teaspoons garlic powder
1 teaspoon baking powder
½ teaspoon baking soda
½ teaspoon onion powder
½ teaspoon Old Bay Seasoning, optional
¼ teaspoon pepper

Hot, Sweet 'n Sassy Drizzle Sauce

¾ cup hot sauce
½ cup honey
¼ cup salted butter, melted
2 tablespoons cider vinegar
1 tablespoon lemon or lime juice
¼ teaspoon liquid smoke, optional
Zest of one orange, finely minced

Canola oil for frying, about 5 cups, or as required

For the Chicken Hot Sauce Brine, in a large bowl, combine the hot sauce, vinegar, salt, and sugar. Stir to dissolve salt and sugar. Add the chicken pieces. Cover and refrigerate for at least 4 hours and up to 12 hours. 6 to 8 hours is ideal. If you have a large Ziploc bag, you could also put the chicken and marinade in that.

Preheat the oven to 425 F. Line two large, doubled-up baking sheets with parchment paper. Place two large sheets of parchment paper on your work surface.

In a medium bowl, whisk the eggs together; set aside.

For the Seasoned Coating Mix, in a large bowl, blend the flour, sesame seeds, cornmeal, salt, garlic powder, baking powder, baking soda, onion powder, Old Bay seasoning and pepper.

Drain the chicken pieces, discarding the brine, and dip each first in the seasoned coating, then in the eggs, and then in the seasoned flour coating again. Coat each piece as generously as you can. Lay each piece out on the parchment paper on the working surface. Repeat until all of the pieces are coated.

Place two 12-inch skillets on the range, and fill each 1/3 full with oil. Heat to 375 F. Place a few pieces of the chicken back in the Seasoned Coating and re-dredge them. Shake off excess coating. Fry each for a few minutes on each side, until golden brown.

Repeat (gently re-flouring a few pieces at a time) and use tongs to remove browned pieces to the prepared baking sheets.

When all of the chicken pieces are fried, place them in the oven for about 15 minutes, until the chicken is cooked through. (Oven finishes the cooking and shortens the frying time).

For the drizzle sauce, combine the hot sauce, honey, butter, vinegar, lemon or lime juice, liquid smoke, if using, and zest in a saucepan. Heat over low heat until just simmering, about 3 to 4 minutes. Remove from the heat and offer as a dipping sauce or drizzle on the cooked chicken pieces.

Serve the chicken in baskets, with carrot sticks, celery, and Mango and Grilled Vidalia Onion Salsa (recipe follows).

Serves 6–8

Mango and Grilled Vidalia Onion Salsa

Delicious with Buffalo Girl Chicken Tenders or any chicken or fish dish. Hot, sweet, tangy flavors make this a great side dish.

¼ cup minced red onion
½ cup very finely minced Vidalia onion
½ cup finely minced tart apples (cored and peeled)
¾ cup coarsely diced mango
1 ½ cups finely diced fresh pineapple, or grilled pineapple, if preferred
¼ cup minced dried cranberries
3 tablespoons red wine, or raspberry or plum vinegar
2 tablespoons canola oil
1 tablespoon brown sugar, plus more to taste
1 tablespoon fresh lime juice
1 tablespoon fresh orange juice
1 tablespoon finely minced cilantro
2 teaspoons finely minced ginger
1 small Scotch bonnet pepper, grilled, and then seeded and finely minced
2 teaspoons Chipotle Tabasco or regular hot sauce
Salt, pepper

In a medium bowl, mix the onions, apples, mango, pineapple, cranberries, wine or vinegar, oil, sugar, lime juice, orange juice, cilantro, ginger, pepper, Tabasco, salt and pepper.

Chill before serving to allow the flavors to meld. Taste and adjust seasonings (add more brown sugar or salt to taste).

Makes 1 ½ cups

Chicken Paprikash

Aromatic and smooth as silk with sour cream and served with potatoes or nockerl (Eastern European pasta), this is Hungarian comfort food in its finest hour. A total blue-ribbon-winner of a recipe. Hungarian paprika comes in a few varieties: sweet, hot, and smoked. Most of us use sweet paprika in just about everything, but smell and taste it to ensure it's fresh and fragrant. I use the famed Sveged brand, imported from Hungary.

1 chicken, cut into 8 pieces
Salt, pepper
Flour for dredging
2 tablespoons oil
2 cups diced onions
2-3 tablespoons sweet paprika
1 cup chicken broth
1 cup sour cream
1 tablespoon white wine
Salt, pepper

Preheat oven to 350 F. Have an ovenproof 5-quart casserole ready.

Season the chicken with salt and pepper and dredge each piece in flour, shaking off excess.

Heat the oil in a large skillet and brown the chicken on each side. Place the chicken in the casserole. Drain most of the fat from the skillet. Brown the onions in the skillet over low heat, then stir in the paprika and a tablespoon of flour. Stir in the chicken broth, sour cream, and wine. Adjust the seasonings and pour the mixture over the chicken in the casserole. Cover and bake for 30 to 45 minutes.

Serves 4

Maple Orange Chicken

This is good enough to make at least twice a week. Leftovers are great cut into chunks for an Asian chicken salad or stuffed into a pita bread sandwich.

4 boneless, skinless chicken breasts
¼ cup Worcestershire sauce
1 tablespoon tamari
2 teaspoons Dijon mustard
2 garlic cloves, finely minced
2 tablespoons balsamic or plum vinegar
3 tablespoons ketchup
1/3 cup pure maple syrup
½ cup orange juice
1/8 teaspoon pepper
2-3 tablespoons canola oil

Finishing Touches
Orange wedges

Using a paring knife, score the chicken pieces with a few shallow crosshatch cuts.

In a medium bowl, whisk together Worcestershire sauce, tamari, mustard, garlic, vinegar, ketchup, maple syrup, orange juice and pepper. Toss the chicken in the marinade and let stand 15 to 20 minutes.

Preheat the oven to 400 F. Have a nonstick shallow roasting dish nearby that will accommodate the chicken pieces.

Over medium-high heat, heat the oil in a 9-inch nonstick skillet.

Using tongs, place the chicken pieces in the skillet, scored side down, and sear about 2 minutes on each side. Place the chicken in the roasting dish.

Place the chicken in the oven and roast until done, about 20 minutes, reducing the temperature to 375 F after ten minutes. Baste the chicken once or twice during roasting.

Drizzle any marinade that has accumulated in the roasting pan over chicken just before serving. Serve garnished with orange wedges. (Great with couscous or wild rice and grilled asparagus).

Serves 4

Beer Can Chicken

This recipe is an urban legend, but one I still attribute to barbecue guru and cookbook author Steven Raichlen who made it famous. Once I made it, it became a staple throughout barbecue season. It is fun, easy and yields incredible, mouthwatering, tender, flavorful chicken. The beer tenderizes the chicken and acts as an automatic stand-up spit device.

1 whole chicken, 3–3 ½ pounds1
12-ounce can of beer
5 tablespoons dry spice rub *
¼ cup barbecue sauce, optional

*You can use any prepared dry rub or seasoning mix for chicken or barbecue meats or, alternatively, a mixture of equal parts paprika, garlic, salt, pepper and 1 teaspoon of sugar.

Pour of ¼ of the beer and discard. Add 3 tablespoons of the dry rub spice mixture to the can of beer. Rub the chicken inside and out with the remaining dry rub. Smear the barbecue sauce on the chicken, if desired (best for oven method).

Refrigerate the chicken while preparing grill.

Heat grill to hot and bank coals or a mixture of coals and briquettes to the side for indirect grilling. For oven preparation, preheat your oven to 425 F and line a baking sheet with foil.

Place the chicken atop or astride the beer can. Place on the grill or on the baking sheet (for oven preparation).

Grill or bake 1 to 1 ½ hours, or until the chicken is thoroughly browned, slightly charred, and tests done with a meat thermometer, around 165 F.

Let the chicken stand 5 to 10 minutes before removing and serving. (Discard the beer, being careful not to spill any as it is quite hot and can scald).

Serves 3–4

American Chicken Smothered in Mushrooms

Everyone starts their adult culinary life with at least one signature dish and this is one of mine, inspired by a recipe in the vintage Time Life Series American Cooking. As a new bride, this was my company dish; years later it still brings raves.

1 3-pound chicken, cut into 8 pieces, or just breasts and legs
Salt, pepper
Flour for dredging
3 tablespoons canola oil
½ cup diced onions
2 medium garlic cloves, finely minced
2–3 cups sliced mushrooms
¾ cup chicken broth
1/3 cup white wine
½ cup light cream or half-and-half

Finishing Touch
Minced parsley

Season the chicken pieces with salt and pepper and dredge them lightly in flour.

Heat the oil in a large, heavy bottomed, ovenproof casserole.

Brown the chicken, skin side down, for about 5 to 7 minutes, turning once to lightly brown the other side (just browning, not cooking thru).

Drain the chicken pieces and set aside. Drain off most of oil and chicken bits and such in the pan. Sauté the onions, garlic, and mushrooms lightly for about 3 minutes.

Arrange the chicken in the casserole. Spoon on the onions, garlic and mushrooms.
Pour the chicken broth, wine, and cream or half-and-half over the chicken. Lightly dust the chicken with salt and pepper. Cover and bake at 350 F, lowering the heat to 325 F after 20 minutes, for 30 to 40 minutes. Adjust the seasonings and dust with minced parsley.

Serve with seasoned potatoes or wild rice.

Serves 4–6

Asian Wings

You may already have a soy-garlic wing recipe, but this one breaks the mold. This dish marinates overnight or at least a few hours ahead. Fermented black beans, easily found in Asian food stores, add tremendous flavor, but if you don't have them on hand, it is fine to make this without them.

1 cup ketchup
2/3 cup hoisin sauce
½ cup soy sauce
½ cup (packed) brown sugar
½ cup honey or molasses
¼ cup Chinese fermented black beans, optional
¼ cup Dijon mustard
¼ cup horseradish
¼ cup rice or cider vinegar
1 tablespoon sesame oil
1 tablespoon minced garlic
½–1 teaspoon Chinese five-spice powder
3–4 pounds chicken wings, split in half, tips removed

The night before, or at least six hours ahead, stir together the ketchup, hoisin sauce, soy sauce, brown sugar, honey or molasses, mustard, horseradish, vinegar, sesame oil, garlic and Chinese five-spice powder. Combine ingredients well and pour over the wings. Refrigerate for at least 6 hours or overnight.

Preheat the oven to 400 F.

Arrange the wings in a single layer on a foil-lined baking sheet and bake for about 45 minutes (basting every 10 minutes) until the wings are well glazed and a deep, rich, reddish brown color.

Serve with stir-fried vegetables and Chinese noodles or rice.

Serves 4–5

Best-Ever Brined Thanksgiving Turkey

Brining turkeys is as old as time, but it came back into vogue a few years ago. Brining inflates and infuses incredible flavor into the turkey (and also chicken), and helps impart the most amazing moistness and taste imaginable in the final bird. What's more, you don't need to brine it for days and days like pickles, but just enough brining forethought, as it were, results in magnificent turkey. When making your turkey this way, choose a regular (not pre-basted turkey) turkey.

Turkey and Brine

1 10–14-pound turkey, not pre-basted
2 cups table salt
¼ cup sugar
Water, preferably spring water, to cover turkey

Pan Stuff

2 carrots, cut up
2 ribs celery, cut up
2 cups water
½ cup white wine or water
½ cup chicken broth
1 cut-up lemon
1 medium onion, peeled and quartered

Herb Slather

1 generous cup minced parsley
2 tablespoons finely minced fresh rosemary
2 tablespoons finely minced fresh sage
4 sprigs crumbled fresh thyme
2 scallions, diced
Zest of 1 lemon
3 large garlic cloves, peeled
7 tablespoons olive oil
4 tablespoons unsalted butter
2 teaspoons salt
1 teaspoon pepper

Roasting Pan Extras

Melted unsalted butter or olive oil, about ¼ cup
Salt, pepper
Bell's Seasoning * or sage
Paprika
Garlic powder

Bell's Seasoning is a New England vintage spice blend that comes in a little yellow box in most supermarkets. I find it indispensable but you can also use regular dried sage.

In a large stock pot, (one that is big enough to fit the turkey), stir the salt, sugar and water together to dissolve the salt and sugar. Place the turkey inside and allow it to sit in the brine, in a cool place (garage under 50 F or fridge), for 4 hours. Drain and pat dry; discard the brine.

Preheat the oven to 400 F and place the turkey in the roasting pan. Add the carrots, lemon, and onion to the pan.

For the Herb Slather, combine the fresh parsley, rosemary, sage, thyme, scallions, lemon zest, olive oil, butter, salt and pepper in a food processor. Process to a paste. Lifting up the skin of the turkey from the area where the cavity is (where you usually put the stuffing), use your fingertips to spread equal amounts of the Herb Slather on the breast area of both sides of the turkey as evenly as you can. Pat the skin down gently.

Place the turkey in the roasting pan. Brush the turkey with melted butter or olive oil and then dust with the Roasting Pan Extras— salt, pepper, the Bell's Seasoning or sage, and some paprika and garlic powder.

Roast the turkey for at least 1 ½ hours and then reduce the temperature to 350 F, basting 3 to 4 times during overall roasting. Roast 20 minutes per pound, or 3 ½ to 4–5 hours, depending on size of the bird. Use an oven thermometer to ensure it is evenly cooked through and is 180 to 185 F.

Do not baste turkey within about 30 minutes of it being done, to allow skin to crisp. If pan juices evaporate, add ½ cup water or more, as required, to the pan. Use the juices that remain to make gravy.

Let the turkey stand about 15 to 20 minutes before carving.

Serves 10–12

Turkey Garden Burgers

I love the lite look and taste of these fragrant, savory turkey burgers. Low-fat turkey is perfect as a beef burger respite. The dashes of carrots and parsley perk up the look and taste. Dress these burgers in garlic mayo, mustard, ketchup or even mango salsa. If you have multi-grain or honey whole-wheat hamburger buns or English muffins on hand, you'll be all set.

1 pound ground turkey meat
¼ cup finely shredded carrots
2 tablespoons minced onion
1 teaspoon garlic powder
½ teaspoon onion powder
½ teaspoon paprika
1/8 teaspoon celery seed powder
1 teaspoon seasoning mix (Mrs. Dash or Lawry's) or salt
Salt, pepper
¼ cup breadcrumbs
1 egg
2 tablespoons barbecue sauce
½ teaspoon hot sauce

In a large bowl, toss the turkey with the carrots, onion, garlic powder, onion powder, paprika, celery seed powder, seasoning mix or salt and a generous dusting of pepper. Stir in the breadcrumbs, egg, barbecue sauce and hot sauce. Gently shape into four patties.

For a barbecue method, over indirect flame (not directly over the coals), cook the burgers for about 12 to 15 minutes or until burgers are hot inside and meat is cooked through (all white without any pink). Alternatively, slow cook them in a touch of olive or canola oil in a nonstick skillet, turning only once, until cooked, 15 to 20 minutes in total time.

Serve on buns or English muffins garnished with slices of onion, stoneground mustard, and tomato.

Serves 4

CHAPTER SIX

It's Beef! It's What's for Dinner

Who doesn't remember the famed "It's Beef, It's What's for Dinner" commercial in the '70s? You can, of course (if you don't remember or weren't born at the time), find it on YouTube, complete with the best score any commercial ever had: Aaron Copland's *Appalachian Spring*. That beef commercial was stirring and showcased succulent shots of superb beef recipes. It had you doing a hoe-down on your way to the kitchen to cook up a batch of beef – and that is just what you have here: simply great beef recipes (hoe down is optional).

Vegetarian entrees and delectable roast chicken can only take me so far and then it's beef time, big time. Perhaps it's the iron inherent in beef because clearly I'm one of those people that need the occasional slam of red beef. Hearty, staying, flavorful and, yes, it's what for dinner - at least once in a while. Nutritionists aside, the American West wasn't won or otherwise settled with tofu chili, sometimes dinner calls for beef and nothing but: real, hearty, red-fat-marbled, stick-to-your-ribs....beef! (And then go for a run and drink plenty of green tea and have kale the rest of the week. Beef, as they say, is rib-sticking food.

Mom's Famous Garlic-Dijon Cross Rib Roast

Not as expensive as a regular rib roast, this is a superb go-to weekday roast. I usually serve it with pan-roasted potatoes. Leftovers are perfect served over warmed, sliced baguettes with extra sauce or a sharp horseradish and Dijon mustard. This is my mother-in-law Shirley Posluns' legendary rib roast, and if you make it half as good as she does, your kitchen will earn a 5-star rating.

1 Cross Rib Roast or any recommended roast (5–7 pounds)
1/3 cup Dijon mustard
10 large garlic cloves, smashed
2 tablespoons light olive oil
1 tablespoon garlic powder
1 tablespoon dry mustard
1 tablespoon paprika, plus more for sprinkling
½ teaspoon pepper
Salt
1 ¼ cup water
½ cup red wine
1 packet beef gravy mix
1 packet dry onion soup
1 10-ounce can condensed golden mushroom soup

Preheat oven to 375 F.

Place the meat in a shallow roasting pan. In a small bowl, make a paste by mixing the mustard with the garlic, olive oil, garlic powder, dried mustard, paprika, pepper and salt. Spread or pat the paste over the top and sides of the roast. Make additional paste if the meat is not well covered. Pour the water, wine, beef gravy mix, and soup mix into the pan around the roast. Sprinkle top of roast generously with extra garlic powder and paprika. Cover roast with foil.

Roast at 375 F. for the first hour. Lower the temperature to 350 F and continue roasting for a couple of hours more, depending on desired doneness, basting every so often. Remove the foil during last half hour of cooking.

Remove the meat and slice thinly. In the roasting pan, stir the mushroom soup with the pan juices, mixing well. Pour some of this over the meat, offering the rest as gravy.

Serve cold (leftovers) sliced thinly on a garlic toasted French hard roll, with Dijon and white horseradish, and a side salad.

Serves 6–8

Guinness Corned Beef

There are hundreds of ways to make corned beef, from deli style to the hearty Irish wash day classic that has become a pub menu classic. This one is definitely a cut above and features a healthy dose of Guinness beer. The corned beef is slowly oven-braised in the beer, resulting in a deeply tender and fragrant beef for slicing. I serve this with steamed cabbage, small boiled potatoes and roast turnips. I love this dish with hunky Irish soda bread.

1 3–5 pound corned beef (already corned with spices and salt)
¾ cup (packed) brown sugar
1 12-ounce can of Guinness or other strong, dark beer
½ cup water or apple juice

Preheat oven to 325 F.

If the corned beef is heavily spiced, brush or lightly rinse off the excess spices. If only a little spice is left on its surface, leave as is.

Place the corned beef in a large roasting pan. Rub with the brown sugar and drizzle a bit of the Guinness or beer over it. Then place the water, apple juice and remaining beer in the bottom of the pan. Cover lightly with foil and roast until tender, 4 to 5 hours.

Serve with braised cabbage, turnips, and mashed potatoes.

Serves 6–7

Irish Beer Stew with Golden Puff Pastry Cover

What could be better than a rib-sticking, deeply flavored, hearty stew with a buttery puff pastry "hat" to tuck into? This is an inspiration from this Irish-spirited, if not authentically Irish chef. Minus the puff pastry crown, this is still one of the best stews around.

8 ounces prepared puff pastry, defrosted
2 pounds lean stewing beef, in small chunks, trimmed of fat
12 ounces (1 ½ cups) dark or medium beer (flat)
½ cup water
2 medium potatoes, peeled and grated
2 grated carrots
1 large onion, diced
4 medium garlic cloves, peeled and bruised, but not crushed
1 tablespoon salt
1 tablespoon Worcestershire sauce
2 teaspoons paprika
2 teaspoons beef bouillon liquid (or one cube)
½ teaspoon onion powder
½ teaspoon garlic powder
¼ teaspoon pepper
2 cups whole baby carrots
2 cups tiny new potatoes or small cubes of larger potatoes

Preheat oven to 350 F.

Place beef, beer, water, potatoes, grated carrots, onion, garlic, salt, Worcestershire sauce, paprika, bouillon, onion powder, garlic powder and pepper in a 4- or 6-quart Dutch oven or casserole. Cook about 2 hours, stirring once in a while. Add the small potatoes and the whole baby carrots and cook until they are tender, about 45 minutes more and beef is tender when you put a fork in it. Adjust seasonings to taste.

Remove the stew from the oven and let cool on the counter. When ready to serve (it can be made ahead and refrigerated or sit on the counter for up to an hour before finishing it with pastry), raise the oven rack to a higher position and preheat the oven to 425 F.

On a lightly floured work surface, roll out the puff pastry, large enough to cover the stew and extend to the sides (inner sides or upper edges of casserole—it is up to you what sort of look you want; on top of the stew is fine). Arrange the pastry sit on the stew or gently adhere by pressing it to the outer edges of the baking dish.

Bake to puff and brown the pastry, 10 to 15 minutes. To serve, use a large spoon to break into the pastry and dole out servings of stew and pastry.

Serves 4–6

Bistro Pepper Steak

Not to be confused with steak and green peppers, this classic French bistro dish is steak at its finest hour. It features a peppercorn-crusted, pan-sautéed rib eye steak (or any prime, thick cut, boneless steak you prefer) with a brandy and red wine sauce, garnered by deglazing the pan. It is absolutely mouthwatering and as good, if not better, than any restaurant could do. Just use the best peppercorns you can find.

Steak

2 1-inch thick premium strip sirloin or fillet steaks, 8 to 10 ounces each, fat trimmed
2–3 tablespoons peppercorns
Sea salt
1 tablespoon each unsalted butter and olive oil

Sauce

¼ cup unsalted butter
1 cup beef broth
¼ cup red wine
½ teaspoon Dijon mustard
1 teaspoon Worcestershire sauce
2 tablespoons fresh lemon juice
Salt, pepper
2–4 tablespoons brandy

Place the peppercorns in a Ziploc bag. Crush them with a rolling pin or use a mortar and pestle. If using a mortar and pestle, cover the pepper with plastic wrap for the initial pounding of the peppercorns so they do not fly out of the bowl. Then remove the plastic and crush gently until they are coarsely ground.

Place the steaks on a sheet of wax paper or parchment and dust the steak with salt. Then press each side of each steak into the crushed peppercorns.

In a nonstick pan, melt the butter over medium heat and then add the steaks. Brown steaks very briefly on each side over high heat. Reduce the heat to medium-low and cook to desired doneness, 15 to 20 minutes. (Alternatively, you can remove the seared steaks from the pan, make the sauce, then cover the steaks with the sauce and finish in the oven for 15 to 20 minutes at 400 F.). Remove the steaks to a warm plate.

For the sauce, add butter to the meat drippings in the pan and cook over medium-low heat, stirring in the beef broth, wine, Dijon mustard, Worcestershire sauce, lemon juice, and some salt and pepper. Cook to meld flavors and reduce slightly. Sauce should thicken. Stir in brandy slowly. You may simmer off alcohol by simmering for 2 to 3 minutes. Spoon the sauce over the steaks and serve immediately.

Serves 2

Best Roast Beef

This is one of those memory-making meals that people will always recall about you, as in, "he/she made the best roast beef on the planet." Forget about leftovers; there aren't any with this recipe.

3–5 pounds any cut roast beef
½ cup red wine
½ cup water
12 garlic cloves,
1 tablespoon paprika
1 tablespoon onion powder
1 tablespoon garlic powder
1 package red wine gravy (any brand)
1 package peppercorn gravy, mushroom gravy,
or roast beef gravy (any brand)
Salt, pepper
¼ cup ketchup
1–2 tablespoons Dijon mustard
½ cup finely minced mushrooms, optional

Preheat the oven to 325 F.

Place the beef in a roasting pan, then douse with the red wine and water. Toss the garlic cloves in around the roast. Dust the top of the roast very generously with paprika, onion powder, garlic powder, gravy mixes (just the dry contents—do not add water), salt and pepper. Spoon on the ketchup, mustard, and mushrooms. Drizzle a bit more water over the top so that the spices and gravy powders do not dry out the top as the beef cooks.

Cover lightly with foil and roast 3 hours. Reduce the temperature to 300 F and roast until tender. If after 6 to 8 hours, the beef is not tender, slice it thin, return it to the pan/gravy (adding more water if needed), and slow roast it at 300 F. This will braise the meet until fork tender.

Serves 6–8

Root Beer and Cola Smokey Ribs

This recipe is outstanding with either long beef ribs or baby back pork ribs. You can oven-roast these from start to finish or put them on the grill at the last minute for some extra charring and grill flavor. Of course, grilled slowly outdoors is the best way, but you will be amazed by how deeply flavored and tender these are straight out of the oven. The dry rub is key as is the slow roasting and the ambrosial glaze or mop (it should have a patent) and what makes these ribs so very special.

Dry Rub

5 teaspoons sea salt

5 teaspoons paprika

1 ½ teaspoons onion powder

1 teaspoon pepper

¾ teaspoon garlic powder

¼ teaspoon celery seed powder

¼ teaspoon cayenne pepper

Ribs

3–4 pounds baby back ribs or long beef ribs

Mop

1 12-ounce can root beer

1 12-ounce can cola

½ cup barbecue sauce

½ cup (packed) brown sugar

½ cup ketchup

2 tablespoons steak sauce

1 bay leaf

½ teaspoon liquid smoke *

* Use only if you are not finishing the ribs on the grill.

The night before or early on the morning of cooking, combine the salt, paprika, onion powder, pepper, garlic powder, celery seed powder, and cayenne in a small bowl and mix to blend. Pat the mixture all over the ribs. Wrap in plastic wrap and refrigerate 12 to 48 hours.

Preheat the oven to 325 F. Place the ribs in a shallow baking dish and bake, uncovered, for 2 to 3 ½ hours, until very tender.

Meanwhile, make the mop. Place root beer, cola, barbecue sauce, brown sugar, ketchup, steak sauce, bay leaf, and liquid smoke, if using, in a 4-quart pot or larger, and bring to a boil over medium-high heat. Once the mixture has come to a boil and the sugar has dissolved, reduce the heat to medium and allow the mixture to reduce to a glaze consistency, about 25 to 30 minutes longer. Reserve and keep warm until ready to use. About an hour before the ribs are ready (they will be almost fully tender), start basting them every 15 minutes with the mop. When you remove them from the oven, drizzle one final basting of mop.

If you are finishing the ribs on the grill,
prepare an indirect fire or put a handful of new
briquettes over a hot fire of gray coals. Sprinkle
on wet mesquite or hickory chips.

Place the ribs on the grill and baste with the
mop as they cook.
Remove the ribs to a platter. Using a sharp knife,
cut the ribs apart or serve a few ribs, connected
to each diner. Serve the ribs with some of the
leftover glaze on the side, if desired.

Serves 3–4

Cowboy Cornbread Lasagna

Take a cornbread base, add taco filling, top with Monterey Jack cheese, and serve with a side of salsa, avocado slices, sour cream, and diced chilies and whoa, Nellie!. If you prefer, replace the meat in the taco filling with minced tofu to make this kosher or vegetarian. Served in generous hunks, with a huge green salad and pitcher of homemade lemonade or iced green tea. It reheats well too.

Cornbread Base
1 ½ cups all-purpose flour
1 cup cornmeal
3 tablespoons sugar
2 teaspoons baking powder
1 teaspoon salt
½ teaspoon baking soda
1 cup buttermilk
1/3 cup oil
1 egg

Middle Layer
1 cup beans, black or kidney, refried, optional
1 batch medium or lean hamburger meat, prepared as taco filling*
½ cup prepared salsa or taco sauce
1–2 cups shredded Monterey Jack or mild orange cheddar cheese

Sides
Corn or taco chips
Salsa
Sour Cream
Diced Chilies
Sliced Avocado

*Prepare 1 pound of taco meat according to seasoning packet, such as Old El Paso brand.

Preheat the oven to 350 F. Spray a 9- by 9-inch baking pan with nonstick cooking spray.

In a bowl, stir together the flour, cornmeal, sugar, baking powder, salt, baking soda, buttermilk, oil and egg to make a soft batter, drizzling in more buttermilk if required to make a pourable or spoonable batter.

Spoon the batter into the prepared pan.

Bake 25 to 35 minutes, until the cornbread is firm to the touch. Remove from the oven, but leave the oven on.

Spoon the beans, if using, over cornbread, then the taco filling. Douse with salsa or taco sauce and top with the cheese. Bake again to melt the cheese, about 15 to 20 minutes.

Cut into squares to serve and offer with sides.

Serves 4–6

Sweet and Sour Cranberry Meatballs

Cranberry sauce is the secret ingredient here, along with one or two other pantry items. These meatballs are zesty and full of bite; no matter how often I make them for dinner, they get hijacked before I serve them!

1 can jellied cranberry sauce
1 can condensed tomato soup
½ cup ginger ale or cola
¼ cup red wine
¼ cup ketchup
¼ cup brown sugar
2 teaspoons fresh lemon juice
1 ½ pounds medium ground beef
½ cup breadcrumbs or fine matzoh meal or soda cracker meal
½ small onion, finely minced or grated
1 egg
¾ teaspoon salt
¼ teaspoon pepper
½ teaspoon citric acid or sour salt *

* Citric acid or sour salt is available in kosher food sections, pharmacies, or online

In a 4-quart saucepan, over low to medium heat, combine the cranberry sauce, tomato soup, ginger ale or cola, wine, ketchup, brown sugar, lemon juice and citric acid. Heat to a gentle simmer for 5-8 minutes.

Meanwhile, in a large bowl, combine the ground beef, breadcrumbs, onion, egg, salt, and pepper. Form into 1-inch balls.

Place the meatballs into the simmering sauce and let simmer over very low heat for an hour.

Serves 4–6

Hamburgers with Balsamic Glaze

A lot of fuss goes into hamburgers, but I tend to think simpler is better, as long as you start with fresh, top quality ground beef, preferably Angus beef. These are great off a barbecue grill or pan-roasted in a nicely seasoned cast iron pan to sear them.

1 pound lean ground beef
1 egg
2 tablespoons barbecue sauce
1–2 small garlic cloves, finely mashed
1 teaspoon Worcestershire sauce
½ teaspoon Dijon mustard
Salt, pepper

Finishing Touches
Olive oil
2 tablespoons flour
1/3 cup beef broth
3 tablespoons red wine
1 tablespoon balsamic vinegar
1 tablespoon unsalted butter, optional
1 small garlic clove, finely minced
Caramelized mushrooms and onions

In a medium bowl, lightly mix the beef with the egg, barbecue sauce, garlic, Worcestershire sauce, Dijon mustard, salt and pepper. Gently form the meat into 3 patties without pressing them too firmly.

Heat your grill or a nonstick or cast iron pan to medium-high and drizzle in a bit of oil. Place the patties in the pan or on the grill and immediately lower the heat to low. Let cook until well browned on one side and cooked half-way through, about 5 to 8 minutes. Turn over and cook the remaining side for another 5 to 8 minutes. Remove from the pan. To the pan, stir in the flour and cook for 2 minutes or less. Slowly drizzle in the beef broth, wine, and vinegar. Add the butter, if using, and the garlic mix to make a quick thin glaze.

Place the patties back in pan and toss in the glaze. Serve on buns with mustard, caramelized onions, horseradish sauce, or whatever condiments you like.

Caramelized onions and mushrooms are optional, but one of my favorite toppings. To caramelize mushrooms and onions, put a few cups of each, thinly sliced, in a nonstick fry pan with a few tablespoons of canola oil. Slowly cook until mixture reduces and is nicely browned (but not burnt), 20 minutes or so. Season with salt and pepper.

Serves 2–3

Caramelized Onion, Garlic and Mushroom Cola Brisket

Not only does this roast beef taste out of this world, it needs only one long, slow bake versus the bake, slice and re-roast approach of most brisket recipes). Who has the time? One day, I simply realized that a long slow roasted brisket doesn't require slicing and a second roasting and it still results in a succulent, tender meat. This is a deeply flavorful brisket that has all the rights notes of wine, garlic and onions, braised to perfection.

4-6 pound beef brisket
2 tablespoons canola oil
4 large onions, sliced
Salt, pepper
10 garlic cloves, finely minced
2 tablespoons paprika
1 tablespoon onion powder
1 tablespoon garlic powder
1 10 ounce can tomato soup
1 cup cola
½ cup ketchup
1/3 cup beef broth
¼ cup red wine
1 package dry mushroom sauce or dry beef gravy mix, optional
2 tablespoons minced fresh parsley
1 cup sliced mushrooms

Preheat oven to 350 F. Place meat on a large piece of foil.

Heat the oil in a large nonstick fry pan, over low heat and slowly sauté the onions until they are softened and barely caramelized, about 15 minutes. Stir in the salt, pepper and garlic and cook to soften garlic, another 5 minutes. Stir in the paprika, onion powder, and garlic powder. Place the beef in a large roasting pan that will hold both it and the gravy/roasting juices. Spread the spice mixture on the meat. Drizzle the tomato soup, cola, ketchup, broth, wine, and sauce or gravy mix around the meat. Sprinkle with the parsley and top with the sliced mushrooms. Cover lightly in foil.

Reduce the oven heat to 325 F and roast the meat for 5 to 7 hours, or until fork tender. (You can time this before the meal in time to serve, or make it a day ahead and reheat, sliced first or reheated as a whole roast).

For the last 30 minutes, remove the foil to allow the top of the meat to crisp slightly. If brisket needs more juices, add ½ cup ketchup and ½ cup each red wine and beef broth.

Serves 8–10

Red Garlic Chili

My version of a bowl of 'red' is a zesty, piquant, deeply flavored chili to warm up a sporty fall weekend, a snowy winter one, or a chilly night between seasons. Texans make a face if you mention tomatoes or beans when it comes to chili; Cincinnatians add cinnamon to theirs and serve it atop spaghetti but chili, in any style, is always a hit. This version offers heat, spice, bold flavor and rib-sticking beefiness with a big smack of garlic.

3 pounds lean ground beef
2–3 tablespoons olive oil
4 large garlic cloves, finely minced
1 cup finely minced onions
2–4 tablespoons chili powder
1–2 teaspoon onion powder
1–2 teaspoons garlic powder
½–1 teaspoon cumin
Pinch cayenne or crushed red pepper flakes, or to taste
Pinch sage, oregano, cinnamon
Salt, pepper
1 28-ounce can stewed, puréed, or ground plum tomatoes
¼ cup water
3 tablespoons tomato paste
1 tablespoon red wine vinegar
1 tablespoon sugar
2 19-ounce cans black beans or kidney beans, drained

Finishing Touches and Garnishes
Sour cream
Colby or cheddar
Minced jalapeno
Minced cilantro

In a large Dutch oven, sauté the meat in the olive oil until it is evenly browned, 5-8 minutes. Move the meat to the side of the pot; add the garlic and onions and sauté just to soften. Add the chili powder, onion powder, garlic powder, cumin, cayenne, sage, oregano, cinnamon, salt and pepper. Stir in the tomatoes, water, tomato paste, vinegar, and sugar. Cook 5 to 10 minutes and then add the beans, if using. Simmer for 30 minutes. Adjust seasonings.

Serve in ceramic bowls with minced herbs, a dollop of sour cream, shredded cheese, minced jalapeno, and a side of corn bread or tortillas.

Serves 6–10

Roasted Garlic Meatloaf

Garlic always makes a meatloaf taste extra special and in this case, double garlic means double good.

1 ½ pounds ground beef (a mixture of lean and medium)
3 tablespoons finely minced mushrooms
2 tablespoons drained and finely minced oil-packed sun-dried tomatoes
2 tablespoons finely minced carrots
2 tablespoons finely minced onions
1 tablespoon garlic oil
1 teaspoon minced garlic
½ teaspoon garlic powder
1 teaspoon hot sauce
Salt, pepper

Roasting Pan Fixins'
½ cup beef broth
1/3 cup red wine
1 bulb garlic, cloves separated, but not peeled

Preheat oven to 350 F.

In a medium bowl, mix together the beef, mushrooms, sun-dried tomatoes, carrots, onions, garlic oil, garlic, garlic powder, hot sauce, salt and pepper together and shape into a loaf. Place in a small roasting pan. Drizzle the broth and wine around the meatloaf along with the garlic cloves. Roast, basting occasionally, until done, about 40 to 50 minutes.

Drain the meatloaf and place it on a platter. Squish the roasted garlic cloves out of their casings into the pan juices and offer the juices on side.

Serves 4–5

Best-Ever Shepherd's Pie

Few things satisfy like this meat-and-potatoes classic. Double this recipe and fill up a slew of individual foil freezer containers for late night or Saturday afternoon instant meals.

2 tablespoons oil
1 small onion, minced
1 ½ pounds medium ground beef
1 tablespoon tomato paste
2 teaspoons garlic powder
2 teaspoons Worcestershire sauce
Salt, pepper
½ cup beef broth
1 tablespoon cornstarch mixed with 2 tablespoons cold water
1 12-ounce can corn, drained
3 cups prepared mashed potatoes

Finishing Touches
Paprika

Preheat the oven to 350 F. Spray a 2- or 3-quart baking dish with nonstick cooking spray.

Heat the oil in a nonstick skillet over medium heat. Sauté the onion until lightly golden. Stir in the ground beef and brown until no pink color remains. Stir in the tomato paste, Worcestershire sauce, garlic powder, salt and pepper. Stir in the beef broth. Add the cornstarch mixture and stir until the mixture bubbles slightly and thickens.

Mash potatoes as per your preferred method. Spread meat as first layer in baking dish. Then spread the corn evenly over the meat. Last, spread the mashed potatoes over the corn. Dust top with paprika.

Bake until casserole is heated throughout, 30 to 35 minutes.

Serves 4–6

CHAPTER SEVEN

Catch of the Day, Fish and Seafood

I used to think people who enjoyed fish (and seafood) were like cat and dog people, i.e. you like fish (and cats) or are a meat person (dog person), much like the coffee versus tea people. There's not much cross-over. Once I was a chicken/pasta person but now even I've learned to enjoy fish and seafood, primarily because I've created fish recipes are appealing and easy, but also because fish is so light and healthy. It pays to become a fan.

Fish dishes, done right, are feel good food. Fish also cooks up faster than anything else and with a couple of great fresh fish and seafood stores around the corner, I now have plenty of reasons to know various types of fish and enjoy it more often.

Fish is so packed with nutrients that dieticians and nutritionists tout without any waffling or changing food trends: fish is always on the good food list – it never goes out of vogue on health advocates' list. Fish, while light, is also protein-packed yet relatively low in

calories (if you're a calorie counter). After a fish meal, you leave the table replete, but not stuffed.

Unless you are already an avid fish fan (in which case, you then are well acquainted with all the wonderful attributes of the treasures of the lakes and seas), let me introduce you to this chapter of fish for fish fanatics and for skeptics. There is not a dish in this collection that that you won't like - that I promise you. Each recipe is rife with flavor, color and texture. You won't think, "Oh, it's fish," with disappointment. Instead, you'll marvel that a veritable feast has landed on your plate, all sizzling and fresh. Moreover, via these recipes, you'll enjoy a variety of fish and seafood, in a rolodex of styles that suit your mood, your particular penchant for spices and with a preparation time that suits your needs. There's everything from single-plate gourmet meals to Salmon for a Wedding which remains my go-to company salmon dish. There's nothing fishy about great food – so just enjoy.

Greek Fish

Sunny, simple and flavorful, what else would you expect from a quick, fragrant Greek fish recipe? Have your fish monger gut and trim the fish if you prefer fillets over whole fish. This is a sublime go-to recipe whether you choose bass, snapper, trout, sole, or even wild salmon.

1 large whole fish (2–3 pounds) such as bass, snapper, or trout, butterflied, boned and gutted
Salt, pepper
2 cups cherry tomatoes, halved
¼ cup extra virgin olive oil
2 tablespoons lemon juice
1 tablespoon white vinegar
1 tablespoon finely minced fresh oregano
4 garlic cloves, thinly sliced
2 teaspoons minced fresh hot chili, such as jalapeno
1 large lemon, thinly sliced
4–6 sprigs fresh thyme or minced parsley

Preheat the oven to 450 F.

Sprinkle the inside of the fish with salt and pepper. Set aside.

In a medium bowl, toss the tomatoes, 2 tablespoons of the oil, lemon juice, vinegar, oregano, most of the garlic, chili and dust with salt and pepper. Let stand 15 minutes.

Heat the remaining 2 tablespoons of olive oil in a large, ovenproof nonstick or cast iron pan. Add the fish and roast in the oven for 15 to 20 minutes. Gently turn the fish, toss on the tomato mixture and the remaining garlic, and cook the other side for 8 minutes. Before serving, adjust seasonings (adding more salt or herbs) and garnish with thyme or parsley.

Serve with a rice dish or Greek potatoes.

Serves 2–3

Beer Batter Fish

This is fish-and-chips, typical pub style. The beer in the batter tenderizes it and adds the right flavor note to the fish. The batter does double duty if you want crisp beer-battered fried onion rings on the side.

4 fish fillets, such as sole, halibut, blue fish, or tilapia
2 eggs
1 cup flat beer
2 tablespoons oil
2 cups all-purpose flour, plus extra for dredging
1 ¼ teaspoon salt
1 teaspoon garlic powder
¼ teaspoon baking powder
Salt, pepper

Canola oil for frying

In a medium bowl, whisk together the eggs, beer, oil, the 2 cups of flour, salt, garlic powder and baking powder until the batter is smooth and thin. Let batter stand, covered, at room temperature for at least 4 hours, or refrigerate overnight. (Remove from the refrigerator one hour before using).

Meanwhile, lay the fish out on parchment paper or a plate. Dust with salt and pepper and lightly dredge with flour.

Fill a deep fryer two-thirds full of oil and heat it to 360 F. (Without a thermometer, test oil by dropping a little batter in. It should immediately begin to sizzle). Dip the fish fillets in the batter. Immediately immerse in the oil and fry until golden brown on both sides. Drain on paper towels.

Serve the fish immediately or keep warm by placing on a wire cookie rack on top of a cookie sheet in a 275 F. oven.

Serves 4

Teriyaki Grilled Tuna

This is the new restaurant and home classic, aka fish meets grill with an Asian spin. This is lean, mean, simple, and totally tasty. What more could you ask for?

1 cup teriyaki sauce
¾ cup olive oil
2 tablespoons finely minced garlic
1 teaspoon pepper
4 6-8 ounce Yellow Fin Tuna fillets

In a large Ziplock plastic bag, combine the teriyaki sauce, oil, garlic and pepper. Place the tuna fillets in the bag. Seal the bag with as little air in it as possible. Give the mix a good shake to coat the tuna fillets well. Marinate for 30 minutes in the refrigerator.

Meanwhile, preheat your outdoor barbecue grill to high. Lightly coat the grill with oil.

Remove the fillets from the marinade and place them on the hot grill. For rare tuna, grill 3 to 5 minutes per side; for medium, grill 5 to 8 minutes per side; and for well done, grill 8 to 10 minutes per side.

Serves 3–4

Wedding Poached Salmon

This is a knockout, elegant dish. If you don't have a poacher, follow the directives for using a large pot instead. This is my go-to, crowd-pleasing salmon dish, wonderful for a summer meal or a wedding buffet.

1 salmon, 5–6 pounds (have your fish monger remove the head)
2 cups white wine
3 carrots, cut in chunks
3 celery ribs, cut in chunks
1 medium onion, sliced
¼ cup minced parsley
2 tablespoons minced dill
2 tablespoons sea salt
1 teaspoon pepper

Place salmon in poacher. If you do not have a poacher, use a large pot. Round the fish in a semicircle in the pot so it looks like it is chasing its own tail. Cover the fish with water until almost submerged. Add the wine, carrots, celery, onion, parsley, dill, salt and pepper. Bring to a boil, reduce the heat, and let gently simmer until done, about 30 to 40 minutes.

Remove the fish from the pot, discarding the poaching liquid and vegetables, and place the fish on a platter. Refrigerate. The next day, gently remove the skin. Garnish with dark green salad greens, parsley, and lemon wedges.

Serves 10–12

Two Buffet Sauces for Salmon

These sauces are lickety-split to make and wonderful served with chilled salmon (as well as cold, sliced turkey). My chef's trick? If you are out of fresh dill or parsley, but have dry herbs, soak the herbs briefly in hot water or lemon juice, drain and use. They won't be the same as fresh, but they'll be a great deal better than straight-from-the-shaker-jar dried herbs.

Quick Dijon Sauce

1 ½ cups mayonnaise
½ cup Dijon mustard
2 tablespoons finely minced parsley
1 tablespoon fresh lemon juice
2 teaspoons finely minced dill

In a medium bowl, combine the mayonnaise, mustard, parsley, lemon juice, and dill. Stir to mix well.

Chill before serving.

Makes 2 cups

Quick Red Sauce

1 cup mayonnaise
1 cup chili sauce
½ cup red or white horseradish

In a medium bowl, combine the mayonnaise, chili sauce, and horseradish. Stir to mix well.

Chill before serving.

Makes 2 cups

Salmon in a Package with Green Herb Slather Marinade

I love this herb coating on fresh salmon steaks or fillets. Make this in the oven or en papillote, in a parchment paper envelope, to quickly cook this in the microwave. Because it's so fast to prepare, this is one of my favorite lunch choices. The marinade lasts for a week or so and is wonderful tossed with boiled new potatoes, added to vinaigrette or slathered on chicken fillets before pan frying or broiling.

3 or 4 salmon fillets or steaks, as required (8- to 10-ounce fillet per serving)
1 medium yellow onion, coarsely chopped
1 cup fresh basil leaves
½ cup fresh flat-leaf parsley
2 tablespoons fresh rosemary leaves
1 tablespoon fresh sage leaves
3 tablespoons fresh dill
½ teaspoon fresh mint
1 tablespoon lemon zest
1 tablespoon lemon juice
4 garlic cloves, peeled
1 cup olive oil
Salt, pepper

Place the onion, basil, parsley, rosemary, sage, dill, mint, lemon zest, lemon juice, juice and garlic in a food processor. Pulse several times to chop. Add the oil, salt, and pepper. Purée and refrigerate or use immediately. (Keeps up to two weeks in the fridge)

To make the fish, coat a piece of salmon in about ½ cup of the marinade. Refrigerate for 30 minutes to 2 hours.

Wrap the fillet in parchment paper, making a sealed envelope. Place on a plate and microwave for 5 to 8 minutes, until the fish easily flakes apart when touched with a fork.

For oven baking, preheat the oven to 425 F.

Place the fish in a casserole or baking dish and place in the oven, as close to the heat source as possible. Bake until done, about 12 minutes or until the fillets flake apart.

Serves 3–4

Blue Plate Special Deluxe Tuna Casserole

This is an amalgamation of about three or four tuna casserole recipe approaches. I took the best elements from each and incorporated them into this, the mother of all tuna casserole recipes. The Ritz Cracker topping is one of those retro things that still has wow appeal.

6 ounces flat egg noodles, cooked according to package instructions, drained
2 tablespoons butter
1 cup chopped celery
1 cup chopped onion
2 cans (6 ½ ounces each) white flaked tuna
1 cup frozen peas
1 cup milk
1 l0-ounce can condensed cream of mushroom or cream or celery soup
½ cup low-fat plain yogurt or light sour cream
4 ounces shredded Brick, Colby, or mild white Cheddar cheese
2 teaspoons minced fresh parsley
1 teaspoon minced fresh dill or ½ teaspoon dried dill
¼ teaspoon Old Bay Seasoning
Salt, pepper
20 Ritz Crackers, coarsely crumbled

Finishing Touches
Melted butter
Paprika

In a small nonstick skillet, sauté the celery and onion in margarine until softened.

Preheat the oven to 350 F. Lightly grease a 9- by 13-inch casserole.

In a large bowl, combine the noodles, sautéed celery and onions, tuna, peas, milk, soup, yogurt or sour cream, cheese, parsley, dill, Old Bay Seasoning, salt, and pepper. Toss well.

Spoon the noodle mixture into the prepared casserole. Sprinkle cracker crumbs evenly over the top and drizzle with l to 2 tablespoons of melted butter (this assists browning). Dust lightly with paprika.

Bake for 30 to 35 minutes, until the top is browned and the casserole is evenly hot throughout.

Serves 6

My Best Deli-Style Tuna Salad

A well-made tuna salad is the stuff of great sandwich legends. I made this in huge batches when I worked in a health food café in the start of my culinary career. The secret here, as it often is with my savory recipes, is Old Bay Seasoning.

2 7-ounce cans of tuna (one white flaked, one light flaked)

½ cup mayonnaise, or to taste

1 tablespoon fresh lemon juice

1 teaspoon minced fresh dill (or ¼ teaspoon dried dill)

1 tablespoon minced parsley

½ teaspoon salt, or to taste

½ teaspoon Old Bay Seasoning *

¼ teaspoon pepper

¼ cup minced celery

4–6 drops hot sauce

* *Old Bay Seasoning* is a special seasoning mix for seafood and for this tuna salad. It usually comes in a yellow tin in the spice section of the supermarket.

Place the tuna, mayonnaise, lemon juice, dill, parsley, salt, Old Bay Seasoning, pepper, celery and hot sauce in a food processor and process briefly. Pulse gently to blend, but not purée the mixture.

Taste and adjust seasonings. Keeps refrigerated for 3 to 4 days.

Makes 1 ½ cups

Deluxe Tuna Melts

There are so many routes to this diner classic, which is essentially a tuna salad sandwich with melted cheese on top. You can use any sort of sliced bread (white, rye, pumpernickel, whole-wheat bread or English muffins. I also make my Tuna Melts, open-faced on sourdough bread.

Tuna Salad Filling (or My Best Deli-Style Tuna Salad)
2 slices bread, lightly toasted
Dijon mustard
Mayonnaise
Pesto (basil or sun-dried tomato, your choice)
Black or green olive tapenade
Sliced pickles or a few capers
Salt, pepper
A few slices cheese such as Havarti, Cheddar, Asiago, or Camembert
Olive oil (for pan)

Smear one slice of the toasted bread with some mustard, mayonnaise and pesto. Spread on about 1 cup of tuna salad. Top with some tapenade and sliced pickles or capers. Dust with salt and pepper. Add cheese and lightly press the top bread slice on top.

Heat a cast iron skillet over medium heat. Coat the pan with a bit of olive oil. Place the sandwich in the pan gently and top it with a few plates to weigh it down.

Gently grill each side of the sandwich, press sandwich down (so you can cut it more easily), until the bread is just brown and the cheese is melted. Serve immediately.

Serves 1

Tuna and Brie Sandwich

This takes a sandwich meal up a notch to gourmet sophistication. Happily, it's still fast and easy. You can also make these sandwiches in an open-faced rendition and just broil briefly to melt the cheese before serving.

Sandwich
4 large slices sourdough or country bread
olive oil or unsalted butter, for smearing bread
1 large garlic clove, finely minced
6–8 thin slices Brie cheese

Filling
3 7-ounce cans white flaked tuna, packed in water
1/3 cup mayonnaise
¼ cup very finely minced celery
1 tablespoon Dijon mustard
1 tablespoon lemon juice
1 tablespoon very finely minced onion
1 tablespoon each minced parsley and dill
1 tablespoon capers, optional
2 tablespoons pitted, sliced black olives, optional
Salt, pepper
Hot sauce, to taste

Smear or brush each piece of bread on both sides with some olive oil or butter. Rub the garlic over each side of the slices. Set aside.

Put the tuna, mayonnaise, celery, mustard, lemon juice, onion, parsley, dill, capers, olives, salt, pepper and hot sauce in a food processor and pulse to combine (do not purée). Adjust seasonings and add a bit more mayonnaise if the mixture is dry.

Divide the tuna filling between two of the bread slices. Top each with some brie and then top with a slice of bread to make the sandwich.

Preheat a nonstick skillet. Add the butter or olive oil and let heat for 20 to 30 seconds. Place the sandwiches in the pan and press down on them firmly. Place 3 or 4 dinner plates on top of the sandwiches to weigh them down. Cook over medium-low heat until lightly browned on the bottom, then turn over to brown the other side. Serve immediately.

Serves 2

Maple-Cured Broiled Salmon

Maple, soy and sesame collide in a West-meets East with Northern Exposure accent. Broiled or grilled, this makes an outstanding light fish entree. The maple brings out the subtle salmon taste and helps it caramelize on the edges just so. Perfect with asparagus and cumin-scented couscous.

1/3 cup pure maple syrup
1/3 cup white wine
3 tablespoons soy sauce
2 tablespoons brown sugar
2 scallions, minced
2 garlic cloves, finely minced
1 teaspoon sesame oil
1 teaspoon minced fresh ginger
Salt, pepper
4 salmon steaks, 6–8 ounces each

In a medium bowl, mix the maple syrup, wine, soy sauce, sugar, scallions, garlic, sesame oil, ginger, salt and pepper. Immerse the salmon in the marinade (a Ziploc bag works well) and marinate, refrigerated, for 1 to 3 hours.

Grill or broil until the fish is cooked through, basting with marinade at first. Once the fish is halfway done, stop basting so that the outside crisps or browns nicely.

Serves 4

CHAPTER EIGHT

The Bistro Italiano, Pasta and Pizza

There are few things, excluding a fancy omelet, that whip up as fast and easy as a great pasta dish. Pasta is so versatile, insofar as it comes in countless shapes and sizes, but also in that it can be sauced or topped with almost anything in the fridge or pantry. Your imagination and your personal taste and palate, is the only higher authority when it comes to the variety of pasta seasonings and add-ins you can choose. In less than 30 minutes, and just a drizzle of extra virgin olive oil and a dusting of sea salt and pepper, you have a meal. Add some crisp pancetta, fresh herbs and a shower of grated cheese and you have a feast. The potential for another great pasta dish (and a solution to lunch, supper, and impromptu guests) is unlimited.

As simple as pasta is, there are a few rules to better pasta dishes.

First, boil pasta in water to which you've added some sea salt and some olive oil. This insures the pasta doesn't stick to itself and the pasta, once cooked, has a bit of flavor which is a totally different flavor than when you add the salt in afterwards (you will add salt in the recipe itself but start with lightly salted pasta nonetheless).

For boiling the pasta, use a nice sized, tall stock pot. A 6- or 8-quart pot is usually sufficient. A pasta pot can be inexpensive and still up to the job. Unlike a stock pot, which needs to be of excellent quality, a pasta or simple water-boiling pot doesn't have to cost a lot. But whatever pot you choose, don't boil pasta in a too-small pot. Pasta needs room to cook properly and keep from becoming starchy or sticky. Add pasta to the water once the water is at a full boil.

You can use fresh pasta or dry but opt for quality no matter what you do. If the fresh pasta is your own, let's assume it's top notch (and use durum wheat flour to make your own pasta). If you use fresh pasta that comes from nearby stores, just try it out and suss out a best brand or supplier. Alternatively, you can ask a local Italian restaurant you frequent if they'll sell you fresh pasta to take out.

If using dry pasta, I find there is De Cecco and there is everyone else. Of course, that's not quite true (there are many gourmet dry pastas that are remarkable), but my point is don't assume that all dry pasta is the same. I would start with imported brands and, as with fresh pasta, try a few brands (and different shapes and sizes) until you find what you prefer. You might also like certain styles or shapes of pasta from one company, but prefer the lasagna noodles or width of the spaghetti from another.

Whole-wheat pasta is another great way to add extra nutrition and fiber to your pasta dishes. That said, test those out, too. Some brands of whole-wheat pasta are amazing, while others are tasteless and gritty.

About Pizza

Is anything as wonderful as yet another homemade pizza, done your way, using simple ingredients and a simple dough base? Homemade bistro style pizza is so it can put a trendy pizza restaurant to shame. Yes, even without a brick oven, you can make outstanding pizza and/or use simple pizza dough to make a ton of other amazing recipes. Trust me. A baker knows about good uses for handy pizza dough. Make your own or, in a pinch, you have my permission to pick up pizza dough at a local pizzeria or bakery and then top it off with wonderful things, that are all fresh and to your own taste. There's no need to order out. Dine in and make your kitchen into a mini pizzeria chez vous. Even an imperfect home pizza, made with quality ingredients and a great dough, bakes up beautiful. And the flavor? Fresh garlic, fresh basil, fresh cheeses? Nothing is better than homemade (and leftovers, while part of pizza making, are most desirable!)

As you will see with these recipes, there's always something extraordinary you can do with a foundation of pizza dough so long as you have some on hand. I think my best advice is to find a pizza dough recipe you prefer, a technique that works for you, and an oven temperature (and oven rack position) that gives you the consistent results that matches your taste and expectations for a great pizza. Once those basics are refined, feel free to invent anything you like with pizza dough.

Cold Rise Rustic Pizza Dough

I can't tell you how many ways I make basic pizza dough and yet how I like each and every recipe I create. But this one is about the easiest and gives you a crisp, bistro style pizza. The cold rise also results in a better-tasting pizza due to the unique development of the dough. Very little yeast and a lot of time does the magic. Everyone needs a basic 'black dress' great pizza dough; this is my latest, current favorite.

1/4 teaspoon instant yeast
1 ½ cups spring water, room temperature
4-5 cups bread flour
1 3/4 teaspoon salt
¼ teaspoon sugar
2 tablespoons olive oil

In a mixer bowl or bread machine, whisk the yeast and water together for 1-2 minutes. Add in most of the flour, salt, sugar and olive oil. Mix, then gently knead, adding in more flour as required to make a soft dough. Cover and let rise 8-12 hours (or after 6 hours if it is later in the day, refrigerate the dough in an oiled plastic bag; punch down if you see it rising and release the gases).

Place the dough in a plastic bag which has been lightly sprayed with non-stick cooking spray. Refrigerate overnight or up until two days.

To bake, divide dough into three.

Pan out as you prefer for pizza (in a pan or on a baking sheet). Smear with olive oil and then put on the toppings you like. Cover lightly with a large plastic sheet and let rise 1-4 hours. Preheat oven to 475 F for a good hour before you bake. Bake on middle shelf of oven (about 9-14 minutes per pizza)

Makes 9-12 inch thin pizzas

Pepperoni and Pancetta Pizza Bread

This specialty pizza features many folds or layers which is why my Italian neighbor calls it centi pelli or "one hundred skins pizza." This is great, cut in generous hunks, warm or cold, and served with sangria or sparkling lemonade. Instant yeast is also known as bread machine yeast and it's what I recommend for this recipe.

Dough

1 ¾ cups warm water
1 tablespoon instant yeast
2 eggs
¼ cup olive oil
2 teaspoons salt
4 ½–5 ½ cups bread flour
Olive oil
Semolina

Filling

4–6 tablespoons olive oil
3 garlic cloves, crushed
2 teaspoons finely minced basil
Salt, pepper
2 cups grated Parmesan cheese
1 small jar marinated-in-oil artichoke hearts, coarsely chopped
½ cup minced sun-dried tomatoes
1 cup black olives, pitted and minced
½ pound spicy pepperoni, thinly sliced and sautéed
3 cups cooked pancetta, drained and chopped

In a large mixer bowl, whisk together the water and yeast and let stand a few minutes. Stir in the eggs, oil and then the salt. Add 4 ½ cups of the flour and knead to make a soft dough, adding more flour as required, up to another cup. Knead for 8 to 10 minutes. Cover and let the dough rise for 30 minutes.

Gently deflate the dough and let it rest for ten minutes.

On a lightly floured board, roll dough out to a large rectangle, about 18 by 24 inches. Line a 15- by 20-inch baking sheet with parchment paper. Coat the parchment with a bit of olive oil and sprinkle with semolina.

Brush the dough surface with the 4 to 6 tablespoons of olive oil, then smear on the crushed garlic, basil and dust with salt, and a generous amount of pepper. Sprinkle the Parmesan cheese on, then the chopped artichokes, sun-dried tomatoes, olives, pepperoni, and pancetta. Press the ingredients into the dough slightly.

Fold the dough from the top down into 3 or 4 folds, almost like you are folding a letter. Gently lift the dough onto the prepared baking sheet. Using a rolling pin, press and roll the dough out (it is now filled) to fit to all corners of the pan. Smear the top of the dough with a bit more olive oil. Insert the baking sheet in a plastic bag and let rise for 20 to 35 minutes.

Preheat the oven to 350 F. Bake for 25 to 35 minutes, until the top is golden brown. Cut into large squares to serve.

Serves 12–16

Muffaletta

Way down yonder in New Orleans they enjoy this great, stuffed sandwich of cold cuts and olive salad, all pressed into a sandwich extravaganza that will make you a legend, no matter where you hail from. This savory treat is easily made ahead for serving at an informal lunch or to tote to your picnic. This recipe makes two rustic stuffed breads (pick up the round breads at your bakery or bake them yourself), as well as roasted peppers, marinated artichokes, and pimento-stuffed olives.

1 pound round rustic, crusty bread, split horizontally into three layers
1 cup red wine vinegar
3 large garlic cloves, finely minced
3/8 teaspoon salt, pepper to taste
1/3 cup olive oil
¾ pound sliced Provolone cheese
1 cup very finely chopped marinated artichokes
1½ pounds sliced salami or pastrami
1 cup pimento-stuffed green olives, very finely chopped
1½ pound sliced mortadella
1 cup roasted sweet red peppers, finely minced
1½ pounds sliced smoked turkey or chicken
1½ pounds sliced cappicolo

First prepare the loaf. Dig out a bit of the breadcrumbs from the upper and lower layers. In a small bowl, mix the vinegar, garlic, some salt and pepper to taste and then the oil. Drizzle a little over each layer of the bread.

On the bottom layer, place a layer of the cheese, then the chopped artichokes, and the salami or pastrami.

Cover with the middle layer of the bread. Top with more cheese, the chopped olives, the mortadella, more cheese, the red peppers, and smoked turkey or chicken.

Press the top layer on the sandwich. Wrap well in foil. Press the sandwich down, using a cast iron skillet or a few plates, and refrigerate to meld the flavors and flatten the sandwich (it does not flatten all that much, but enough).

Slice to serve.

Serves 6–8

Double Garlic Pizza

Only a vampire would refuse this incredible, savory garlic pizza that is thin, crisp and appetizingly laced with herbs. This takes both dry and fresh basil.

Garlic Dough
1 1/3 cups warm water
1 ¾ teaspoons instant yeast
1 ½ teaspoons salt
1 tablespoon sugar
2 tablespoons extra-virgin olive oil
5 medium garlic cloves, finely minced
1 ½ cups bread flour
1 ½ cups all-purpose flour, or more
Cornmeal or semolina
Olive oil

Topping
1/3 cup olive oil
6 large garlic cloves, finely minced
Salt, pepper, oregano, and basil
1 cup shredded mozzarella
½ cup grated Parmesan
½ cup grated American Asiago
Fresh minced basil
Fresh minced parsley

For the dough, in a mixer bowl, hand whisk the water and yeast together. Briskly blend in the salt, sugar, olive oil, garlic, bread flour and most of the all-purpose flour. Mix and then knead for about 8 to10 minutes, dusting in additional all-purpose flour as required to get a soft dough. Spray the dough with nonstick cooking spray or coat it with a bit of olive oil. Cover lightly with a large plastic bag and let rise for 45 minutes to 2 hours, until almost doubled in size. Alternatively, you can refrigerate the dough and let it rise slowly overnight (which is a cool rise) to use it the next day.
Divide the dough in three equal portions and shape into three thin (9 inches or so) pizzas.

Line a large baking sheet (you might need two depending on how thin you stretch the pizzas) with parchment paper, smear with olive oil, and dust with cornmeal or semolina. Place each pizza on the sheet (if they don't all fit, use a second pan; essentially, use your largest pan that fits your oven and place 1, 2, or all 3 pizzas on it. Bake in one bake or in batches).

Brush each pizza with some oil and then spread the garlic on, dividing equally between the pizzas. Dust with salt, pepper, oregano and basil. Top each pizza with the cheeses, and then dust with the fresh basil and parsley.

Cover lightly with plastic and let rise until puffy on the edges, 30 to 45 minutes (but longer is fine too). If you are in a hurry, you can forgo the rise and bake the pizzas right away, which results in a crisper pizza.

Preheat the oven to 425 F. Bake the pizzas until they are crisp around the edges and bubbling on top, 10 to 15 minutes. Dust with basil and parsley.

Makes 3 small pizzas

White Pizza with Artichoke Hearts, Ricotta, and Roasted Garlic

This is a light, beautiful white pizza with touches of green that brings instant raves. The recipe features easy, classic pizza dough (it's not quite pizza, not quite focaccia), topped with herbs, ricotta cheese, garlic, the best virgin olive oil you can find and marinated artichoke hearts.

Classic Pizza Dough

2 teaspoons instant yeast

1 ½ cups warm water

4 teaspoons sugar

1 ½ teaspoons salt

3 tablespoons light olive oil

4 cups all-purpose flour, approximately

1/3 cup panko

White Pizza Topping (per pizza)

1-2 tablespoons extra virgin olive oil

2 tablespoons minced basil

2 tablespoons minced parsley

3–4 garlic cloves, finely minced

Salt, pepper

¾ cup Ricotta cheese

1 cup Fontina or Chevre cheese, in bits

1 cup or a small jar marinated artichoke hearts, drained and patted dry, quartered

8–10 cloves roasted garlic, coarsely chopped

½ cup grated Parmesan cheese

Finishing Touches

Fresh lemon juice

White balsamic vinegar

Hot sauce

For the dough, in a mixer bowl, hand whisk the water and yeast together briefly. Briskly whisk in the sugar, salt, olive oil, and about half of the flour and mix/knead to form a soft, but not too sticky dough, 8-10 minutes. Add the remaining flour or a bit more as required for the right consistency, which is a soft, bouncy dough. Allow to rest, covered with a large plastic bag, for about 45 minutes.

When the dough is ready, gently deflate it and allow it to rest for 15 minutes before using. Alternatively, refrigerate the dough in an oiled plastic bag for up to two days.

Divide the dough into three equal portions. Line a large baking sheet with parchment paper. Drizzle some olive oil on the parchment and scatter on a light dusting of panko.

To make a pizza, gently stretch out one of the dough portions into a round. Smear some oil on it, and dust it with basil, parsley, garlic, salt and pepper. Cover with a sheet of plastic and let rest for 30 minutes. Top each pizza with the ricotta and Fontina cheeses. Place the artichoke hearts around the sides and middle and finish with the roasted garlic cloves.

Top with the Parmesan cheese and another dusting of salt, pepper, basil and parsley. Cover lightly with a plastic bag and let rise for 1 to 3 hours, as you wish (less for crisp pizza, longer for puffier ones). Repeat with the remaining dough portions.

Preheat the oven to 475 F. Bake the pizzas on the upper rack of the oven for 12-16 minutes until crisp and the cheese is bubbling and the edges of the pizza are medium brown. As each pizza comes out of the oven, sprinkle it with a few drops of fresh lemon juice or white balsamic vinegar and hot sauce.

Makes 3 9-inch pizzas

Pizza Quiche

Whether you use your own pie shell or a store-bought one and add a bit of spice, cheese, tomatoes and cream in this recipe, you'll be rewarded, big-time. This is pizza flavor with a dash of French sophistication. This is a brown bag gourmet treat or a fall brunch hospitality dish. The taste says pizza; the presentation says you're a genius.

1 9-inch pie shell, unbaked
1 cup whipping cream
1 cup finely ground canned tomatoes
3 eggs
2 ½ cups shredded Mozzarella cheese
2 tablespoons olive oil
1 teaspoon garlic powder or 2 teaspoons minced fresh garlic
½ teaspoon onion powder
1 teaspoon finely minced fresh oregano or ½ teaspoon dried oregano
1 teaspoon finely minced fresh basil or ½ teaspoon dried basil
Salt, pepper

Finishing Touches
Grated Parmesan cheese
Minced parsley

Preheat the oven to 375 F. Line a baking sheet with parchment paper and place the pie shell on it.

In a mixer bowl, blend the whipping cream with the tomatoes, eggs, Mozzarella cheese, oil, garlic powder, oregano, basil, salt and pepper. Pour the mixture into the pie shell. Dust the top with parsley and Parmesan cheese.

Lower the temperature to 350 F and bake until just set, 35 to 45 minutes. Quiche will start to puff up around the edges and appear set in the middle. That is when it is done. Cool for at least 20 minutes before serving. Serve with a tossed green salad and minestrone or hunks of fresh Italian bread and assorted olives.

Serves 5–6

Deluxe Marinara Pasta Toss Sauce

This is a hot and spicy topping for pasta and pizza. Commercially (it's imported and comes in jars) it's called La Bomba, and it's always good but I love making my own. Three dimensions of tomatoes tease your palate: fresh plum tomatoes, piquant sun-dried tomatoes and marinara sauce. This is also great for a quick dinner when you can reinvent the leftovers by adding some of this zesty topping to grilled fish or chicken.

½ cup boiling water
¾ cup sun-dried tomatoes, packed in oil, slightly drained
¼–1/3 cup olive oil
½ medium onion, finely minced
1 large carrot, shredded
1 medium stalk celery, finely minced
3 garlic cloves, finely minced
3 pounds trimmed, diced plum tomatoes
Salt, pepper
¼ cup red wine
2 tablespoons fresh lemon juice
1 cup prepared spaghetti sauce
2 tablespoons finely minced oregano
2 tablespoons finely minced parsley
½ cup vegetable or beef broth
½ teaspoon garlic powder
¼ teaspoon onion powder
½ teaspoon mixed Italian spices
¼–½ teaspoon red pepper flakes

Place the boiling water and sun-dried tomatoes in a food processor and process until smooth. Set aside.

In a large pot, heat the olive oil over low heat and sauté the onion, carrot, celery and garlic until softened, about 5 to10 minutes. Add the plum tomatoes and season with salt and pepper. Heat until the tomatoes start to soften, about 15 minutes, and then add the wine, lemon juice, spaghetti sauce, oregano, parsley, bouillon, garlic powder, onion powder, Italian spices, red pepper flakes, and the puréed sun-dried tomato mixture.

Simmer until thickened to a sauce-like consistency, about 1 hour. Add some more liquid (water or broth) for desired consistency and adjust seasonings.

Serves 6–8

California BBQ Chicken Pizza

Barbecued chicken slivers (your own or left-over take-out chicken), a fusion of melted cheeses, and the perk of red onion make this a zesty pizza meal. This amount of topping is for three small pizzas.

Olive oil
1 recipe Classic Pizza dough (or store-bought dough)
3 boneless, skinless chicken breast halves, cooked and slivered or cubed
¾ cup hickory-flavored barbeque sauce
½ bunch fresh cilantro, chopped
½ cup shredded smoked Gouda cheese,
½ cup shredded sharp Cheddar cheese
1 cup thinly sliced red onion
Salt, pepper

Stack two baking sheets together and line the top one with parchment paper. Place the pizza dough rounds on the baking sheet. Cover lightly and let rise 30 minutes to 2 hours (depending on how risen you want them; more rise is a chewy pizza; less rise is a crisper one).

Preheat the oven to 450 F.

Brush the pizza dough with olive oil. Arrange some chicken pieces on top. Drizzle on some barbecue sauce, then sprinkle on cilantro, some of each of the two cheeses and top some red onion. Dust with salt and pepper.

Bake until the cheese is bubbling, 12 to 18 minutes.

Makes 3 pizzas

Pasta Primavera

There are various ways of preparing this classic, which is essentially linguine tossed with fresh, springy vegetables in a light cream sauce that includes Parmesan, pine nuts and then crowned with fragrant, fresh basil. Chefs tirelessly revamp this classic recipe; this is my own best version. Take it up a notch with a shaving of truffles and some dots of creamy Chevre.

1 pound box linguine or spaghetti
1 cup fresh or frozen green peas
1 cup snap peas
1 cup asparagus spears, in 1 ½ inch pieces
2 cups small diced broccoli florets
1 cup carrots, in fine matchsticks
1/3 cup cream, any type
¼ cup minced Brie or Camembert cheese
2–3 tablespoons extra virgin olive oil
2 garlic cloves, finely minced
1 finely minced teaspoon capers
½ teaspoon crushed red pepper flakes
Salt, pepper
¼ cup grated Parmesan cheese
¼ cup grated Asiago cheese (American type)
2 cups grape-sized tomatoes, cut in half
¼ cup finely minced parsley
6 fresh basil leaves, finely minced
1 teaspoon finely minced oregano or ¼ teaspoon dry

Cook the pasta according to the package instructions, then drain and toss with a touch of oil. Set aside in a covered casserole and keep warm in a 300 F oven.

Meanwhile, bring 4 cups of salted water in a 3-quart sauce pan, blanch (immerse for 2 to 3 minutes) each type of vegetable, drain, place in a bowl, and rinse with cool water to stop cooking.

Place the pasta in a large serving bowl. Add the cream, Brie or Camembert, oil, garlic, capers, red pepper flakes, salt and pepper.

Add the Parmesan and Asiago cheeses. Toss the pasta a bit and then add the tomatoes, parsley, basil, and oregano. Dust with salt and pepper.

Serves 3–4

Pasta Puttanesca

So much is written about the roots of this dish, the name of which translates to "prostitute's pasta," attributable (depending on the source) to either its spiciness or the "tarted up" quality of the dish or to the fact that prostitutes could quickly whip up a batch between clients. I don't much pay much mind to either explanation; I just think this is one of the best ways to make a fine dish of pasta.

Pasta

1 pound box pasta (spaghetti or linguine), cooked, tossed with a bit of olive oil, and kept warm

Sauce

2–3 tablespoons extra virgin olive oil
6 garlic cloves, finely minced
1 32-ounce can crushed plum tomatoes
1 cup marinara sauce, homemade or canned
1 tablespoon white or red wine
1 tablespoon balsamic vinegar
¼ cup finely minced parsley
½ teaspoon each dried basil and oregano (or 1 tablespoon each finely minced fresh)
½ teaspoon, more or less to taste, red pepper flakes
Tiny pinch sugar
Salt, pepper
½ cup coarsely minced capers
1 cup pitted and coarsely minced Kalamata olives
1–2 cups grated Parmesan cheese

To make the sauce, in a large skillet, warm the olive oil and sauté the garlic for a few minutes to barely soften. Stir in the crushed tomatoes, marinara sauce, wine, vinegar, parsley, basil, oregano, red pepper flakes, sugar, salt and pepper.

Cook to meld the flavors, about 6 to 10 minutes, over low heat.

Remove from the heat and let cool for a minute. Toss the sauce with the cooked pasta. Then fold in the capers and olives, and dust generously with the cheese. Season to taste with salt and pepper.

Serves 4–6

Pumpkin Ravioli with Sage Butter and Shitake Mushroom Béchamel

Make as many of these pumpkin ravioli as you like, freeze them, and pop them in simmering water when you want a special meal. You can use fresh pasta sheets to make the ravioli (and cut with a paring knife into small squares or a round or square ravioli cutter) or, handier still, store-bought wonton wrappers. Canned pumpkin is a noble shortcut but just make sure you purchase plain pumpkin (not sugar and spiced pumpkin puree). You can also use pureed butternut squash instead of pumpkin.

Pumpkin Filling
1 ½ cups canned pumpkin or well-mashed pumpkin
¾ cup Ricotta cheese, well drained
1/3 cup Chevre cheese
½ cup grated Parmesan cheese
¼ cup whipping cream
1 egg
2 teaspoons balsamic vinegar
Pinch of freshly grated nutmeg
Salt, pepper
1/8 teaspoon cayenne
1 teaspoon finely minced sage
1 pound fresh pasta sheets or wonton wrappers, as required, and 1 egg for forming ravioli

Shitake Mushroom Béchamel
1 cup shitake mushrooms, very finely diced
1 cup white button mushrooms, very finely diced
2 tablespoons olive oil
1 tablespoon unsalted butter
2 tablespoons all-purpose flour
1 small garlic clove, finely minced
1 cup milk
Salt, pepper

Sage Butter Sauce
4 tablespoons unsalted butter
6 sage leaves, chopped

Finishing Touches
Minced parsley and sage
Grated Parmesan cheese
4 whole large sage leaves

For the filling, combine the pumpkin, Ricotta, Chevre, Parmesan, cream, egg, vinegar, nutmeg, salt, pepper, cayenne, and sage. Taste and adjust seasonings as needed. Refrigerate.

To make the ravioli using wonton wrappers, place them on a sheet of parchment paper. Deposit a small spoonful (about half a tablespoon) of pumpkin filling on each wonton wrapper. Using a small pastry brush, moisten the edges with a little beaten egg and cover with another wonton wrapper. Press the edges to seal. Repeat until you run out of wrappers or filling.

To make the ravioli using sheets of fresh pasta, deposit rows of pumpkin filling mounds on the fresh pasta, leaving a border of ½ inch around each mound. Brush the beaten egg around the outer edges of the mounds of filling. Place another sheet of pasta dough on top and press lightly over mounds. Cut with a paring knife into squares or using a ravioli cutter (even a cookie cutter is fine, especially if you have one with a fluted edge). You can freeze these uncooked raviolis, in a single layer, for 1 to 2 months.

For the Shitake Mushroom Béchamel, heat the oil in a medium nonstick skillet and add the mushrooms. Slowly cook the mushrooms until they are reduced to one-third and are very dark in color. Remove the cooked mushrooms from the pan and set aside.

Add the butter to the pan and heat for a minute. Add the flour and cook, stirring, for a few minutes to cook the flour. Add the garlic and then slowly stir in the milk, salt and pepper.

Cook over low heat to thicken mixture slightly, about 2 to 3 minutes. Fold in the cooked mushrooms. Set aside.

For the Sage Butter, melt the butter and chopped sage leaves with a pinch of salt until the butter foams and just begins to brown. Remove the sage leaves and then slowly cook the butter sauce until it turns amber brown.

To cook the ravioli, bring 3 quarts of water to a gentle boil. Cook a few ravioli at a time for 2-3 minutes. Drain and place on a platter.

To serve, arrange a few ravioli on each plate, drizzle with the sage butter and a few tablespoons of the béchamel. Dust with parsley, a whole sage leave in center of each plate, and grated Parmesan cheese and top each mound of ravioli with a whole sage leaf.

Serves 6

Sun-Dried Tomato-Stuffed Chicken Tortellini

Serve these tender, zesty morsels with an arabica, Alfredo, or marinara sauce, or simply with quality extra virgin olive oil, a dusting of Parmesan and fresh basil. Use wonton wrappers or very thin, fresh pasta for the tortellini.

Chicken Tortellini

1 pound boneless, skinless chicken breast or 1 pound ground chicken

1 egg

½ cup grated Parmesan cheese

¼ cup seasoned breadcrumbs

3 garlic cloves, very finely minced

3 tablespoons sun-dried tomato pesto

2 tablespoons minced parsley

2 tablespoons ice water

2 tablespoons extra virgin olive oil

1 tablespoon balsamic vinegar

1 teaspoon dried oregano

1 teaspoon dried basil

¾ teaspoon salt

¼ teaspoon pepper

60 won ton wrappers or 1 pound of fresh pasta sheets (about 60 squares, 2 ½–3 inches each)

1 egg, lightly beaten

Finishing Touches

Olive oil and garlic or marinara sauce

Grated Parmesan cheese

Minced parsley

If you are using whole chicken breasts, place the meat in a food processor and pulse to grind. Transfer to a large bowl and add the egg, cheese, breadcrumbs, garlic, pesto, parsley, ice water, oil, vinegar, oregano, basil, salt and pepper. Mix well.

Lay several wonton wrappers or pasta squares out on a large sheet of parchment paper. Put about 2 teaspoons of mixture in each one. Using a small pastry brush, paint the edges of each square with some beaten egg. Fold the pasta or won ton over to make a triangle, and then fold the ends backwards to meet each other, forming a tortellini.

Bring a large pot of salted water to a simmer. Simmer a few tortellinis at a time for 5 to 8 minutes, until tender and cooked through, and remove with a slotted spoon to a serving platter. Repeat with the remaining tortellini. Serve hot, with the desired sauce and garnishes. You can also serve it as a casserole by saucing the cooked tortellini, topping with mozzarella cheese, and baking until the cheese bubbles.

Serves 5–6

Italian Sausage and Peppers Rustica

Sausage-and-peppers is a rustic Italian dish that you can find in Italy as well as in the American Northeast, wherever there is a vibrant Italian community. Most times, it's comprised of onions, peppers, and sausages sautéed together and then tossed with pasta and finished with Parmesan cheese. This is totally wonderful and soul-satisfying, especially when you are hankering for a casserole or need a good potluck recipe. You can also use turkey sausage if you like, but this dish is best with a mix of hot and sweet Italian sausages.

1 box (12–16 ounces) pasta, such as rigatoni
½ cup plus 1 tablespoon olive oil
6-7 hot or sweet, Italian sausages (6 ounce sausages)
1 large green pepper, cored and sliced
1 large orange pepper, cored and sliced
1 large red pepper, cored and sliced
1 large yellow pepper, cored and sliced
1 large onion, thinly sliced
2 14-ounce cans crushed, oven-roasted tomatoes with roasted garlic
1 14-ounce can tomato sauce or marinara sauce
3 tablespoons sun-dried tomato pesto
1 tablespoon balsamic vinegar
5–7 garlic cloves, finely minced
Salt, pepper
½ cup, or more, combination of grated Pecorino and Parmesan cheeses
¼- ½ teaspoon dried oregano
¼ teaspoon dried basil

Preheat the oven to 350 F.

Bring a large pot of salted water to a boil and cook the pasta until al dente. Drain and set aside.

Meanwhile, heat the tablespoon of olive oil in a nonstick skillet. Over medium-low heat, cook the sausages, turning every so often, until they are nicely done (about 15 to 20 minutes). Prick them and let fat drain out as they cook for another 2 to 3 minutes. Remove from the pan and cool; slice into ½-inch thick slices.

Add the peppers to the skillet and cook slowly until softened, adding in a bit of olive oil if mixture sticks, 6 to 8 minutes. Add the onion and cook to soften, 5 to 8 minutes. Taste and adjust seasonings if needed.

In a 4- or 5-quart casserole, add the crushed tomatoes, tomato sauce, pesto, the remaining ½ cup of olive oil, vinegar, garlic, salt and pepper.

Place the sausage-onion-pepper mixture in a casserole dish and stir. Fold in the pasta and cheese. Dust with oregano and basil. Bake, stirring occasionally, until the mixture is stew-like, about 45 to 55 minutes.

Serve with additional cheese on the side and hard Italian rolls.

Serves 4–6

Bistro-Style Garlic Lasagna

You can use regular dry, imported lasagna noodles or fresh-made lasagna sheets for this hearty dish. This is sumptuous or as one of my testers put it, it's a total sensory experience. Homemade marinara is best but prepared marinara is fine if you're pressed for time.

Pasta
Regular or garlic flavored nonstick cooking spray
10–12 ounces cooked green spinach lasagna noodles (about 9 strips 2 ½ inches by 8 inches or so)

Garlic Béchamel
2 tablespoons olive oil
3 tablespoons flour
½ cup chicken broth
1 tablespoon white wine
2 garlic cloves, finely minced
3/8 teaspoon salt
¼ teaspoon white pepper
1 ½ cups milk
4 tablespoons Chevre

Marinara Sauce
2 ½ cups prepared marinara sauce
2 garlic cloves, finely minced
1 tablespoon balsamic vinegar

Filling
1 10-ounce bag fresh spinach, steamed, drained and finely chopped
1 tablespoon sun-dried tomato pesto
1 tablespoon basil pesto
1 cup fresh basil leaves, finely minced
¼ cup finely minced parsley

¼ teaspoon dried oregano
½ teaspoon dry basil
2 cups finely shredded skim milk Mozzarella
1 cup low-fat Ricotta cheese
2 tablespoons grated Parmesan cheese

Finishing Touches
Minced fresh parsley
Paprika

Preheat the oven to 350 F and spray an 8 by 11-inch rectangular baking dish roasting pan lightly with the cooking spray.

Prepare the lasagna noodles according to package instructions, leaving them just slightly undercooked. (Fresh is best or then a good quality imported dry lasagna noodle. No-boil lasagna is not recommended as it can be gummy in the final result)

For the Garlic Béchamel, in a 3-quart saucepan, over low heat, warm up the olive oil for one minute. Stir in the flour and cook, stirring, until flour is pasty. Slowly pour in the chicken broth, whisking all the while, and then quickly, whisk in the wine, garlic, salt and pepper. Whisk in the milk, stirring all the while. Increase the heat and cook, whisking, until mixture thickens to a thin milkshake consistency, 1 to 2 minutes. Stir in the chevre and remove from the heat.

For the Marinara Sauce, stir marinara sauce, garlic and balsamic vinegar together in a medium bowl.

To assemble the lasagna, spoon about ½ cup of marinara sauce into casserole. Lay down a layer of pasta. Smear on some more marinara, about ½ cup of the béchamel, then the spinach. Top with another layer of pasta. Smear on more marinara, béchamel, and dot with the pestos. Scatter on some parsley, basil, oregano and basil. Sprinkle on about 1 cup of mozzarella. Top with another layer of pasta, then marinara, béchamel, and drop the ricotta in dollops over this layer. Top with more pasta, and use up the remaining marinara, béchamel, spices, and mozzarella. The final layer should be pasta, marinara, a drizzle of béchamel, a pinch of spices, basil leaves, and dusting of the Parmesan.

Bake 35 to 45 minutes, until mixture seems hot through and through and the top is bubbling slightly.

Sprinkle parsley and paprika over the top just before serving.

Serves 6

Triple-Cheese Macaroni with Buttered Breadcrumb Topping

A toasty, buttery crumb topping plus tons of real cheese and a nip of hot mustard upgrade this cafeteria classic to a whole new level. Nothing out of a box can touch this. This reheats like a charm, but it's unbeatable hot and bubbling from the oven.

2 ½ cups elbow macaroni, cooked to taste (perhaps slightly on the firm side)

Cheese Sauce
3 tablespoons unsalted butter
3 tablespoons all-purpose flour
1 ½ cups milk
2 ½ cups shredded Cheddar cheese
1 ½ cup shredded Havarti or Monterey Jack cheese
1 teaspoon dry mustard
Salt, pepper
¼ teaspoon paprika
Pinch cayenne

Buttered Breadcrumb Topping
1 ½ cups finely minced, slightly stale breadcrumbs
¼ cup butter, melted
Salt, pepper

Preheat the oven to 350 F and butter a 4-quart casserole. Have prepared (cooked) pasta ready, nearby.

For the Cheese Sauce, in a 4-quart saucepan, melt the butter over low heat. Add the flour and cook to brown flour slightly, 2 to 3 minutes. Slowly pour in the milk and let it warm briefly. Add the cheeses, mustard, salt, pepper, paprika and cayenne and cook over low heat to melt the cheeses.

Place the cooked, drained macaroni in the prepared casserole. Pour in the cheese sauce and toss gently to cover the pasta with sauce.

For the topping, toss the breadcrumbs with the butter, salt, and pepper. Evenly distribute over the topping over the pasta.

Bake for 35 to 40 minutes.

Serves 4–6

Restaurant-Style Spaghetti and Meatballs

When was the last time you made a great meat sauce, replete with spicy meatballs? Sometimes the simplest meals are the most memorable. This is one of those extraordinary versions of an Italian blue plate special. It's restaurant-worthy but with unrivaled homemade, wholesome taste. I prefer a combo of lean and medium ground beef.

Sauce
8 oil-cured sun-dried tomatoes, drained
2–3 tablespoons extra virgin olive oil
1 ½ pounds ground beef
½ pound Italian sausage
2–3 garlic cloves, finely minced
Salt, pepper
2 tablespoons tomato paste
1 28-ounce can ground plum tomatoes
1 cup prepared marinara sauce
2 tablespoons finely minced onion
½ teaspoon dry oregano
½ teaspoon dry basil
1 tablespoon minced parsley
¼ cup beef broth
1 tablespoon balsamic vinegar
2 tablespoons red wine
2 pinches crushed red pepper flakes

Meatballs
1 pound ground medium beef
1 tablespoon finely minced onion
1 teaspoon finely minced garlic
1 teaspoon garlic powder
½ teaspoon onion powder
2 tablespoons very finely shredded carrots
2 eggs
¼ cup breadcrumbs
½ teaspoon crushed red pepper flakes

1/3 cup grated Parmesan cheese
2 tablespoons cold water
½–1 teaspoon salt
Pepper
1–2 tablespoons light olive oil

Finishing Touches
Minced parsley
Minced basil

Cover the sun-dried tomatoes with boiling water and let stand a few minutes to plump them. Drain and finely chop.

For the Sauce, heat the oil in a heavy bottomed 6-quart saucepan. Crumble or break up the ground meat and sausage and brown lightly, breaking up the meat so that it cooks evenly, 10 to 12 minutes. Add garlic and sauté 1 to 2 minutes. Season with salt and pepper. Stir in tomato paste, tomatoes, marinara sauce, the sun-dried tomatoes, onion, oregano, basil, parsley, broth, balsamic vinegar, wine and red pepper flakes. Adjust seasonings or add more tomato liquid or beef broth if needed.

Simmer for 30 to 45 minutes over low heat.

Meanwhile, prepare the meatballs. In a medium bowl, use your hands to mix together the meat, onion, garlic, garlic powder, onion powder, carrots, eggs, breadcrumbs, red pepper flakes, cheese, water, salt, and pepper. Mix well and then shape into small balls (or whatever size you prefer).

Add 1 to 2 tablespoons of oil to a nonstick fry pan set over low heat. Add the meatballs and cook until done, about 8 to10 minutes. Drain and add to the meat sauce.

As the sauce simmers, prepare the pasta according to package directions.

Serve the meat sauce over hot pasta. Dust with cheese and fresh herbs.

Serves 4

Fettuccine Alfredo

Make this once and it will become a staple in your pasta repertoire. This is lightly infused with garlic, creamy, and simply delicious. It is also my middle son's favorite pasta dishes of all time—so much so that I initially called it After School Alfredo because he enjoyed it daily from grade two through high school graduation. Any pasta shape thrives with this easy, zesty sauce provided you opt for freshly grated Parmesan and lots of fresh garlic.

½ pound pasta
2–3 tablespoons unsalted butter or olive oil
3 tablespoons flour
1 ¼ cups milk
1 garlic clove, finely minced
Pinch fresh nutmeg
Salt, pepper
½ cup grated Parmesan cheese

Finishing Touches
Grated Parmesan
Minced parsley
Freshly ground pepper

Cook pasta according to package directions. Drain and set aside.

While the pasta is cooking, set a medium saucepan over medium heat, add the butter and allow it to melt or add the oil and allow it to heat. Stir in the flour. Using a whisk, let the flour mixture 1-3 minutes, until it browns just a little.

Slowly pour in the milk, whisking all the while to incorporate it. Increase the heat to thicken the mixture or leave it on medium if it begins to get saucy. Stir in the garlic, nutmeg, salt, and pepper. Toss in the cheese and stir with a whisk or wooden spoon. Ladle generously over the cooked pasta.

Garnish with cheese, parsley and pepper.

Serves 2–3

Encore Pasta

Consider the amazing punch of ingredients (creamy cheeses, sun-dried tomatoes, chunks of Calabrese salami, spices, and garlic) and you can see why this recipe rocks. It is gourmet good and tastes like a chef stepped into your kitchen to create a signature dish.

Pasta

1 pound dry linguine (or any shape pasta)
2/3 cup olive oil
1 cup cubed eggplant
2 ounces (about 10 thin slices) pancetta, chopped
2 ounces (about 10 thin slices) Calabrese dry salami, chopped
2 hot Italian sausages, slow cooked and coarsely chopped
1 Scotch bonnet pepper, cored and finely minced
2 large garlic cloves, finely minced
1 ½ teaspoons salt
Pepper
Juice of ½ a small lemon
2 tablespoons each minced parsley, basil
1 tablespoon grated Parmesan cheese
8 sun-dried tomatoes, plumped and finely sliced
2 cups freshly grated Parmesan cheese
4 tablespoons St. Andre cheese (or Brie), in small pieces
4 tablespoons Chevre, in small pieces

Finishing Touches

Grated Parmesan cheese
Minced parsley
Salt, pepper

In a 6-quart stock pot, start water boiling for pasta.

Meanwhile, heat 1/3 cup of the olive oil in a skillet and sauté the eggplant until it appears slightly crisp and cooked, 6 to 8 minutes. Drain and set aside. Skim off most of the oil in the pan and then sauté the pancetta, salami, and sausage. When almost crisp, add the Scotch bonnet pepper and sauté to soften. Using a mortar and pestle, mash the garlic with the salt, pepper, lemon juice, the remaining 1/3 cup olive oil, parsley and basil. Use some of the Parmesan cheese to help make a paste. Stir in the sun-dried tomatoes.

Place the drained pasta in a serving dish. Toss with the eggplant, pancetta, salami, and sausage. Add the garlic-herb paste and the cheeses. Toss well. Garnish with additional shavings of Parmesan cheese, parsley, salt, and pepper.

Serves 6-8

CHAPTER NINE

Great Sides, Vegetables and Vegetarian

I am not surprised vegetables and other non-meat things are just called "sides," as if they were afterthoughts. But it is undeserved under-billing because sides, aka vegetable dishes, especially superlative ones, are more like the framing to a great meal just as a great frame showcases great art. There are so many wonderful ways with the common potato, a few beans, rice and some other carbs of the garden that 'sides' should get far more attention or at least, far more care and respect.

Here are some of my best sides; they are so good they can stand alone and hold their own. But match them up with a main dish, and you have a memorable meal.

Ancho and Maple Syrup Sweet Potatoes

These are delectable, deeply braised sweet potatoes. Ancho is a smoky, sweet chili powder. Together with the maple syrup, the ancho infuses a remarkable flavor into these sweet potatoes. A perfect side anytime but especially welcome at Thanksgiving. If you don't have ancho spice, you can use smoked paprika. (Ancho powder is not hot so beware of unauthentic ancho powder- it is probably more likely smoked chili powder. I get mine at The Spice House)

3 pounds sweet potatoes, cut into long wedges, (washed but not skinned)
½ cup maple syrup
3 tablespoons unsalted butter or light olive oil
1/3 cup brown sugar
½ cup orange juice
1-2 tablespoons ancho spice
Salt, pepper

Preheat oven to 350 F.

Wash and prepare the potatoes and place in a large roasting pan. Cover potatoes with maple syrup, butter or oil, brown sugar, orange juice, ancho spice; dust with salt and pepper. Toss with a spoon to coat potatoes with all ingredients. Cover lightly with foil

Bake 45 minutes and then remove the foil cover. Continue to bake until potatoes are well-roasted, soft and caramelized (the skins will almost blacken), another 45-60 minutes.

Serves 4-6

Sweet Potato, Parsnip and Carrot Casserole

As you can tell, I am a huge fan of sweet potatoes and invent a new way to make them every other week. This particular recipe is a great side for any meal, but it's especially for holiday meals such as Thanksgiving or whenever a nice rustic, harvest type of casserole would be especially welcome.

3 large sweet potatoes, about 3 pounds
2 medium carrots, shredded
Salt, pepper
¾ cup (firmly packed) brown sugar
1 large parsnip, peeled and shredded
1 cup orange juice
½ cup olive oil or unsalted butter, melted

Preheat oven to 350 F. Generously spray a 5-quart casserole with nonstick cooking spray. It should be a large, deep casserole that you can also use to serve in.

Place the sweet potatoes in a large pot and just cover with water. Bring to a boil and parboil the sweet potatoes until barely softened. Immediately drain and rinse with cold water, peel off the skins, and slice ½ inch thick.

Layer the sweet potatoes in the casserole, dusting between layers with salt, pepper, and a bit of the brown sugar. Drizzle the layers with orange juice and olive oil or butter. Top with the shredded carrots and then the parsnips. Drizzle on remaining splash of orange juice, brown sugar, olive oil and a final light dusting of salt and pepper. You will have 3 to 4 layers in the end but it doesn't have to be perfect or exact.

Cover with foil or casserole cover. Bake until the casserole is bubbling and the vegetables seem softened and cooked through, 60 to 90 minutes. Remove cover and bake about 15 minutes more, until it is slightly browned on top and the liquid is mostly evaporated.

Serves 5–7

Potatoes Rustica

Potatoes lightly browned in olive oil, with a smattering of wine, pancetta, Parmesan cheese and a taste that leaps out of the pan.

6–8 medium-large red-skinned potatoes (not sweet potatoes)
¼ cup extra virgin olive oil
Salt, pepper
3 garlic cloves, finely minced
Juice of ½ lemon
3 tablespoons white wine
1/3 cup finely minced parsley
½ cup fresh Parmesan cheese
½ cup pancetta, cooked, drained, and finely minced

Finishing Touches
Minced parsley
Lemon slices

Peel the potatoes and par boil until barely tender, about 10 to 12 minutes. Drain and rinse with cold water. Cut into quarters.

Heat the oil in a large nonstick skillet and gently fry the potatoes, dusting with salt and pepper, and tossing to cook evenly over medium-low heat. As they brown, add the garlic.

When the potatoes are almost all browned and fork tender, add the lemon juice and wine and cook until the liquid has evaporated. Just before serving, toss with the parsley, cheese and pancetta.

Garnish with a dusting of minced parsley and lemon slices.

Serves 3–4

Greek Restaurant Potatoes

Why do Greek restaurants always make such great potatoes? Simple things, done right taste divine as any savvy cook, Greek or otherwise, will tell you. This is a great, easy potato dish that pairs well with kebabs of any sort with grilled chicken, fish or steak.

8 large potatoes, cut into 4–6 wedges each
½ cup olive oil
1/3 cup water
3 tablespoons white wine, optional
Juice of 1 lemon
4 garlic cloves, coarsely minced
1 tablespoon oregano
Sea salt, pepper

Preheat the oven to 425 F. Generously spray a 9- by 13-inch or 4-quart casserole with nonstick cooking spray.

Place the potatoes, olive oil, water, white wine and lemon juice and garlic, in the casserole and toss. Season the potatoes with the oregano, salt and pepper.
Place potatoes in the oven and immediately lower the temperature to 400 F. Bake for 45 to 60 minutes, tossing every so often to distribute the spices and ensure that the potatoes are cooking evenly.

If the potatoes get dry while baking, add ¼ cup water at a time so they continue to cook without drying out before they are properly cooked through. When the potatoes are soft (when a fork or knife is poked through) inside and crusty on the outside, they are done.

Serves 6

Restaurant-Style Rancher's Potato Wedges

Use large Idaho-style potatoes for these show-off wedges. This side dish is bursting with flavor and is a natural alongside a classic roast beef Sunday dinner or Western omelet.

4–6 potatoes (Yukon Gold or Idaho), washed and cut into wedges
¼ cup olive oil
1 cup buttermilk ranch dressing
1 cup grated Parmesan cheese
1–1 ½ cups seasoned breadcrumbs

Preheat the oven to 350 F. Spray a large roasting pan generously with nonstick cooking spray and then drizzle in the olive oil.

Place the dressing in a shallow bowl that will accommodate the potato wedges. Place the cheese and breadcrumbs each in similar bowls or on pieces of waxed paper.

Dip each potato in the dressing to coat. Next, press each side firmly in the cheese, and then the breadcrumbs. Place the coated potatoes in the roasting pan.

Bake until done, turning once or twice, to brown the potatoes, about 45-65 minutes.

Serves 6

Hungarian Scalloped Potatoes

A hearty spud dish that will become a classic in your repertoire. I acquired this recipe ages ago from a cousin who married a Hungarian mathematician. It's become a legendary potato dish that I consider a must for anyone's repertoire.

8–10 red-skinned potatoes, boiled, cooled, and sliced
Salt, pepper
Paprika
2 large, spicy, dry sausages, diced, optional
1 cup sour cream
½ cup unsalted butter, melted
½ cup fresh grated Parmesan cheese
4–6 hard-boiled eggs, crumbled or sliced, optional
1 cup shredded cheddar cheese
4 scallions, finely minced
1 cup milk

Finishing Touches
Paprika
Breadcrumbs
Grated Parmesan
Preheat oven to 350 F.

Place one layer of sliced potatoes in a large baking dish. Sprinkle generously with salt, pepper, and paprika. Continue to layer and sprinkle each layer. Reserve enough potatoes for a final layer. On the second-to-last layer, toss on some of the sausage, dollops of sour cream, melted butter, hard cooked eggs, Parmesan cheese and scallions. On the final layer, sprinkle the cheddar cheese and paprika and pour milk through the gaps in the dish (milk is to keep dish moist).

Bake for 45 minutes. Let rest 10 minutes before serving.

Serves 8–10

Olive Oil Pasta Toss

Who doesn't want a fool-proof side dish that goes with every and anything? I make this with a quality imported pasta, extra virgin olive oil, a touch of garlic, sea salt and pepper. In minutes I have a perfect side, good for an informal family meal or in case an unexpected (but welcome) guest drops by. Just make sure each element is of great quality because this is one of those 'more than the sum of the parts' recipe.

1 pound pasta, such as spaghetti or linguine, cooked according to package directions
Juice of ½ lemon
2 medium garlic cloves, finely minced
¼–1/3 cup extra virgin olive oil
Salt, pepper
Grated Parmesan cheese
Minced fresh herbs, such as basil or oregano

Prepare the pasta and drain. Place in a medium serving bowl and toss with the lemon juice. Then add the garlic and olive oil and dust with salt, pepper, and Parmesan.

Serves 4–6

Roasted Eggplant Zucchini Caponata

This is the simplest, sunniest dish you can imagine. Layer on the ingredients, don't bother stirring, slow roast, and dip into Mediterranean heaven.

1 large eggplant, trimmed, partially skinned, and diced into 1-inch cubes
4 medium zucchini, trimmed and sliced into ½-inch slices
1 small lemon, washed and thinly sliced
1/3 cup extra virgin olive oil
1/3 cup pitted black olives, sliced
¼ cup pitted or pimento-stuffed green olives
¼ cup red wine
2 tablespoons balsamic vinegar
5 garlic cloves, finely minced
½ bunch parsley, finely minced
½ teaspoon Italian spices
1 28-ounce can ground San Marco or plum tomatoes
Salt, pepper

Preheat oven to 325 F.

In a 4- or 5-quart Dutch oven, combine the eggplant, zucchini, lemon, olive oil, olives, wine, vinegar, garlic, parsley, Italian spices, tomatoes, salt and pepper and sauté over low heat, 5-10 minutes, stirring often.

Cover the casserole and place in oven, and roast for 2 to 3 hours, until the vegetables are softened and cooked down. Adjust seasonings.

Serve hot or cold with French bread or focaccia, an omelet or quiche, or as a bruschetta topping.

Serves 4–6

Crispy Zucchini Sticks

Spare the spuds. Zucchini is just as crisp and a tad lighter.

4 tablespoons melted butter or olive oil
4 or 5 medium zucchini, trimmed
½ cup fresh grated Parmesan cheese
1/3 cup breadcrumbs
½ teaspoon garlic powder
Salt, pepper
2 eggs, beaten

Preheat the oven to 425 F. Line a large baking sheet with parchment paper. Drizzle on 2 tablespoons of the melted butter or olive oil.

Mix the cheese, breadcrumbs, garlic powder, salt and pepper together in a bowl.

Cut the zucchini lengthwise into ½-inch wide sticks (as for French fries). Pat dry, then dip in the beaten egg and then press in the breadcrumb mixture.

Place on the prepared baking sheet. Drizzle on remaining melted butter or olive oil. Bake until crisp and golden, about 12 to 15 minutes, turning to cook evenly. Serve warm.

Serves 4

Blue Ribbon Turkey Stuffing

I created this peerless turkey stuffing recipe because I wanted a stuffing that hit all the right notes: flavorful, fragrant, moist and good enough to eat even without turkey – on its own! Why people use boxed stuffing mix, I don't know because a great homemade stuffing is both easy and a thing of beauty. I add both diced apples and cranberries but if you prefer your stuffing exclusively savory, just leave them out. You can stuff the turkey or as I do more often, prepare it in a casserole. Apparently, it's a safer way to cook stuffing.

2–3 tablespoons canola or light olive oil
2 cups shredded carrots
1 cup finely minced onions
1 cup finely minced celery
2 garlic cloves, finely minced
Salt, pepper
2 tablespoons minced parsley
1–2 teaspoons poultry or stuffing seasoning (I adore Bell's)
1 teaspoon sage, optional
¼ teaspoon celery seed powder
6–8 cups cubed bread, such as challah or French bread
2¼ cup white wine
2 cups chicken broth
3 eggs
2 teaspoons gravy browning *
½ cup raisins, optional
½ cup dried or coarsely chopped fresh cranberries, optional
1 cup minced tart apples

* Gravy browning is also known as Kitchen Bouquet. It and comes in a small bottle and is most often found near the soups section in the supermarket. It is essentially burnt sugar (but a liquid) and used to color up gravies to a beautiful mahogany hue.

In a large nonstick skillet, heat the oil. Add the carrots, onions, celery and garlic and brown lightly, 5 to 7 minutes. Season with salt and pepper and add the sage, celery seed powder, cubed bread, wine, gravy browning, chicken broth, eggs, raisins and cranberries, if using, and apples. Stir well to combine ingredients and cook for 5 to 8 minutes over low heat.

Remove stuffing from heat and let cool 15 minutes before stuffing a turkey, or spoon stuffing into a prepared, greased 4 quart casserole to bake. (If baking in a casserole, allow 45 to 60 minutes at 350 F, otherwise cook with the turkey)

Serves 8–12

Thanksgiving Roasted Sweet Potato Casserole

You can omit the miniature marshmallows but it's so traditional (and camp), I would leave them in. Thanksgiving is only once a year.

3 pounds sweet potatoes, peeled and cubed
1 cup (firmly packed) brown sugar
1 cup orange juice
1/3 cup unsalted butter, melted
¼ cup maple syrup or honey
Salt, pepper
2 cups miniature marshmallows

Preheat the oven to 350 F.

Place the potatoes in a large casserole. Add the sugar, orange juice, butter, and maple syrup; dust with salt and pepper and toss to coat. Top with the marshmallows.

Cover with foil and bake for about 1 ½ hours or until tender, removing the foil for the last 20 minutes of cooking.

Serves 6–8

Roasted Garlic Mashed Potatoes

This was a trend years ago and it's now a classic that's here to stay. I choose different potatoes each time I make this and I haven't had a batch that wasn't sublime. This is a side that goes with everything; it's even good alone or warmed up, as a midnight snack.

6 garlic cloves, peeled
1 tablespoon olive oil
1 ½ pounds potatoes
5 tablespoons butter
1/3—2/3 cup warm milk
Salt, pepper
½ cup Parmesan, grated

Preheat the oven to 400 degrees.

Place the garlic cloves on a small square of aluminum foil and drizzle with olive oil. Wrap garlic with the foil and bake for 20 minutes or until golden. Remove from the oven, but leave the oven on.

Quarter the potatoes and cover with water in a large pot. Bring to a boil and simmer until tender, about 15 minutes. Drain the potatoes and cover in cold water. Slip off the skins.

Return the potatoes to the hot pot and mash with masher or hand held mixer. Mash in the roasted garlic. Mix in the butter, milk, salt, and pepper. Transfer the mashed potatoes to an ovenproof dish and sprinkle the top with Parmesan. Bake for 15 minutes or until the top is golden

Serves 4–6

Harvest Curried Apple Sweet Potatoes

I noticed this recipe once in a newspaper and didn't jot it down, but remembered the major elements – curry, apples, and sweet potatoes. Good thing I did because this dish outstanding. I served it once and now it's my standard potato side dish at my holiday dinners.

2 pounds peeled sweet potatoes (about 8 large potatoes)
2 cups peeled, shredded apples
½ cup unsalted butter, melted
1/3 cup honey
2–3 teaspoons curry powder
Salt, pepper

Boil the sweet potatoes until fork tender. Rinse and drain.

In a large bowl, mash the potatoes and stir in the apples, butter, honey and curry powder. Season to taste with salt and pepper.

Serves 6–8

Greek Restaurant Lima Beans

Trust me, you'll love these lima beans. I was introduced to this lovely, simple, appetizer at a Greek restaurant when a business colleague and I enjoyed a power lunch of broiled snapper and this memorable dish. Serendipitously, the restaurant recipe appeared in the food section of the local newspaper the very next day. I adapted the recipe (the original recipe called for 4 cups of olive oil; I've reduced it a great deal). There's no way I can convey how good this dish is, you'll just have to try it.

2 cups dry jumbo lima beans, also called fava beans
5 large ripe tomatoes, quartered
1 large Spanish onion, chopped
½ bunch parsley, stems trimmed, coarsely chopped
6–8 garlic cloves
1 28-ounce can ground tomatoes
2 tablespoons tomato paste
1 1/3 cups extra virgin olive oil
Sea salt, pepper

Have a 4- or 5-quart roasting pan ready.

Fill a 6-quart stock pot or Dutch oven with salted water to about two thirds full and bring to a boil. Stir in the lima beans, bring back to the boil, and then simmer until the beans are just tender, about 1 to 1 ½ hours.

Meanwhile, place the fresh tomatoes in a food processor and process to make a chunky purée. Remove to a bowl and then coarsely chop the onion, parsley, and garlic in the processor. Mix the onion mixture with the fresh and canned tomatoes and the tomato paste. Stir in the olive oil.

Preheat oven to 350 F.

Drain and transfer the beans to a large baking pan. Stir in the tomato mixture and season with salt and pepper. Cover lightly with foil.

Bake for 1 to 2 hours, until the beans are very tender. Adjust seasonings.

Serve at room temperature as an appetizer or a side dish.

Serves 5–6

Garlic-Lemon Middle Eastern Fried Eggplant

There are a zillion eggplant dishes and being an eggplant fan, I would enjoy any one of them. But this one is sliced (versus mashed) eggplant and nicely marinated in a tangy, garlic-lemon vinaigrette. It would be at home on a summer table, a picnic, or with grilled, cold chicken.

2 medium eggplants, sliced very thin
4 eggs
1 ½ cups all-purpose flour
Salt, pepper
Canola oil for frying (or half canola, half olive oil)

Lemon Vinaigrette
½ cup fresh lemon juice
2–3 garlic cloves, minced
1–2 teaspoons cumin
Salt, pepper

Trim the eggplants and slice thin. Dip each in the beaten eggs and then lightly dredge in flour. Lay out on a baking sheet, lined with parchment. Dust with salt and pepper.

Meanwhile, heat up two frying pans with about ½ inch of oil. Fry the eggplant slices, turning once, until tender, a few minutes per side, taking care to brown, but not burn the slices.
Drain the slices on paper towels. Arrange all the slices on a large platter.

In a small bowl, whisk together the lemon juice, garlic, cumin salt and pepper. Drizzle this over the eggplant.

Refrigerate at least 2 hours and up to 5 or 6 days.

Serves 6–8

Asparagus and Herb Quiche

April-in-Paris Quiche is probably a better name for this younger-than-springtime recipe with its delightful herb and cheese mix. You could substitute tender, sautéed chopped leeks for the asparagus if you prefer.

1 9-inch refrigerated pie crust, or homemade
2 cups asparagus, cut in 1-inch pieces, blanched, and drained well
1 cup shredded Swiss cheese
1 cup shredded sharp white Cheddar or Colby
2 scallions, finely minced
5 eggs
1 ¼ cups half-and-half or light cream
1 tablespoon all-purpose flour
2 teaspoons Dijon mustard
¼ teaspoon garlic powder
¼ teaspoon onion powder
¼ teaspoon salt
1/8 teaspoon white pepper
2 teaspoons each, finely minced chives, dill and parsley

Preheat the oven to 425 F.

Place the unbaked pie crust in a pie pan on top of a parchment-lined baking sheet and cover or press it down with another pie pan the same size (but empty). Bake for about 7 minutes or until the crust is set. (That is another great baker's trick, by the way, to pre-bake a pie shell without it neither buckling up nor fussing with pie weights. Remove from the oven and reduce the heat to 350 F.

Line a baking sheet with parchment paper and place the pie pan on it.

In medium bowl, toss the asparagus, cheeses, and scallions and then arrange them in the pie crust. In a bowl, whisk the eggs, half-and-half or cream, flour, mustard, garlic powder, onion powder, salt, pepper and herbs until mixed well. Pour over the cheese and asparagus mixture.

Bake 25 to 35 minutes or until just set and a knife inserted about 1 inch from the edge or near the center comes out clean. Remove from the oven and let stand 10 minutes to set. Cut into wedges and serve. This is also good cold or gently reheated.

Serves 6-8

Garlic, Goat Cheese Artichoke Spinach Strata

This make-ahead casserole is an awesome brunch classic of incredible flavors and textures. It's a meal in itself, paired up with a salad and some orange juice-champagne spritzers. Reheated, it is a rustic Sunday afternoon snack. The nicer the serving dish, the better the impression this dish makes, but it is a showstopper no matter what.

2 tablespoons light olive oil
1 medium red bell pepper, minced
3 garlic cloves, finely minced
1 10-ounce package frozen chopped spinach, thawed
8 eggs
2 ¼ cups milk
½ cup whipping cream
½ cup grated Parmesan cheese
8 ounces diced Chevre
½ cup small curd cottage cheese
3 cups shredded medium or sharp white Cheddar
2 6-ounce jars marinated artichoke hearts, drained and coarsely minced
1 pound loaf of slightly stale Italian or rustic French bread, cut in 1 ½-inch cubes
3 scallions, finely minced
½ teaspoon dry mustard
½ teaspoon salt, more to taste
Pepper
2–3 tablespoons butter, cut into small pieces

Extras
½ cup crisp-fried, minced pancetta
1–2 tablespoons minced fresh herbs, such as parsley, thyme, oregano, or basil
A few tablespoons pesto or sun-dried tomato pesto

The night (or 8 hours before), heat the olive oil in medium skillet over medium-low heat. Add the peppers and sauté until tender, about 6 minutes, and then stir in garlic to soften, while peppers just finish cooking. Then set aside. Meanwhile, drain the spinach in a colander lined with a paper towel.

In a large bowl, whisk the eggs well and then add in the spinach, milk, cream, Parmesan cheese, Chevre, cottage cheese and Cheddar. Mix in the mustard, salt, pepper, and the bits of butter. Fold in the peppers and artichokes.

In a 9- by 13-inch or similar ovenproof casserole, layer half the bread cubes, the scallions, then half the egg-vegetable mixture, and then repeat with remaining bread cubes and egg-vegetable mixture. You can top last layer with some extra cheese of your choice.

Cover and refrigerate for 4 hours or overnight. Remove from the refrigerator and uncover 30 minutes prior to baking. Preheat the oven to 350 F.

Bake for 60 to 75 minutes or until golden brown on the top and firm in the center. A knife inserted in center will come out clean.
Let rest 15 minutes before serving.

Serves 6–8

Falafel

The fast food of Israel and fast food courts of North America all tout this healthy (albeit fried) vegetarian snack made with canned chickpeas. Find fresh pita breads to go with them.

Chickpea Batter
1 19-ounce can chickpeas, drained
6 garlic cloves, finely minced
¾ cup breadcrumbs or matzoh meal
2 tablespoons lemon juice
1 ½ teaspoons salt
1 teaspoon cumin
1/8 teaspoon pepper
A few squirts of hot sauce

Tahini Dressing
½ cup sesame seed paste or tahini*
¼ cup lemon juice
1 tablespoon finely minced parsley
1 large garlic clove, finely minced
1 teaspoon salt, or to taste
2 tablespoons olive oil

Oil for frying
Pita breads, warmed

* Tahini is available in health food stores or Middle Eastern markets

For the batter, blend the chickpeas and garlic in a food processor to make a thick, coarse mixture. Fold in the breadcrumbs or matzoh meal, salt, cumin, pepper, hot sauce and lemon juice. Chill for 20 minutes. Using wet hands, form the mixture into 1 ½-inch balls.

Heat up about a cup or a bit more of oil in a large skillet to 325 or 350 F (i.e. frying temperature). Add a few balls at a time and fry until all the balls are browned on all sides. Drain on paper towels.

For the dressing, place the tahini, lemon juice, parsley, garlic, salt and olive oil in a food processor and whiz until smooth. Add a touch more lemon juice or water if it needs to be thinned out.

To serve, place a few falafels in each pita with shredded lettuce, minced tomatoes, and Tahini Dressing.

Serves 4–6

World's Best Vegetarian Paté

This is a superlative sandwich filling for everyone—vegetarian or not. It's an ideal sandwich pita bread stuffing. I learned this recipe when I was head baker in a Californian-style sandwich café. It calls for nutritional yeast, not to be confused with baker's yeast and looks like a wheat germ. It adds a ton of flavor and nutrients.

1 cup sunflower seeds
2–3 tablespoons olive oil
1 cup finely minced carrot
½ cup finely minced onion
½ cup finely minced celery
1 cup mashed potatoes
½ cup nutritional yeast*
¼ cup minced parsley
¼ cup whole-wheat flour
¼ cup corn flour or all-purpose flour
¼ cup fresh lemon juice
2 teaspoons basil
1 ½ teaspoons minced garlic
1 teaspoon paprika
1 teaspoon salt
½ teaspoon garlic powder
¼–½ teaspoon pepper
A few drops of Kitchen Bouquet** (optional)

* Nutritional yeast is available in health food stores (this is not bread yeast).

** Kitchen Bouquet, usually sold in the soup section, is a natural ingredient that is often used to brown gravies. Add some to this vegetable pate and you will get an appealing, meatier tint.

Lightly toast sunflower seeds by baking them in a 350 F oven for a few minutes until they brown slightly. Remove from the oven and set aside. Leave the oven on.

In a nonstick fry pan, over medium heat, sauté the carrots, onions and celery in the oil until softened, 5 to 10 minutes.

In a large bowl, blend the toasted seeds, sautéed vegetables, mashed potatoes, nutritional yeast, parsley, flours, lemon juice, basil, garlic, paprika, salt, garlic powder and pepper. Mix well. If you like, add a few drops of Kitchen Bouquet to tint to a meaty color.

Pack into a 9- by 5-inch loaf pan or a 9-inch square pan. Bake until set, 30 to 45 minutes. Chill very well before slicing for salads and sandwiches.

Makes enough to fill 5-6 sandwiches

Nacho Layered Dip

You dump and layer ingredients. You scoop 'em. You eat 'em. What could be simpler or more manly? To make this girl food, or new age guy food, opt for low-fat sour cream.

2 large avocados, mashed
1 tablespoon mayonnaise
2 teaspoons fresh lemon juice
Salt, pepper
½ teaspoon garlic powder
1 cup salsa
½ cup pitted, sliced black olives
½ cup canned black beans, drained
1 cup canned diced green chilies, drained
1 small onion, finely chopped
1 ½ cups shredded Monterey Jack or mild orange Cheddar cheese
1 8-ounce container sour cream
1/3 cup finely minced cilantro

In a large bowl, mash the avocados with a fork and stir in the mayonnaise, lemon juice, salt, pepper, and garlic. Spoon this mixture into a shallow 2-quart serving dish. Layer on the salsa, olives, black beans, green chilies, onion, cheese and sour cream. Sprinkle the cilantro over the top.

Chill at least one hour (or up until a few days). Serve with tortilla chips on the side.

Serves 6

CHAPTER TEN

Sweets for the Sweets, Desserts or Sweet Finales

To a baker, dessert usually is an occasion to show off one's winning ways with flour. But sometimes, all you really need is something simple and light, especially after a big dinner or simply as a nice change of pace from more elaborate desserts. These sweet finales are my *from-a-baker*, ultra-special desserts that also happen to be my personal favorites. Many of them are updated classics that I believe are important for anyone's repertoire but they are delicious, sweet offerings in their own right and timelessly appealing.

Desserts can be anything sweet and many of these recipes don't even call for or use flour or baking powder, so for me these recipes definitely fall in the "cooking" category. Most cooks in the professional kitchen are also called upon to make these in a full service restaurant where there might not be a resident pastry chef.

However you define them, these recipes are always most welcome. We forget sometimes that dessert can be smooth and spoon-able versus something that is baked in a pan and gets sliced up, put on a plate, and offered with a fork.

I've carefully honed these recipes and while they are elegant, they are also nicely homespun and use ingredients you're likely to have in your pantry or fridge. You don't have to break the bank or go on a special shopping mission and you will still be rewarded with magical results.

Once in a while, let go of the big chocolate cake, the cheesecakes, tortes and tarts and revisit glorious silky custard, a cinnamon-infused country baked apple, or one of the most unctuous, luscious rice puddings you will ever enjoy. These are all-spoon, no fork required, wonderful recipes.

Old-Fashioned Apple Dumplings with Warm Vanilla Sauce

Pie dough, some rosy apples and the gentle heat of your oven makes for lovely retro apple dumplings, kissed with cinnamon and crowned with a delectable warm vanilla sauce. Pure and simple, no wonder it's a comfort dessert winner.

Dumpling Filling

3 tablespoons raisins or dried cherries
3 tablespoons finely chopped walnuts
6 tablespoons brown sugar
½ teaspoon cinnamon
2 tablespoons honey
1 pound prepared pie or puff pastry dough
3 large apples, peeled, cored, and quartered
1 egg, beaten
Sugar for dusting

Warm Vanilla Sauce

5 tablespoons unsalted butter
2 tablespoons brown sugar
2 cups confectioners' sugar
1 teaspoon pure vanilla extract
2 tablespoons dark rum or apple juice
Preheat oven to 375 F.

Stack two baking sheets together and line the top one with parchment paper.

To make the Dumpling Filling, in a small bowl, combine the raisins (or cherries), walnuts, brown sugar and cinnamon. Stir in the honey. Divide the pie dough into 6 pieces. On a lightly floured work surface, roll each portion into a 6-inch circle, about ¼ inch thick. Place 2 to 3 apple quarters on each piece of dough. Spoon on some of the filling. Bring up the ends of the dough and seal on top/over the apples. Pinch to seal. Brush the dumplings with egg wash and sprinkle with sugar.

Place the apple dumplings on the prepared baking sheet, lower the oven temperature to 350 F, and bake until the apples are softened (you will see juices bubbling out), 20 to 25 minutes.

For the sauce, melt the butter with the brown sugar over medium heat in a saucepan or in a microwave. Remove from the heat once melted and add the confectioners' sugar and vanilla. Stir in the rum to make a pourable glaze. Add more rum if required. Drizzle some sauce over each dumpling before serving.

Serves 6

Deluxe Banana and Toffee Cream Pie

I like this with either a graham or vanilla wafer crust, but it's especially sublime with a classic basic pie pastry crust. This is a deluxe version of that diner classic but made homemade wonderful.

1 baked 9 inch pie crust or 1 prepared graham or vanilla wafer crust

Custard Filling
1 cup sugar
½ cup all-purpose flour
1/8 teaspoon salt
2 cups milk
4 egg yolks
1 teaspoon pure vanilla extract
1 tablespoon unsalted butter

Topping
1 package (any size) instant vanilla or butterscotch pudding
2 cups whipping cream
2 tablespoons confectioners' sugar
1 cup miniature marshmallows
1 cup vanilla wafer cookies, coarsely chopped
2–3 ripe bananas, peeled and sliced into 3/ 8 inch slices
¼ cup toffee or butterscotch bits

Finishing Touches
Whipped cream
Miniature marshmallows
Have the 9-inch pie crust ready.

For the Custard Filling, combine the sugar, flour, and salt in a small bowl and whisk to blend. Set aside.

In a heavy 3-quart saucepan, over low heat, add ½ cup of the milk, the egg yolks, and the flour mixture. Increase heat to medium and stir while adding in the rest of the milk and the vanilla extract, stirring constantly. Bring to a gentle boil and when the mixture begins to thicken, add the butter, continuing to stir. Keep boiling and stirring until mixture reaches a nice pudding consistency. Remove from the heat and chill for 30 minutes.

For the topping, prepare the pudding mix as per the package directions and chill for 20 minutes. For the whipping cream, whip the cream with the confectioners' sugar until stiff and chill 20 minutes.

Remove the three chilled mixtures from the fridge. To the custard filling, fold in the whipping cream, marshmallows, and the chopped wafers.

To assemble, spoon half of the custard mixture into the pie shell. Top with the bananas and sprinkle with the toffee bits. Cover with the remaining custard and then mound on the instant pudding. Chill for 2 to 4 hours.

Before serving, preheat the oven to 400 F. Top the pudding with the additional miniature marshmallows, and bake on top rack just to brown the marshmallows. Remove and serve (adding some whipped cream on top if you like).

Serves 8–10

Pumpkin Pie Brown Sugar Crème Brûlée

This is too special to wait for fall or a Thanksgiving meal; make this anytime of year when you want a smooth, gently spiced treat.

Melted butter for brushing the custard cups

1 15-ounce can pure pumpkin puree (not pie filling)
½ cup white sugar
½ cup (packed) brown sugar
5 egg yolks
2 teaspoons pure vanilla extract
1 teaspoon cinnamon
½ teaspoon allspice
¼ teaspoon cloves
1/8 teaspoon nutmeg
Tiny pinch salt
3 cups whipping cream
½ cup raw or brown sugar

Preheat oven to 325 F.

Fill a large roasting pan two-thirds full with water. Spray 8 small ceramic soufflé or custard cups generously with nonstick cooking spray or brush with unsalted butter. Place the custard cups in the prepared roasting pan.

In a large bowl, whisk together the pumpkin purée, white and brown sugars, egg yolks, vanilla extract, cinnamon, allspice, cloves, nutmeg and salt.

In a 2-quart saucepan, heat the whipping cream to a gentle simmer. Gently and gradually pour the cream into the pumpkin mixture (gradually because you don't want to cook the egg yolks), stirring all the while.

Pour the mixture equally into the prepared custard cups. Bake until just set 30-35 minutes.

Sprinkle a tablespoon of the raw or brown sugar over each custard top. Before serving, broil the custard cups to liquefy the sugar tops (2 to 3 minutes; watch carefully). Refrigerate the custards before serving (which will harden the topping).

Serves 8

Crème Brûlée

Rice pudding may be comfort food, but crème brûlée is solace for the sensualist. Call it perennially trendy or constantly classic, but don't confuse it with Crème Caramel (where the crackling sugar is on the bottom). Crème Brûlée is enduring, decadent and elegant.

Melted butter for brushing the custard cups

2 cups whipping cream
5 egg yolks
2 whole eggs
½ cup sugar
1 teaspoon pure vanilla extract
½ cup white or light brown sugar , for the glaze

In a 2 ½-quart pot, heat the cream to a simmer.

Meanwhile, in a medium bowl, briskly whisk together egg yolks, whole eggs and sugar. Cool the cream slightly and add a few tablespoons to the egg yolk mixture and whisk. Then, straining through a fine sieve, drizzle the rest of the cream into the egg yolk mixture, whisking to combine. Strain again into another bowl. Stir in vanilla extract.

Preheat the oven to 300 F.

Fill a roasting pan two-thirds full with water.

Spray 6 small ceramic soufflé or custard cups generously with nonstick cooking spray or brush with unsalted butter. Place the custard cups in the prepared roasting pan.

Pour the cream mixture evenly into the prepared custard cups. Place in the oven and immediately lower the heat to 250 F.

Bake 60 to 90 minutes, until the custard is set, but still quivering. Remove the cups from the water bath and cool to room temperature. Cover with plastic wrap. Refrigerate at least 6 hours or up to two days.

Before serving, preheat the broiler. Using a paper towel, blot up any moisture on the top of the custards. Distribute the sugar over the top surface of each custard. Place the custard cups on a baking sheet. Broil until sugar caramelizes, 2 to 3 minutes. Watch carefully.

As the custard cools, the sugar will crack. Serve immediately or refrigerate and served chilled. The caramelizing is best done just before serving.

Serves 6

Roasted Rhubarb with Blood Oranges

This is a new spin on stewed rhubarb which marries well with sweet blood oranges that also tint the rhubarb a deep rose color, but any oranges you have are just as perfect.

6 cups diced rhubarb
3 blood oranges, peeled and thinly sliced
1 large apple, such as Granny Smith, peeled and shredded
½ cup white sugar
½ cup (packed) brown sugar
½ teaspoon pure vanilla extract
2 tablespoons pomegranate molasses *

*Available in Middle Eastern food shops or sections. You can substitute honey.

Preheat oven to 350 F.

Place the rhubarb, oranges, apple, white and brown sugars, vanilla extract, and pomegranate molasses in a 4- or 5-quart Dutch oven or ovenproof casserole with a cover.

Mix and then bake, stirring every so often, for 60 to 90 minutes or until tender.
Serve warm or chilled.

Makes 4–5 cups

Stovetop Coconut Cream Rice Pudding

A classic that is the ultimate sweet comfort food. Just make sure you use a heavy-bottomed pot so there's no scorching the rice. Canned Cream of Coconut is generally a thick mixture and can be found in Asian or Indian markets or most supermarkets (sometimes near the mixed drinks ingredient area). It adds a wonderful creamy taste and velvety texture. The trick to this recipe is a slow simmer; the reward for your patience is an ambrosial taste experience.

2 cups water
¼ teaspoon salt
1 cup medium grain rice
2/3 cup sugar
3 cups half-and-half or light cream
2 cups milk
1 5.6-ounce can creamed coconut
1 egg
1 tablespoon unsalted butter
1 ½ teaspoons pure vanilla extract
1 tablespoon cornstarch
2 tablespoons water
½ cup raisins
½ cup slivered coconut, optional

Finishing Touches
Ground cinnamon and nutmeg for dusting
Whipping cream

In a 2-quart saucepan, bring the water and salt to a boil. Stir in the rice and sugar. Cover and simmer, stirring once or twice, for 20 to 25 minutes, until the water is almost absorbed and the rice is tender.

Stir in the cream, milk, cream of coconut, egg, butter and vanilla extract. Simmer, partially covered, over medium-low heat, allowing the mixture to cook 35 to 50 minutes, stirring often, until most of the liquid is absorbed and seems thickened.

Meanwhile, in a small measuring cup, mix the cornstarch and water together.

When rice is completely tender, add the raisins and coconut and then stir in the cornstarch mixture. Cook a few more minutes until it thickens a touch more.

Remove from the stove and dust the top with cinnamon and nutmeg. Serve warm, at room temperature, or chilled with extra cream.

Serves 6–8

Apple Fritters with Warm Toffee-Maple Sauce

Serve warm, with maple syrup or a dusting of confectioners' sugar. Big chunks of apple in a golden batter with a touch of spice— can anything taste better than this? This is great for breakfast, brunch, or a summery, post-barbecue dessert.

4–6 large apples, peeled, cored, and sliced into ½-inch rings

Fritter Batter
2 ¼ cups all-purpose flour
¼ cup sugar
1 tablespoon baking powder
¼ teaspoon nutmeg
1/8 teaspoon cinnamon
½ teaspoon salt
2 eggs
1 cup milk
1 ½ teaspoons pure vanilla extract
Canola oil, for deep frying

Finishing Touches
¼ cup pure maple syrup
Confectioners' sugar

Prepare the apples, cover and set aside.

In a medium bowl, mix together the flour, sugar, baking powder, nutmeg, cinnamon and salt. In a separate bowl, beat together the eggs, milk, and vanilla extract. Stir the milk mixture into the flour mixture until smooth.

Heat the oil to 375 F in a deep fryer or heavy-bottomed pot, such as a wok.

Dip the apple slices in the batter, letting the excess batter drip off a bit. Fry a few fritters at a time, turning once, until golden. Drain on paper towels and dust with confectioners' sugar or drizzle with maple syrup.

Serves 3–4

Farmhouse Baked Apples

Nothing beats the fragrance of these slow-baked apples, unless it is the taste of them, replete with, honey and a kiss of brown sugar. Choose your favorite apple for this or experiment with a new apple each time. As I like to say, when I'm not near the apple I love, I love the one I'm near.

6–8 large apples, peeled and cored
½ cup raisins or dried cranberries
Brown sugar
Honey
Cinnamon

Finishing Touches
1 cup sweet red wine or black cherry soda

Preheat oven to 350 F.

Generously spray a 9- by 13-inch baking dish with nonstick cooking spray. (For the baking dish, you can use anything that will be good to nest and contain apples in. Alternatively, prepare individual baking dishes the same way so that each diner has one apple).

Prepare the apples by slicing off a ¼-inch slice to form a top or cap. Make a wide hole through the middle of the apple and fill it with a spoonful of raisins and some brown sugar and honey. Dust each apple with cinnamon.

Replace the top apple section back on each apple. Drizzle with the red wine or soda.

Bake until softened, about 30 to 55 minutes, depending on size and variety of the apples.

Baste the apples with the pan juices as they bake. Cool or serve warm.

Makes 6–8

White Chocolate, Raspberry and Vanilla Bread Pudding

Pure decadence: chunks of challah or similar egg bread pulled together in a creamy batter of eggs, cream, vanilla, cinnamon and studded with chunks of white chocolate. This recipe can be made one or two days ahead and refrigerated until needed. Good warm or chilled. Sometimes, I serve this recipe as a dessert square (provided the pudding has been refrigerated).

10 cups slightly stale challah or brioche, in chunks or cubes

1 ½ cups half-and-half or light cream

1 ½ cups milk

l/2 cup whipping cream

7 eggs

¾ cup sugar

½ cup unsalted butter, melted

¼ cup flour

2 teaspoons baking powder

2 teaspoons pure vanilla extract

1 teaspoon cinnamon

Pinch salt

1 ½ cups chopped white chocolate, coarsely chopped

1 ½ cups fresh or frozen raspberries

Finishing Touches
Confectioners' sugar
Cinnamon

Preheat oven to 350 F. Spray a 9- by 13-inch pan or baking dish with nonstick cooking spray.

Place the bread cubes in a very large bowl.

In a separate medium bowl, mix together the half-and-half, milk, whipping cream, eggs, sugar, butter, flour, baking powder, vanilla extract, cinnamon and salt. Pour over the bread cubes and let stand 10 minutes to absorb. Fold in the white chocolate and raspberries.

Spoon the mixture into the prepared pan and dust the top with a little confectioners' sugar and cinnamon.

Bake until the top turns golden, 45 to 55 minutes.

Serves 10-12

Apple Crisp

If you can't remember the last time you had this, it's time to make it again. Simple, nutritious – no wonder it's always gobbled up! This is a nice, quick dessert and a perfect ending to an informal lunch or dinner.

Filling

4 large apples, peeled, cored, and sliced
3 large sweet apples, peeled, cored and sliced
3 tablespoons (packed) light brown sugar
2 tablespoons white sugar
2 tablespoons fresh lemon juice
1 teaspoon pure vanilla extract
¼ teaspoon cinnamon
Pinch each of cloves, allspice, nutmeg

Oatmeal Crisp Topping

1 cup rolled oats or quick oatmeal
1/3 cup flour
1/3 cup (packed) light brown sugar
¼ cup white sugar
¼ teaspoon cinnamon
Pinch of salt
½ cup unsalted butter, in bits
¼ cup finely chopped, toasted walnuts, optional

Preheat oven to 375 F.

Line a baking sheet with parchment paper. Generously spray a 3-quart baking pan (such as a ceramic oval or round baking dish that is ovenproof) with nonstick cooking spray (or lightly butter the dish).

For the filling, add the apples to a large bowl and toss with the brown and white sugars, lemon juice, vanilla extract, cinnamon, cloves, allspice, and nutmeg. Spoon apple filling into the prepared pan.

For the Oatmeal Crisp Topping, in a medium bowl, combine the oats, flour, brown and white sugars, cinnamon and salt and mix briefly. Cut the butter into the dry ingredients to make a crumbly topping. You can do this by hand or, if you prefer, in a food processor. It will be slightly clumpy. Stir in the walnuts, if using.

Distribute the topping as evenly as possible over fruit. Bake 35 for 45 minutes or until the fruit begins to bubble and it smells great. Serve warm or at room temperature.

Serves 5–6

Cuban Flan

A classic Latin sweet that is the most unctuous, smooth, heavenly concoction you will ever experience. Curses, it's also incredibly easy, so you're forewarned—it's decadence without sweat. Serve with fresh berries and homemade butter cookies or shortbread.

1/3 cup pure maple syrup
1 tablespoon unsalted butter
1 14-ounce can sweetened condensed milk
½ cup milk
½ cup half-and-half or light cream
1 ½ teaspoons pure vanilla extract
4 eggs
2 egg yolks
Pinch salt

Preheat the oven to 350 F.

Fill a roasting pan with water, into which a 2-quart dish will fit. Put the roasting pan in the oven. Meanwhile, spray a 2-quart dish (like a soufflé dish) with nonstick cooking spray. (You can also make about 8 to 10 ramekins for individual flans).

In a small saucepan, gently boil the maple syrup and butter until it reaches the soft ball stage, about 8 to 14 minutes. Soft ball stage is reached when a about half a teaspoon of the mixture becomes like taffy when dropped into cold water or when it reaches 235 F on a candy thermometer. Take care not to let it boil too quickly or it will foam over the sides of the pot. It will be slightly thickened. Spoon or pour the mixture into the prepared dish. Let stand 10 minutes to set.

In a food processor, blend the condensed milk, milk, cream, vanilla extract, eggs, yolks and salt to about 1-2 minutes. Gently pour this into prepared baking dish over the maple syrup mixture. Place the dish in the roasting pan and cover the whole thing snugly with foil.

Bake for 55 to 70 minutes, until the flan is just set. Cool at room temperature for 1 hour, and then refrigerate until nicely set and scoopable. Keeps refrigerated 3 to 5 days.

Serves 5–6

Crème Caramel

I make my crème caramel with a touch of fleur de sel, a specialty salt that gives caramel an extra luscious salty-sweet hit. Of course, if you prefer classic crème caramel, just leave it out. The long slow bake ensures this is the silkiest, most luxurious crème caramel ever.

Caramel
½ cup sugar
¼ teaspoon fleur de sel

Custard
Melted butter for brushing the ramekins
2 cups whipping cream
1 cup milk
1 cup sugar
3 egg yolks
2 eggs
1 teaspoon pure vanilla extract
Very tiny pinch salt

Preheat the oven to 350°F.

Line a large baking sheet with parchment paper. Place a large roasting pan on the baking sheet and fill it halfway with water. Generously brush six 6-ounce ramekins with unsalted butter and place them in the roasting pan.

For the custard, in a 2-quart saucepan, heat the cream, milk, and ½ cup of the sugar over medium heat until it is gently simmering (small bubbles will form on the inner sides of the pan). Let simmer.

Meanwhile, in a medium bowl, beat the egg yolks and eggs together, and then slowly whisk the remaining ½ cup of the sugar into the mixture. Slowly whisk the hot cream-milk into the egg mixture. Strain the mixture through a fine sieve into a 4-cup measuring cup. Stir in the salt and vanilla extract. Set aside.

For the caramel, put the ½ of cup sugar in a clean saucepan. Carefully add just enough water, 2 to 4 tablespoons, to dissolve the sugar. Set the pot over medium heat. Once the mixture comes to a gentle but consistent boil (which should take a few minutes), reduce the heat to very low and let it slowly continue to heat. Add the salt. The water in it will evaporate and it will start to turn color. As this is happening, wash down the inner sides of the pan with a brush dipped in cold water (to prevent crystals from forming).

Once the sugar has started to caramelize, watch it carefully. It takes just seconds for caramel to go from perfectly done to burnt or scorched. Let it get almost done (almost the color you think it should be, as from that point on it will cook very fast) and remove from the heat.

Pour a bit of caramel into the bottom of each ramekin. If it seizes up, add a touch of boiling water and stir, taking care not to let any bubbling or steam burn or splatter onto you. Then divide the custard evenly among the caramel-lined ramekins.

Place in the oven, immediately reducing temperature to 325 F, and bake until just set, 60 to 90 minutes. A knife dipped gently into the custard should come out somewhat clean. This is a wide range because, depending on the custard cups, the custard can set sooner or a bit later.

Remove the roasting pan from the oven and let the ramekins cool in the water bath. Remove the ramekins, cover with plastic wrap, and refrigerate for at least 2 hours or up to 2 days.

Run a thin knife around the edge of the custard and invert onto a dessert plate, scraping any caramel from the ramekin onto the custard.

Serves 6

Poached Pears in Earl Grey Tea, Greek Honey and Vanilla

Pears are often overlooked in autumn as beloved apples usually steal top billing. It's a pity because pears are so elegant. Smaller pears (such as Comice or Forelle), poached in Earl Grey tea, Greek honey, and vanilla are sublime. A variation would be to poach the pears in pomegranate juice with some orange zest.

6–8 medium pears, washed and cored (stems left on)
4–5 cups brewed Earl Grey tea
1 teaspoon pure vanilla extract or 1 vanilla bean, split up the middle
1/3 cup Greek honey

Preheat oven to 350 F.

Place the pears in a shallow baking dish that will hold them and the poaching liquid.

In a medium saucepan, simmer the tea with the vanilla extract or vanilla bean and the honey. Pour over the pears. The pears should be almost, but not quite covered with the liquid.
Bake, basting every so often, for about 45 to 60 minutes or until tender. Remove the vanilla bean, if used. Serve warm or cold.

Serves 4–6

CHAPTER ELEVEN

Baker's Bonus, or A Little Decadence

I couldn't write a cookbook—a *cooking* book—without including some very special *baking* recipes for you to try. I'm delighted to share a few new unique baking recipes to remind you of my culinary roots. Besides, who can say *no* to sweets?

I'm always working on new recipes and usually they go into a new baking book or are published on my website, www.BetterBaking.com. But we bakers love to spoil people, so here you go—a bonus offering of a slew of very special baking recipes as a sweet counterpoint to the savory recipes that preceded them. Enjoy!

Brownie-Stuffed Tollhouse Cookies

These are enormous, crisp, classic chocolate chip cookies surrounding a huge center of a gooey fudge brownie. The contrast of crisp cookie and dense, moist brownie is magical. My testers agreed that these are bold and exceptional. As with many an exceptional recipe - no ordinary recipe headnote would ever do them justice. In a hurry? Use a quality brownie mix (but this homemade brownie recipe is far better and super quick).

Chocolate Chip Cookie Dough

1 cup unsalted butter
1 cup (packed) brown sugar
½ cup white sugar
2 eggs
2 ½ teaspoons pure vanilla extract
2 ¾ cups all-purpose flour
1 teaspoon baking soda
¼ teaspoon salt
2 cups semisweet chocolate chips

Brownies

1 cup unsalted butter, melted and cooled
1 cup white sugar
¾ cup (packed) brown sugar
1 ½ teaspoons pure vanilla extract
3 eggs
1 cup all-purpose flour
½ plus 3 tablespoons unsweetened cocoa powder
1/8 teaspoon baking soda
¼ teaspoon salt

Preheat the oven to 350 F.

To prepare for baking the brownies, line a baking sheet with parchment paper. Generously spray a 9- by 9-inch or 8- by 11-inch pan with nonstick cooking spray and line with parchment paper. Place the pan on the baking sheet.

To prepare for baking the cookies, stack two baking sheets together and line the top one with parchment paper.

To make the cookies, in a mixer bowl, blend the butter with the white and brown sugars until well mixed. Add the eggs and vanilla extract and blend well. Fold in the flour, baking soda and salt and blend well. Add the chocolate chips and mix. Wrap and chill the dough while preparing the brownies.

To make the brownies, in a mixer bowl, blend the melted butter with the white and brown sugars and blend well. Add the vanilla extract and eggs and blend well on slow speed until well combined.

In a separate bowl, stir together the flour, cocoa, baking soda and salt. Stop the mixer and the fold dry ingredients into the batter and blend well, on low speed, scraping the bottom of the mixing bowl often to ensure that the ingredients are evenly combined. Spoon into the prepared pan.

Place the pan on top of the baking sheet (to protect the bottom from over baking). Bake until done, 30 to 35 minutes. Brownies will appear set (versus wet) and will be slightly firm to the touch, but not dry. Cool and then place the pan in the freezer for 1 hour before cutting the brownies.

To cut, unmold the brownies and peel off the parchment paper. Cut the brownies into 1 ½-inch squares.

To make each cookie, break off about 3 tablespoons or more of cookie dough and press a brownie square into the center. Seal the edges whatever way you can and press gently onto the prepared doubled-up cookie sheet.

Bake until the cookies are done (the edges will be browned, and the center just set), about 16 to 18 minutes, depending on the size.

Makes about 12–16 large cookies or 30 smaller ones

Greek Yogurt Cheesecake

A sumptuous little cheesecake you can whip up in no time flat. This is ideal when you want a smaller cheesecake along with the nutrition and smoothness of a thick Greek yogurt. It still results in the luxurious taste of a classic, decadent cheesecake. I serve simply dusted with confectioners' sugar or you can top it with fresh berries. This recipe works well with low fat Greek yogurt too.

Bottom Crust
1 ¼ cups graham cracker crumbs
3 tablespoons brown sugar
3–4 tablespoons unsalted butter, melted
Pinch cinnamon

Filling
2 ½ 8-ounce packages (20 ounces total) cream cheese, softened
½ cup plus 2 tablespoons sugar
3 eggs
1 ½ teaspoons pure vanilla extract
1 tablespoon lemon juice
1 cup plain, thick Greek yogurt

Finishing Touches
Berries
Confectioners' sugar for dusting

Preheat the oven to 350 F. Line a baking sheet with parchment paper.

For the bottom crust, mix the graham cracker crumbs, brown sugar, butter, and cinnamon together well and pat into a 9-inch layer cake or springform pan. Place the pan on the prepared baking sheet.

For the filling, in a food processor, cream the cream cheese with the sugar until smooth. Add the eggs, vanilla extract, lemon juice and yogurt. Process until smooth, about 1 to 2 minutes. Pour into the prepared cake pan.

Bake until just set, about 35 to 40 minutes.

Chill for 6 hours or overnight. Top with berries or dust with confectioners' sugar before serving.

Serves 8–10

Milk Chocolate Chip Banana Bread

A mellow and classic banana bread with just enough sweetness, moistness and warm banana flavor. The best banana breads feature hand-mashed bananas and hand-blending. This is not a recipe for a mixer or food processor but rather a wood spoon. Use really ripe, spotted-skin bananas, slow bake the loaf and cut in thick, fragrant, comforting slices. This is aromatherapy of the highest order.

1 cup hand-mashed very ripe banana
1 cup sugar
2 tablespoons brown sugar
½ cup unsalted butter, melted
2 eggs
1 teaspoon pure vanilla extract
½ cup buttermilk
1 2/3 cup all-purpose flour
1 teaspoon baking soda
¼ teaspoon salt
Pinch each cinnamon, nutmeg
½ cup milk chocolate chips

Preheat oven to 325 F. Stack two baking sheets together and line the top one with parchment paper. Spray a 9 by 5 inch loaf pan or 8 by 4 inch loaf pan with non-stick cooking spray and place on the baking sheet.

In a small bowl, hand mash (a fork or potato masher) the bananas and set aside. In a mixer bowl, cream the white and brown sugar and butter until well-blended. Add in the eggs, vanilla, buttermilk and bananas. Fold in the flour, baking soda, salt, cinnamon, nutmeg and chocolate cups. Blend well but don't beat.

Spoon into the pan and bake 60 minutes and then lower temperature to 300 F and bake until cake springs back when lightly pressed with fingertips, about 45-50 minutes. Cool well.

Serves 10

Caramel Oatmeal Spice Apple Pie

This is like a caramel spice oatmeal cookie that landed on top of an apple pie. Just imagine mounds of juicy, baked apples under a sweet and crisp crown. If it's true that people eat with their eyes, this pie is love at first sight.

Crust
Prepared pie dough for 1 9-inch single-crust pie

Spice Caramel Crumb Topping
1 cup oatmeal
½ cup flour
½ cup chopped pecans, optional
1/3 cup caramel or butterscotch chips
¼ cup white sugar
3 tablespoons light brown sugar
1 teaspoon pure vanilla extract
½ teaspoon cinnamon
1/8 teaspoon cloves
Pinch nutmeg
½ cup unsalted butter, cut into chunks

Filling
8–12 large apples, cored, peeled, and cut into wedges
3 tablespoons unsalted butter
1 cup sugar
2 tablespoons cornstarch
¼ teaspoon cinnamon
Pinch cloves
Pinch nutmeg

Preheat the oven to 400 F. Line a baking sheet with parchment paper. Line a 9-inch pie pan with pastry dough and place on the baking sheet.

For the Spice Caramel Crumb Topping, combine oatmeal, flour, pecans, if using, caramel or butterscotch chips, white and brown sugars, vanilla extract, cinnamon, cloves and nutmeg in a food processor. Add the butter and process to make a mealy, clumpy mixture. Set aside.

For the filling, prepare apples. In a large nonstick fry pan, melt the butter. Over medium heat, stir the apples with the white and brown sugars and cook to soften the apples, stirring often, about 15 to 20 minutes. Stir in the cornstarch and water and cook 2 more minutes. Cool to room temperature or refrigerate for 30 minutes. Stir in the cinnamon, cloves, and nutmeg.

Mound the apples in the pie shell. It should be very high with apples. Pat on the oatmeal crumb topping, patting and/or pressing slightly to make it adhere.

Place on the baking sheet and bake for 15 minutes at 400 F, then reduce the temperature to 350 F and bake for another 35 to 50 minutes, until it smells more like pie than fresh apples and you see juices bubbling out the sides a bit or through the streusel. Cool to room temperature.

Serves 8–10

Carrot Cake Biscotti

This is an inspired sweet and sassy biscotti that features a mellow vanilla, cinnamon and orange batter, calico-ed up with shredded carrots, walnut chunks and raisins. The "cream cheese" frosting is actually melted white chocolate. This is a reputation-maker biscotti.

Carrot Cake Biscotti Batter

1/2 cup canola oil
½ cup unsalted butter, melted
1 ½ cups sugar
3 eggs
1 tablespoon pure vanilla extract
1½ teaspoons orange oil or 1 teaspoon orange extract
1 tablespoon fresh lemon juice
3 ½ cups all-purpose flour
1 tablespoon cinnamon
1 ¼ teaspoons baking soda
1 teaspoon baking powder
½ teaspoon salt
2 cups shredded carrots
1 ½ cups chopped walnuts
1 ½ cups raisins, plumped and dried

Glaze

1 cup chopped white chocolate, melted

Preheat oven to 350 F. Line a 9- by 13-inch pan with parchment paper. Place pan on a parchment paper-lined baking sheet.

For the biscotti batter, in a large mixer bowl, blend the oil, butter, sugar, and eggs together (stirring by hand is fine). Add the vanilla extract, orange oil or orange extract and lemon juice. Fold in the flour, cinnamon, baking soda, baking powder and salt. Then fold in the carrots, walnuts, and raisins to make a thick batter. If the batter is very gloppy, add a few more tablespoons of flour to firm it up.

Spread the batter into the pan (it should go out to the sides like cake batter). Alternatively for small biscotti, make two logs of batter and place on a parchment paper-lined baking sheet.

Bake 45 to 55 minutes, or until set. Put the pan in the freezer for 3 to 4 hours.

To bake biscotti for the second time, preheat the oven to 325 F. Turn the frozen biscotti out onto a cutting board and cut the horizontally in half, then cut into sticks about ½ inch wide.

Place on a baking sheet and bake 15 to 20 minutes on each side, until they dry out and are crisp. Smear white chocolate on one side of each biscotti.

Makes 2 –2 ½ dozen, depending on size.

Cake Mix Cinnamon Buns

I once heard about a bakery that combined yellow cake mix into their sweet yeast dough to make apparently legendary cinnamon buns that brought customers to their knees. I made my own version using that cake mix trick and now I see why they're so good.

Sweet Dough
2 ½ cups warm water
2 tablespoons instant yeast
1 1 pound box yellow cake mix
2 cups bread flour
3 ½ cups all-purpose flour

Filling
½ cup unsalted butter, softened
1 cup sugar
1 cup raisins, plumped and dried
1 cup chopped walnuts, optional
1 tablespoon cinnamon

Glaze
2 cups confectioners' sugar
3 to 4 tablespoons milk
1 teaspoon pure vanilla extract

Line a baking sheet with parchment paper. Generously spray a 9- by 13-inch pan with nonstick cooking spray and place on a baking pan.

For the Sweet Dough, in a mixer bowl, whisk together the water and yeast and let stand 2 to 3 minutes. Stir in the cake mix, the bread flour, and most of the all-purpose flour. Knead with a dough hook until smooth and elastic, about 8 to 12 minutes, adding more all-purpose flour if required. Form into a ball and place in a lightly greased bowl. Cover and let rise until doubled, about 30 to 45 minutes. Gently deflate the dough and remove from the bowl. On a lightly floured work surface, roll the dough out to a rectangle of about 15 by 20 inches.

For the filling, spread the softened butter evenly over the dough. Dust with the sugar, raisins, walnuts, if using, and cinnamon. Roll into a large log and cut into one-inch slices.

Place the pieces touching each other (i.e. quite snugly) in the pan. Cover lightly with a large plastic bag and let rise until almost doubled in size, 60 to 90 minutes, or refrigerate for a cool rise, 8 to 12 hours. Preheat oven to 350 F.

Bake 30 to 35 minutes, until lightly browned and the center seems baked (not too mushy), otherwise continue baking, ensuring it does not dry out on the edges. You can lower the temperature and bake a little longer for even baking.

Cool the buns 15 minutes. Make the glaze by whisking together the confectioners' sugar, milk, and vanilla extract until you have a thick glaze that can be poured or spread over the buns. Drizzle or spread the glaze over the buns.

Makes 1 dozen buns, or more, depending on size

Decadent French Mint Cookies

The irresistible combination of mint and chocolate never fails to impress or seduce. These are decadent fudge cookies with crackly tops and a texture midway between a cookie and a brownie (think crisp edges and fudgy interior). Warm out of the oven, they are anointed with a peppermint patty that sits a few minutes before it melts into a beautiful mint marble topping. With cookies like this, life is good.

½ cup unsalted butter, softened
½ cup (packed) brown sugar
¾ cup white sugar
1 egg
1 teaspoon pure vanilla extract
¾ cup semisweet chocolate chips, melted and cooled
1 ¾ cups all-purpose flour
½ teaspoon baking powder
¼ teaspoon baking soda
½ cup semisweet chocolate chips
2 packages or about 24 small peppermint patties

Preheat the oven to 350 F. Double up two sets of baking sheets and top each set with parchment paper.

Melt the chocolate in the microwave and set aside to cool.

In a mixer bowl, with the paddle attachment, cream the butter, brown sugar and white sugar. Blend in the egg and vanilla extract, and then blend in the melted chocolate. Fold in flour, baking powder, and baking soda and blend until almost smooth. Fold in the chocolate chips.

Form the dough into walnut sized balls and place, evenly spaced, on the baking sheets. Bake until just set, about 12 to 14 minutes.

Remove from the oven and immediately place a peppermint patty on top of each cookie and press gently. A few minutes later, gently smear the melting mint to ice the top of the cookie.

Chill slightly or leave at room temperature to set.

Makes 30–40 cookies, depending on size

Banana Caramel Streusel Muffins

These muffins are extraordinary no matter how you bake them, but making them using unbleached Melitta coffee filter papers puts them over the top. Alternatively you can use tulip shaped, bigger muffin baking cups (EBay is super for all sorts of paper baking supplies). Taste? Smooth bananas with caramel, pecans, brown sugar, and vanilla—a bouquet of pure autumnal sweetness.

Caramel Pecan Streusel

6 tablespoons unsalted butter
½ cup (packed) brown sugar
½ cup chopped pecans
1/3 cup butterscotch chips
½ teaspoon cinnamon
½ cup butterscotch or caramel sundae topping

Muffin Batter

¾ cup unsalted butter
1 cup (packed) brown sugar
½ cup white sugar
2 eggs
2 teaspoons pure vanilla extract
2 ½ cups all-purpose flour
1 cup mashed (very ripe) banana (about two large)
2 teaspoons baking powder
½ teaspoon baking soda
½ teaspoon salt
¼ teaspoon cinnamon
½ cup buttermilk

Preheat oven to 375 F.

Generously spray a 12-cup extra-large muffin pan with nonstick cooking spray and place on a parchment paper-lined baking sheet. Into each muffin well, place a #4 coffee filter paper (or extra-large muffin liners) and spray the interior with nonstick cooking spray. Position the oven rack to the upper third position.

For the Caramel Pecan Streusel, place the butter, brown sugar, pecans and butterscotch chips, and cinnamon in a food processor and pulse to make a coarse, grainy mixture. Keep the caramel sauce nearby.

For the muffins, in a mixer bowl, cream the butter with the brown and white sugars until well blended. Add the eggs and vanilla extract and mix well. Fold in the flour, banana, baking powder, baking soda, salt, and cinnamon, and drizzle in the buttermilk.

Blend the batter well, scraping the bottom and sides of the bowl to ensure that the batter is evenly mixed.

Scoop the batter halfway into each coffee filter paper or muffin liner, top with some of the streusel mixture, 1 to 2 teaspoons of the caramel topping, and then more muffin batter. Top with more of the streusel and a touch of caramel sauce on top. If you have more batter than muffins to fill (it can depend on the size of the muffin cups), scoop the batter and top with some streusel onto the parchment lined baking sheet and bake the extra as "muffin tops."

Place in the oven and immediately lower the temperature to 375 F. Bake for 15 minutes, then lower temperature to 350 F and bake until the muffins are gently browned around the edges and seem set when touched, another 15 minutes. If the muffins appear to be browning on the top, but not baked completely through, reduce the oven temperature to 325 F and bake a little longer. Cool well before removing from the pan and let finish cooling on a cake rack.

Makes 12 (or more, depending on size)

Greek Yogurt Lemon Blueberry Muffins

A coffee and teatime treat that one visitor to my website claimed as the best muffin recipe ever. Greek yogurt makes these sublime and tender but the flavor of lemon, vanilla and gorgeous blueberries is riveting stuff.

Streusel Topping
½ cup finely ground walnuts
1/3 cup white sugar
3 tablespoons unsalted butter, softened
2 tablespoons all-purpose flour
1 teaspoon cinnamon
1/8 teaspoon nutmeg

Muffins
½ cup unsalted butter
1 cup sugar
1/3 cup water
1 egg
1 teaspoon pure vanilla extract
Zest of 1 lemon, finely grated
Juice of 1 lemon
1 cup thick plain Greek yogurt
2 ¼ cups all-purpose flour
½ teaspoon baking soda
2 teaspoons baking powder
¼ teaspoon salt
1 ¼ cups frozen or fresh blueberries

Preheat oven to 375 F. Spray the bottoms and top surface of a 12 cup muffin tin with nonstick cooking spray. Line the muffin tin with paper liners. Line a baking sheet with parchment paper and put the muffin tin on it.

For the Streusel Topping, combine the walnuts, sugar, butter, flour, cinnamon and nutmeg in a small bowl by tossing with a fork or rubbing with your fingertips to achieve a crumbly mixture. Set aside.

For the muffins, in a mixer bowl, cream the butter with the sugar until well blended. Add water, egg, vanilla extract, lemon zest, and lemon juice. Stir in the yogurt. Fold in the flour, baking soda, baking powder, and salt and blend well. Gently fold in the berries by hand. Scoop into prepared muffin cups (batter should almost to the top).

Sprinkle the tops with equal portions of the streusel topping. Place in the oven and immediately lower the temperature to 350 F. Bake until done, 32 to 34 minutes.

Makes 10–12 muffins

233

Mazurka Bars

These are a triumph. I never heard of Mazurka Bars, purportedly of Polish origin, until I read Bread Alone, a novel by Judith Hendricks. There's no recipe in the book, but I swooned for the description of bars made of a tart or shortbread bottom, a smack of tart apricot spread or filling, and a luscious topping of caramelized walnuts. I use my own apricot jam, but you can also use a quality imported apricot jam.

Brown Sugar Tart Crust

2 cups all-purpose flour

1/3 cup white sugar

3 tablespoons dark brown sugar

¼ teaspoon salt

¼ teaspoon baking powder

¾ cup unsalted butter, cut into chunks

1 egg

2–4 tablespoons whipping cream

Caramel Walnut Filling

1 cup apricot filling or jam

½ cup unsalted butter, melted

1 cup (packed) light brown sugar

¼ cup corn syrup

¼ cup honey

1 teaspoon pure vanilla extract

2 tablespoons whipping cream

2 eggs

Tiniest pinch salt

2 cups walnuts, coarsely chopped

Line a baking sheet with parchment paper. Generously spray an 8- by 11-inch or 9- by 13-inch rectangular pan with nonstick cooking spray. Place pan on baking sheet.

Preheat the oven to 350 F.

For the Brown Sugar Tart Crust, in a food processor, blend the sugars, salt and baking powder briefly. Add the butter and pulse to break in the butter until the mixture just barely begins to hold together. Turn out into a bowl and mix in the egg and whipping cream, mixing you're your hands to make the mixture really hold together. Press into the prepared pan and chill for 15 minutes. Bake for 20 minutes. Remove from the oven and let cool for 10 minutes. Reduce the oven temperature to 325 F.

Spread the apricot jam over the crust.

To make the filling, in a medium bowl, using a whisk, blend the butter, brown sugar, corn syrup, honey, vanilla, whipping cream, eggs, and salt well. Fold in the walnuts. Pour onto the slightly cooled crust.

Bake for 25 to 35 minutes, or until the filling is just set. Cool well or refrigerate before cutting into bars.

Makes 2–3 dozen, depending on size

Sour Cream Chocolate Cake with Pure Fudge Icing

Mellow flavored chocolate with a delectable crumb, this is as old-fashioned (and reliable) as chocolate cake gets. White and brown sugars combine to offer a subtle caramel afterglow to this moist, hunky cake, but the piece de resistance is the thick fudge-like frosting.

Cake

1 ¾ cups white sugar
¼ cup (firmly packed) brown sugar
1 cup unsalted butter, melted
¼ cup canola oil
3 eggs
2 teaspoons pure vanilla extract
2 ½ cups all-purpose flour
1 cup unsweetened cocoa powder, measured then sifted
1 ½ teaspoons baking powder
1 ¼ teaspoons baking soda
½ teaspoon salt
1 ¼ cups cola, flat, room temperature
¼ cup sour cream

Marshmallow Fudge Frosting

3 cups miniature marshmallows
¾ cup semisweet chocolate chips
¼ cup unsalted butter, softened
1–2 cups confectioners' sugar
¼ cup cold butter, in small pieces
1 teaspoon pure vanilla extract
¼ cup half-and-half or cream, or more, as required

Preheat the oven to 350 F. Line a baking sheet with parchment paper. Generously spray a 9- by 13 inch rectangular pan with nonstick cooking spray and place on the baking sheet.

For the cake, in a large mixer bowl, cream the white sugar, brown sugar, melted butter and oil together. Blend in the eggs and vanilla extract and mix well.

In a separate bowl, stir together the flour, cocoa, baking powder, baking soda and salt. Fold the flour mixture into the butter mixture, adding the cola and sour cream as mixture blends. If using an electric mixer, use slow speed for about 3 minutes, scraping down the sides and bottom once to incorporate all of the ingredients evenly.

Pour the batter into the prepared baking pan and bake for 42 to 45 minutes, until the cake springs back when gently pressed with fingertips.

For the Marshmallow Fudge Frosting, in a small saucepan, slowly melt the marshmallows with the chocolate chips and butter. Remove from the stove and mix until smooth. Let cool for 5 minutes. Place the mixture in a food processor and add the confectioners' sugar, cold butter, and vanilla extract and blend. Drizzle in just enough cream to make a thick, glossy frosting (it will seem almost shiny). Spread on the cooled cake. Let set 1 to 2 hours until quite firm.

Serves 10–14

Scandinavian Sour Cream Cardamom Rusks

Rusks are much like biscotti and mandelbrot. These are gently spiced and fragrant in the way only something made with almonds, sour cream, butter and cardamom could be.

Dough
½ cup unsalted butter, softened
1 ¼ cups sugar
2 eggs
½ cup sour cream
2 teaspoons pure almond extract
½ teaspoon pure vanilla extract
3 ½ cups all-purpose flour
½ cup chopped almonds
1 ½ teaspoons cardamom
1 teaspoon baking powder
½ teaspoon baking soda
3/8 teaspoon salt

Finishing Touches
1 egg, beaten
1 cup slivered almonds

Preheat oven to 350 F. Stack two baking sheets together and line the top one with parchment paper.

In a mixer bowl, cream the butter and sugar until well blended and then blend in the eggs. Add the sour cream and almond and vanilla extracts and blend well. Fold in the flour, almonds, cardamom, baking powder, baking soda and salt.

Divide the dough in two and place on the baking sheet, spaced apart. Pat into 2 logs, approximately 10 to 12 inches long and 3 to 4 inches wide. Brush the tops with beaten egg and sprinkle the slivered almonds over.

Bake until nicely browned all over, about 30 to 35 minutes. Cool well; lower oven temperature to 325 F. Cut the logs into ¾-inch wide slices. Place the slices back on the baking sheet and bake for about 15 to 20 minutes per side, turning once.

Makes 2 ½ –3 ½ dozen

Acknowledgments

My volunteer testers come from all parts of Canada and the United States. My test kitchen ranks include a couple of lawyers, an engineer, a teacher, a nurse, a marriage counselor, a minister, a few food entrepreneurs, a culinary student but overall, bright, talented capable individuals with wonderful palates. Some testers are old friends and some are new ones that segued from being subscribers to my website or came to know me via my other published cookbooks. The common element is that my testers are the nicest, most generous people I've been blessed to collaborate with. They are also especially adept in the kitchen and uniquely skilled when it comes to testing and replicating a recipe for accuracy. Their passion for food is contagious and their input helped make the recipes that much more fun and lively. Without these fine people, this cookbook could not have blossomed neither as it did nor would the recipes be as clear, exacting and (hopefully) sumptuous. With appreciation and special fondness to,

Cookbook Kitchen Testers

Ellen Fuss, Test Kitchen Manager

Batya Anteby	Ann Harste	Michele Meiner
Janice Bell	Christian Hudon	Jill Moncarz
Lynn Caplan	Louise Jacowitz Allen	Sheila Moore
Betsy Carey	Hye Kam	Adrienne Nelson
Emily Carrara	Heidi Kaplan	Wendy Offman
Vicki Gensini	Leone Lamb	Linda Raden
Jonathan Goldman	Yvonne Lachance	Deborah Racine
Janet Goldstein	Joanna Lamprecht	Laurie Rosenthal
Marla Gottlieb	Joyce Leitman	Ellen Silver
Janice Guimond	Judith Lessler	Amy Stromberg
Susan Hatch	Diane Loeffen	Joelle Stromberg

Editing, Proofreading, Indexing

I have had an astonishing and capable editorial team that ensured that *When Bakers Cook* is lyrically, grammatically and editorially wonderful. My thanks to:

Robin Donovan, Senior Copy Editor
Erica Caridio, Indexer
Gene Escherline
Ellen Gold
Cheryl Goldberg

Jonathan Goldman
Janet Goldstein
Louise Jacowitz

Corporate Friends

To the supportive companies and people I've worked with, some since the beginning of my culinary career. These companies have graciously and generously provided products that not only enhanced my test kitchen but made the creation of recipes that much more of a joy. They have, in varying ways, expressed faith and respect in me as a culinary professional that has more than helped me on my publishing journey.

All-Clad
Beehive Kitchenware
BellaViaOrchards.com
BG Foods
Breville
Bodum
Boyajian Inc.
Chemex
Christopher Ranch Garlic
Clabbergirl
Costco
Cutco
Elehost Web Design (Paul McKenzie, Jeff Kemp)
Emile Henri
Garland Range Canada

Jenn-Air Whirlpool Corporation (Brian Maynard)
JS Public Relations (Julia Stambules)
KitchenAid (Justin Newby, Kim Roman, Tandy Ulleg)
King Arthur Flour
Krups
Lamson Sharp
Mauviel USA
Nielsen Massey Vanillas (Matt Nielsen)
Peppermill Imports
Saco Foods
Saffron.com
Simplex Kettles
The Spice House
Viking Cookware
Zojirushi

To Friends, Both Personal and Professional

There are kindred spirits I am most grateful for; individuals who have gifted me with warm encouragement on the creative, culinary pathway. The following people have listened, offered gentle suggestions, and/or generously shared information throughout this book's journey. They deserve a public thank you.

Bonnie Benwick, *The Washington Post*; Daniel Braddock, Roy Francia, John Reick and the editorial, production (Design Team 2) at *Create Space/Amazon*, Jonathan Cheung of *Bon Appetit for Books*, Montreal; Ashley Finestone and *Team Buy*, Sandy Gluck, *Martha Stewart Sirius*, Jennifer Kenney Sendrow, *Martha Stewart Sirius*, Betsy Kuralnick, *Martha Stewart Sirius*, Robert McCollough, *Random House*, Lisa Mantineo, *Martha Stewart Sirius*, Hana Medina, *Costco Connection*, Pam Meeks, *Clabbergirl*; Stephanie Ponder, *Costco Connection*, Tod Jones, Tim Tavitch, *Costco Connection*; Joe Wikert of *Olive Software*; Meredith Williams of *Clabbergirl*, Joe Yonan, *The Washington Post*.

A Special Thank You to My Readers

To readers of my cookbooks and visitors to my site, www.BetterBaking.com, thank you for your warm support over the years. This book is an endeavor of love and faith; it is also my hug of appreciation to you all for keeping me company in the kitchen and at the keyboard. I could not have written and completed this book without you *all*, my gentle readers and baking companions, cheering me on. Thank you from the bottom of my heart.

Marcy Goldman

Index

Vinaigrette(s)
  for Bosc Pear, Blue Cheese and Bibb Salad, 89
  Greek Restaurant Vinaigrette, 78
  for Layered Picnic Icebox Salad, 80
  Lemon, 199
  No Fat, All Flavor Vinaigrette, 77
  for Tuscany Bread Salad, 81

W
Waffles
  Belgian, Buttery, 13
  Buttermilk Pecan, 97
  Red Velvet, with Cream Cheese Glaze, 11
Walnuts
  in Mazurka Bars, 234

Wedding Poached Salmon, 148
White Chocolate, Raspberry, and Vanilla Bread
  Pudding, 215
World's Best Vegetarian Paté, 203

Y
Yogurt
  Greek Yogurt Cheesecake, 225
  Greek Yogurt Lemon Blueberry Muffins, 233

Z
Zucchini
  Caponata, Roasted Eggplant and, 192
  Sticks, Crispy, 193